BEFORE THE SINGING

Before the Singing

STRUCTURING CHILDREN'S CHOIRS FOR SUCCESS

Barbara M. Tagg

OXFORD
UNIVERSITY PRESS

Oxford University Press is a department of the University of Oxford.
It furthers the University's objective of excellence in research, scholarship,
and education by publishing worldwide.

Oxford   New York
Auckland   Cape Town   Dar es Salaam   Hong Kong   Karachi
Kuala Lumpur   Madrid   Melbourne   Mexico City   Nairobi
New Delhi   Shanghai   Taipei   Toronto

With offices in
Argentina   Austria   Brazil   Chile   Czech Republic   France   Greece
Guatemala   Hungary   Italy   Japan   Poland   Portugal   Singapore
South Korea   Switzerland   Thailand   Turkey   Ukraine   Vietnam

Oxford is a registered trademark of Oxford University Press
in the UK and certain other countries.

Published in the United States of America by
Oxford University Press
198 Madison Avenue, New York, NY 10016

© Oxford University Press 2013

All rights reserved. No part of this publication may be reproduced, stored in a
retrieval system, or transmitted, in any form or by any means, without the prior
permission in writing of Oxford University Press, or as expressly permitted by law,
by license, or under terms agreed with the appropriate reproduction rights organization.
Inquiries concerning reproduction outside the scope of the above should be sent to the
Rights Department, Oxford University Press, at the address above.

You must not circulate this work in any other form
and you must impose this same condition on any acquirer.

Library of Congress Cataloging-in-Publication Data
Tagg, Barbara.
Structuring children's choirs for success : before the singing / Barbara M. Tagg.
pages cm
Includes bibliographical references and index.
ISBN 978–0–19–992070–9 (alk. paper) – ISBN 978–0–19–992068–6 (alk. paper)
1. Children's choirs.   I. Title.
MT88.T35 2013
782.7'145—dc23
2012040878

9 8 7 6 5 4 3 2 1
Printed in the United States of America
on acid-free paper

In memory of Barbara F. Marble

Contents

Acknowledgments ix
Foreword *by Francisco J. Núñez* xi
About the Companion Website xv
Introduction xix

1. *Getting Started* 1
2. *Organizational Structure* 14
3. *Beyond the Board* 30
4. *Leadership Transition* 43
5. *Finances* 60
6. *Rehearsals and Parents* 83
7. *Musical Matters* 99
8. *Promotion and Fundraising* 111
9. *Concerts* 128
10. *Building Community* 149
11. *Performing with Professionals* 168
12. *Touring* 187
13. *In the Words of Others* 203
14. *Suggested Treble Repertoire* 215

Notes 245
Bibliography 253
Index 261

Acknowledgments

THE WRITING OF this book is possible because of the community of people with whom I have had the privilege of working, studying, collaborating, and sharing in the choral art.

Special thanks to the choristers and their families, and the board of directors of the Syracuse Children's Chorus (SCC), who believed in our mission, supported the chorus, and collaborated in the shared vision for the organization. My appreciation goes to the staff and volunteers of the SCC, both artistic and administrative, during my thirty-year tenure there. I offer thanks to the choral music educators of the Syracuse City School District and the Onondaga County public schools and surrounding counties' public and private schools, who inspire young singers daily in their classrooms and choirs.

Two professional choral organizations deserve thanks. The American Choral Directors Association, including all my colleagues on the National Committee on Children's Choirs and the National Committee on Repertoire and Standards, provided years of collaboration and volunteer efforts. Much inspiration and knowledge came from Chorus America under the executive leadership of Ann Meier Baker, my colleagues on its national board of directors, and the organization's capable staff. The national conferences and management institutes provided data, knowledge, and resources that were invaluable in developing and sustaining a nonprofit choral organization. Many people are grateful for their strong commitment to children's and youth choirs.

Special thanks go to Jean Ashworth Bartle for her encouragement throughout this project. Gregg Smith challenged, inspired, and encouraged me throughout my tenure with the SCC. Many are grateful for his long-time support of children's singing. Sincere gratitude goes to Dr. Doreen Rao, mentor, colleague, and friend, and to all the colleagues involved in the early years of Choral Music Experience. We laughed, studied, planned, and dreamed together about a world where all children would have an opportunity to sing, and we taught and worked many hours to that end.

My gratitude also goes to the National Endowment for the Arts, which provided both administrative and artistic support for many years to the SCC. The National Endowment for the Arts understood the importance of funding the work of children's choirs, both administratively and artistically, for the future of choral singing in America.

Arts consultants who worked with the SCC included Dr. Sherry Schiller, Douglas Kinzey, John Wessel, and Joan Welles. We were forever grateful for their knowledge and guidance at critical times in the chorus's development.

My sincere gratitude goes to Todd Waldman and Norman Hirschy of Oxford University Press for their support and belief in this book from the beginning. Special thanks go to Timothy J. DeWerff and Janice F. Holbrook for their formidable editing skills.

My deep appreciation is extended to the Syracuse Symphony Orchestra for its many years of inspiration, and in particular to conductors Daniel Hege and Fabio Mechetti, for their numerous collaborations with the SCC. Additional thanks go to Richard Decker, vice president and general manager of the orchestra, who took a chance on a new children's choir performing with the orchestra and subsequently facilitated many collaborative performances over the years.

Other individuals who deserve special thanks include the following: James Abbott, Paul Caldwell, Courtney Chiavara, Shawn Crouch, Allan N. Culbertson, Deborah A. Cunningham, Mary Deissler, G. Fred Holbrook, Glenn Kime, Robert S. Kotcher, Libby Larsen, John F. Marsellus, Stephanie Mowery, Alice Muzquiz, Brent Paris, David Patrick, Rosalind Rees, Annette Riposo, James Schunck, Jamie Sutphen, and the late James Dash and Calvin Custer, each of whom contributed in significant ways.

Syracuse University colleagues who deserve thanks include the deans of the College of Visual and Performing Arts, listed chronologically: Arthur Freundlich, Donald Lantzy, Carole Brzozowski, and Anne Clark; and university colleagues Dr. Robert Bodgan, Dr. John Coggiola, Dr. Bradley P. Ethington, Dr. Hope Irvine, Dr. Patrick M. Jones, George Pappastavrou, Alice Randel Pfeiffer, Dr. Suzanne Thorin, Dr. Vincent Tinto, Dr. Toni Toland, Dr. Cornelia Yarbrough, and the late M. Douglas Soyars and Helen Boatwright.

My appreciation goes to C.V. (Major) and Diane Bowes for offering the cozy cabin on the inspiring Adirondack mountain lake where much of the book was written, and I am also thankful for my mountain retreat near Lake Placid. The final thank you goes to my family; without them the SCC and this book would not have been possible. My mother, Barbara F. Marble, loved music and inspired my life's work. My father, James W. Marble, taught me to always "walk with a purpose," as he did throughout his life, particularly in community leadership and service, passions both my parents shared. My husband, David J. Tagg, was always there for me with love, support, advice, and encouragement, as was our son, D. James Tagg who sang in the chorus as a child.

Foreword

IN 1988, I had just graduated from college. I was a pianist, organist, and composer. But what did I know about children's choruses? All I knew was that serious young people studied privately to see whether they had what it took to be great artists. Once they or their teachers realized they were not prodigies, some continued to practice, but most gave up. Given the odds, how could an entire group of young people—a children's choir—fare any better? How could they attract a recording contract, a fan base, or a touring schedule—especially if they had to be in school the next day? As far as I knew, the children's choir was not ready to be considered a viable musical institution outside of the educational setting.

Regardless, upon graduating from college, I formed the Young People's Chorus of New York City, but with a unique idea: I would create a choir with a dual mission of diversity and artistic excellence. I was thoughtful in creating a chorus with a strong social mission to bring together children from all walks of life to sing at the highest artistic level so that they could learn about each other and create a multicultural community.

From my own experiences, I knew that taking children from the barrio and combining them with children from the upper echelons of New York City would change their lives. I also knew that, in order to keep the children coming back, I had to offer a high-quality musical experience. But my early training had not shown me how to do this. In college, I was taught conducting patterns, ear training, classroom management, and overall basic musicianship skills. I remember speaking about this to one of my colleagues, a doctoral education major at the time, who told me that young children aged eight to twelve are incapable of being musical, as their brains are not fully formed and they cannot understand the concept of musical beauty. I relied on audiotapes and recordings of girls' and boys' choirs from Eastern and Western Europe singing the music of Bartók and Kodály to form my choral palette. Despite what I had been told, I learned that children could be very artistic, even if they were not prodigies. But I had yet to find a model to follow in North America.

In 1991, I attended a workshop in New Jersey with Barbara Tagg and the Syracuse Children's Chorus. These singers, most of them in high school, walked onto the risers looking eager and fresh in their white shirts, red bows, vests, skirts, and pants. Their first sound was a simple breathing exercise, a held "CH" sustained for sixteen beats. I felt like I was in the middle of that classic Maxell TV commercial: There I was sitting in the front row with my hair being blown back as though I was in a wind tunnel. They had incredible power. Next, they sang an arrangement of "Shenandoah." They had a pure tone and artistry like no other I had heard. I was shocked to learn that a children's chorus could sound so incredible. I was inspired. Barbara and I became close friends. She introduced me to her colleagues, and my ideas began to transform.

The community children's choir movement is very young in North America. At one time, music education was an integral part of a child's school curriculum, and choral singing was strong in churches. Therefore, there was no need for additional music education unless a child wanted to study privately.

Until recently, the public perception of a children's chorus in North America was as a fundamental classroom activity, where young people could learn to be expressive, keep time, and acquire basic musicianship skills. The choir programs in pre-college conservatories and music camps were formed primarily for instrumentalists to further their ear-training and sight-reading abilities.

As government funding began to dissipate for school programs, music was slowly phased out, and the need for communities to start choirs became crucial. This movement started in the late 1960s, and a select few choirs were formed in some of the larger metropolitan areas. During this time, the audiences for children's choirs were mainly families and friends of the choristers. The general concert patron was fascinated with instrumental wunderkinds, but rarely would they choose to hear a children's choir. Of course, there were exceptions, such as the Vienna Boys' Choir.

The past fifty years have seen a dramatic shift in the children's chorus movement, and the future continues to be bright. New music continues to be written specifically for children, and the general concertgoer is starting to understand the character and the incredible ability of a children's choir. We are ascending into the next level and creating *wunder-chören*.

Barbara Tagg's influence has become invaluable during this period of change. It is exciting that she has decided to write this book because it addresses what I was looking for as a young conductor: how to do it. The children's chorus movement in North America may still be young, but we have had a handful of dedicated conductors who have made it their life's work to help young people reach a high artistic level. Barbara was one of those pioneers, and now she has put all of her experiences into this incredible book to inspire, just as I was inspired. This is a culmination of her life's work, from scratch to the endgame, a how-to for creating and maintaining a viable, artistic, and exciting organization that can change a community through song.

Francisco J. Núñez
2011 MacArthur Fellow
Artistic Director/Founder
Young People's Chorus of New York City
Conductor, University Glee Club of New York City

About the Companion Website

www.oup.com/us/beforethesinging

Oxford University Press has created a companion website for *Before the Singing: Structuring Children's Choirs for Success*, and readers are invited to visit it frequently to view the following appendices:

Chapter 1—None

Chapter 2
- 2.1 Sample Bylaws
- 2.2 Chorister Representative Monthly Board Reports
- 2.3 Conflict-of-Interest Policy
- 2.4 Whistleblower Policy
- 2.5 Sample Board Agenda

Chapter 3
- 3.1 Sample Organizational Charts
- 3.2 Syracuse Children's Chorus Mission, Beliefs, Values, and Visions
- 3.3 Sample Job Descriptions and Staff Responsibilities
- 3.4 Personnel Forms
- 3.5 Staff Evaluations
- 3.6 Staff Recognition Survey

Chapter 4
- 4.1 Sample Job Description
- 4.2 Sample Candidate Itinerary
- 4.3 Sample Chorister Candidate Audition Evaluation Form

Chapter 5
- 5.1 Sample Budget Worksheet
- 5.2 Sample Balance Sheet
- 5.3 Sample Monthly Budget Report
- 5.4 Sample Application for Choir Tuition Scholarship
- 5.5 Sample Grant Timeline
- 5.6 Record Retention Guidelines

Chapter 6
- 6.1 Audition Timeline
- 6.2 Audition Room Setup
- 6.3 Materials for Staff to Bring to Auditions
- 6.4 Chorus Registration Floor Diagram
- 6.5 Confidential Chorister Information Form
- 6.6 Permission To Be Photographed/Recorded
- 6.7 Chorister Camp Packing List
- 6.8 Staff Packing List—Chorister Summer Camp
- 6.9 Chorister Camp Schedule
- 6.10 Chorister Camp Confidential Medical and Personal Information Form
- 6.11 Chorister Day Camp Schedule
- 6.12 Chorus Attendance Sign-in Sheet
- 6.13 Chorister Music Distribution Form
- 6.14 Parent Volunteer Form
- 6.15 Parent Volunteer Assignments
- 6.16 Chaperone Concert Responsibilities

Chapter 7
- 7.1 Sample General Music Classroom Seating Chart
- 7.2 Sample Audition Form

Chapter 8—None

Chapter 9
- 9.1 Sample Concert Titles
- 9.2 Diagrams and Logistics for a Concert (*The Nine Lessons and Carols*)
- 9.3 Dress Rehearsal Schedule for *The Nine Lessons and Carols*

Chapter 10
- 10.1 A Fall Festival of Choirs Dress Rehearsal and Concert Schedule
- 10.2 Logistics for Benefit Concert with Five Choirs
- 10.3 Sharing the Choral Experience Schedules

Chapter 11—None

Chapter 12
- 12.1 Sample Tour Working Budget for Staff and Board Use
- 12.2 Fundraising Overview for Staff and Board
- 12.3 Agenda for Tour Announcement Meeting for Choristers and Parents
- 12.4 Tour Commitment Agreement
- 12.5 Tour Payment Strategy
- 12.6 Tour Countdown Calendar
- 12.7 About Chaperoning
- 12.8 Chaperone Application
- 12.9 About Family Groups
- 12.10 Sample Tour Handbook Topics
- 12.11 Tour Medical and Personal Information Form

Chapter 13—None

Chapter 14—None

Introduction

CHILDREN'S CHOIRS ARE IMPORTANT. Access to choral singing must exist for *all* children. This book was written for those who wish to start, continue to develop, or expand a children's or youth choir in a school, church, or community context. The comprehensive content is based on teaching and conducting experience at all levels from elementary school through university graduate students. It is based on founding various types of choirs in public schools where none existed or increasing enrollment in existing school choirs. It is based on founding a nonprofit community-based children's choir and serving as the managing artistic director for thirty years through transition to new artistic leadership.

Lessons learned and skills developed throughout years of teaching, managing, conducting, and being involved in professional choral organizations informed this book. It is about the skills necessary to successfully nurture and sustain children's choirs. It is not about the voice or conducting, but rather the organizational matters that allow the music-making to be supported and to thrive. It is about setting up a nonprofit organization, boards of directors, mission statements, budgets, fundraising, planning a season, staffing, strategic planning, communication, touring, collaborating, transitioning to new artistic leadership, and more.

Music matters discussed in the book include how to organize auditions and rehearsals; how to develop music libraries, timelines, and programs; how to plan repertoire for touring; how to work with a symphony orchestra; how to record choirs; and how to commission new works. Seating students in an elementary general music class to improve singing ability and voicing a choir to improve the unity of sound are also discussed. A repertoire list of approximately seven hundred titles is included, reflecting titles appropriate for treble singers, ages eight through seventeen. The appendices include many forms, timelines, models for concert logistics, schedules, organizational charts, and additional materials that reflect the day-to-day organization of ongoing chorus activities.

The book concludes with essays by sixteen distinguished colleagues with whom I have had the privilege of collaborating in various contexts. They contribute their thoughts about why organizational excellence is important for children's choirs, and why the sustainability of children's choirs is important for the future of choral singing.

It is hoped that college students will use this book as a text for learning about structuring future choral organizations. It is also hoped that music educators, conductors, artistic directors, church choir directors, board members, administrators, and non-profit arts leaders will read this book and find something useful to strengthen, better organize, stabilize, sustain, or expand their choirs. May these same people be inspired to explore and implement new ideas, or structure in improved ways how things are done in their own organizations.

My dissertation was based on studying excellence in a diverse inner-city public school music program. The elementary music teacher had grade-level choirs at every level and an additional select choir. The choirs sang folk songs and the music of Bach, Schubert, Brahms, and Copland. They sang in many styles and languages, and they enjoyed African *gahu* (singing, dancing, and drumming). In the same district, this comment was frequently made: "That's great for *her*, but I couldn't do that in *my* school." Her school *was* their school. It was her choice to make decisions about what would be taught and how to structure her program. It was the teacher's choice as to what would be sung each day; how she built the collaborative community of parents, staff, and administrators within the school to support her goals; and how the children would be taught in the general music classes and choral ensembles.

Excellence is a choice we make. We can strive to be excellent and practice how to be excellent each day, or we can settle for mediocrity. By sharing knowledge and skills in a collaborative environment, we can empower administrators, artistic leaders, staffs, boards, volunteers, choristers, and all those involved to be excellent. It is my sincere hope that *Before the Singing: Structuring Children's Choirs for Success* will make a difference and inspire you to strive for organizational excellence, as well as musical excellence.

Although my experience is primarily with treble choirs, many of the ideas presented in this book will apply equally well to adult choirs. We must continue to seek the organizational and musical skills necessary to support and sustain our important choral music programs in our schools, churches, and communities. The joy of participation in the choral art, for both singers and listeners, is worth the commitment and collaborative effort.

Begin with the end in mind.
—STEPHEN COVEY

1

GETTING STARTED

A STATEMENT OFTEN heard among choral musicians is "I want to start a choir, but I don't know where to begin." One also hears "I really want to know how other choirs deal with this topic," or "I'm overwhelmed with the nonmusical workload, so what should I do?" Or "I just became director of this choir and I want to make some changes, so where do I start?" The journey for everyone is different, but there are elements that are similar for all choirs where the creation of beautiful choral singing and excellence is the goal. Establishing a solid structure for a choir, whether it is a school choir, a church choir, or a community choir, allows the music-making to flourish under the direction of the conductor-teacher who leads the ensemble. A smoothly running organization matters.

Often there are individuals or musical moments that inspire our own professional lives. Sometimes life takes us in a direction we never dreamed we would go. Do you think you will conduct on the stage of Carnegie Hall? Do you think you will take a choir to China for an extended tour? Do you think you will commission a major living composer? Do you think you will conduct a professional symphony orchestra and produce a fully staged opera?

If we are lucky, we find ourselves in a position to create something that did not exist before, such as starting a choir in a school where no choir existed in the past, or putting together a chorus of classroom teachers to sing for a student assembly. Sometimes we have an opportunity to increase the size of an existing school choral program. One might be hired as the new director of music in a worship setting where a traditional structure of weekly rehearsals and weekend services exists. One might assume a position as a professional choir director of an organization with a long history of excellence. Or one might assume a position of a choir that has been newly formed. Each director will bring his or her life experiences, expertise, and artistry to the choir. And for each, the journey will be unique.

The Syracuse Children's Chorus (SCC) will be referred to throughout this book as an example of one choir's structure. Its story is one choir's unique journey from founding through the transition to a new artistic director thirty years later. For each person the journey of founding a choir or serving as a managing artist director, artistic director, choral music educator, church choir director, or professional choral conductor will be unique. The model of this choir is just that, one model. What works for one choral organization may or may not work for another, but lessons learned from one context may assist in thinking creatively or differently about another choir in a different context. Other models appropriate for community, school, and church choirs will be discussed.

CHORUS BACKGROUND

SCC began formally in September 1981, although the initial motivation to found the community-based choir in Syracuse, New York, had its earliest roots years earlier in an all-city festival chorus. For those students selected to participate in an all-city festival, the experience of having a dynamic female conductor, barely five feet tall, transform one hundred sixth graders into an outstanding choir in two days of rehearsals was profound. What was unique about the experience was that all the singers could match pitch, something not typical of school music classes or volunteer church children's choirs. This experience set the standard for personal expectations for future choral experiences and would be revisited years later when SCC was founded.

In 1975, the suggestion for a community-based choir in Syracuse came from Doreen Rao, the conductor of the Glen Ellyn Children's Chorus. Rao was a lecturer at a national symposium in music education held at Syracuse University. A community-based children's choir typically draws students of varying ages from many schools in a wide geographic area who gather to engage in the art of choral singing. The students study vocal technique, sight reading, score analysis, and musicianship; are challenged to develop the skills inherent in the age-appropriate repertoire selected for study; and perform treble music of varying styles and languages in rehearsals and concerts. No such choir existed in Syracuse. At that time, there were few community-based children's choirs in the country, and most of those choirs existed in major cities.[1] Rao suggested that Syracuse would be an ideal place to start such a choir and referred to the model established by her own choir, the Glen Ellyn Children's Chorus.

Five years later on March 9, 1981, the first formal meeting of the American Choral Directors Association (ACDA) National Committee on Children's Choirs was held at the ACDA national convention in New Orleans.[2] Chaired by Rao and assisted by seven division chairs, the National Committee on Children's Choirs began the work that would influence American choral music for years to come. Over the next twenty years, with the assistance of dedicated and highly motivated children's choir conductors, the children's choir movement became the fastest-growing area of choral singing in America.[3]

Following the ACDA event in 1981, the time was right to take on the project of forming a community-based children's choir in central New York. Permission to create such a choir was sought from the director of the School of Music at Syracuse University and the dean of the College of Visual and Performing Arts.[4] With the concept readily accepted, the children's chorus would become part of the preparatory division of the School of Music at the university. The next steps needed to be planned.

One month later, the director of the Syracuse University School of Music announced the formation of the choir in a letter that was mailed to all public school music teachers and church choir directors in the central New York area. With already-strong music education programs in schools across the region, the new community-based children's choir would be enrichment for those with demonstrated skills and abilities, and a place where children could share a love of singing with other singers of similar capabilities. It would be similar to my all-city experience years earlier, but a more permanent arrangement for those who had good singing skills and loved to sing.

To ensure the strong relationship between the local school music teachers and the university continued, it was determined that the students who auditioned would need to be recommended by their school music teachers. Once the children were accepted into the chorus, they were required to remain as active participants in their school music programs (if available) to maintain their eligibility in the new community-based choir. Where school programs did not exist or children were home-schooled, a private music teacher, school principal, or church choir director was encouraged to recommend the student. This policy has been maintained to the current day. The chorus has always supported the important work that public school music teachers do each day in the classroom, where the joy of choral singing is shared with *every* child.

Now the challenge was how to make the community-based chorus a reality. An April mailing announced that auditions would be held five months later in September, and that more complete information would be available at that time. This timeline allowed for late spring and summer preparation for early fall auditions and a late September starting date for rehearsals.

Once the announcement letters were mailed, individual phone calls were made to as many music teachers and church choir directors as possible to explain what the community-based children's choir would be, and to answer any questions they had about the fall auditions. It was also an opportunity to generate excitement about the new arts organization in Syracuse, the first of its kind in central New York.

It was a challenge trying to define a community-based children's choir to those unfamiliar with choirs of this type in the United States. Mentioning the Vienna Boys' Choir, an internationally recognized youth ensemble, gave an impression of a serious organization with a high standard of musical artistry. One former public school colleague said, "You can't do that. No one will pay tuition to bring their child to the university to sing!" Other former colleagues said, "I like this idea—kind of like an extended all-county choral festival." With a lot of faith, hope, optimism, determination, support, and hard work, the choir was slowly taking shape.

MORE QUESTIONS THAN ANSWERS

Still, in these earliest phases there were more questions than answers:

- Why start the choir?
- Who will be the singers?
- Will there be enough singers to make a choir?
- What will be the mission of the choir?
- What will we need to begin?
- How long will it take?
- Will teachers recommend students?
- What will you do first?
- What will the budget be?
- What will the singers wear?
- What music will they sing?
- How many parts will we sing—unison, two parts, three parts, or four parts?
- Will there be volunteers?
- What needs of the choir could be delegated to volunteers?
- Where will rehearsals be held?
- When will rehearsals be held?
- Who will accompany the choir?

To form a new choir, you must begin with a vision of the ideal in mind. For SCC, the goal was to establish a community-based, auditioned, treble choir that performed music of exceptionally fine quality with a pure tone and extraordinary beauty; that taught proper singing technique, music-reading skills, ear-training skills, musicianship, analytical skills, a focused work ethic; and that sang music of many styles, cultures, and periods of music history, and shared the joy of choral singing. In the choir's third year, the first premiere of a new work was given. Premiering and commissioning new works annually would become a signature of the ensemble.

A BRIEF HISTORY OF AMERICAN CHILDREN'S CHOIR DEVELOPMENT

At the time of the formation of SCC, there were few published resources related to children's choirs, and most were written prior to the 1960s. By interviewing conductors who had already established community-based children's choirs, much could be learned.

Because print resources were limited at the time, interviews with directors of recently formed or historic choirs were a place to start gathering data. My first interview was with Dr. Milford Fargo, founder of the Eastman Children's Choir at the Eastman School of Music, University of Rochester. Although the choir was no longer functioning,

Dr. Fargo provided details from the first announcement of the choir and the formative years. Topics included size of choir, how singers were recruited, repertoire, rehearsal schedule, and availability of programs and recordings. The music library at the Eastman School of Music provided sample programs and limited recorded examples of the children's choir, such as Alec Wilder's *The Children's Plea for Peace*.

Several useful resources available at the time were consulted. Lois Choksy's book, *The Kodály Context*, discussed teaching methods from the Children's Chorus of Maryland and its founder, Betty Bertaux. A visit to the choir, located in Baltimore, provided rich examples of the organizational structure of the choir, scheduling, and rehearsal models. Ethelyn Sparfeld, founder of the St. Louis Children's Choir, was interviewed at the Organization of America Kodály Educators national conference. It became very clear that although the context of each choir varied, certain organizational characteristics were consistent among all these community-based choirs.

Attendance at a summer workshop, with conductor and founder Jean Ashworth Bartle of the Toronto Children's Chorus in residence, provided an opportunity to observe a model Canadian program during the chorus's annual summer camp.[5] Doreen Rao, founder of the Choral Music Experience Institute for Choral Teacher Education (CME), held summer performance and professional development programs in the United States. Rao's annual weeklong sessions contributed greatly to the expanding body of knowledge about children's choirs as children, university students, conductors, teachers, and experts in the field gathered from across America, and eventually internationally, each summer for study. The CME Institutes, along with the strong leadership of the ACDA National Committee on Children's Choirs and other professional organizations, continued throughout the 1980s and 1990s.[6] The number of children's choirs in the United States increased dramatically during this time.[7]

For the CME Institutes held each summer under the artistic direction of Rao, colleagues with community-based choirs, school choirs, church choirs, and university students would gather to study, share, teach, conduct, and perform. Initially, nine professional music educators, university faculty, and children's choir conductors assisted Rao in developing her vision for a creative and inspiring summer institute where children and professional musicians could gather to study and learn. This included Kathy Armstrong, Lori-Anne Dolloff, Linda Ferreira, Janet Galván, Henry Leck, Rebecca Rottsolk, Timothy A. Sharp, Ethelyn Sparfeld, and myself.

Choristers from various children's choirs, and often an invited choir, formed the chorus for the conducting master classes and open rehearsals lead by Rao. Artist-teachers who attended the summer institutes included beginning through advanced conductors, as well as undergraduate and graduate university students, who were challenged by studying, analyzing, singing, conducting, and performing the varied repertoire selected by Rao. Guest artists and instructors included paid and volunteer staff. Invited composers who were in residence for the week provided further enrichment for participants, faculty, and the resident children's choir.

The Choral Music Experience Institutes for Choral Teacher Education, along with the work of the ACDA National Committee on Children's Choirs, as well as other choral organizations, including the Choristers Guild, the Organization of American Kodály Educators, the American Orff Schulwerk Association, and the Music Educators National Conference throughout the 1980s and 1990s, resulted in significant changes within the profession.

An increased number of community children's choirs were rapidly being established across the country. The number of music publishers printing treble music of high quality also increased. Recordings of American children's choirs on cassette tapes transitioned to compact discs and became more readily available. More articles were being published on the topic of children's choirs in professional journals such as *Music Educators Journal*, *Choral Journal*, and the Kodály *Envoy*, among others. The number of children's choir performances increased at professional conferences. The first performance of American children's choirs at Carnegie Hall was held in 1990.[8] (This performance also included two Canadian children's choirs and a children's choir from Finland.) The first research and poster session at an ACDA national convention was devoted to the topic of children's choirs. The number of commissions for new works written for children's choirs increased. Performances of American children's choirs began to be heard on National Public Radio's *Performance Today* and *The First Art*. Children's choirs increasingly began to tour nationally and internationally. The first ACDA national honors children's choir, and the first International Society of Music Education world honors children's choir in which the ACDA national honors children's choir participated, were held in the United States, and domestic children's choir choral festivals were established.

The state of the art of children's choirs, in its early history in ACDA, is documented in the March 1989 and March 1993 issues of the *Choral Journal* and the annual reports of the ACDA National Committee on Children's Choirs.[9] The ongoing work of the Organization of American Kodály Educators, the American Orff Schulwerk Association, and Helen Kemp's exemplary leadership in the Choristers Guild also contributed to the growing interest in young singers in school, church, and community contexts.

THE CHALLENGES OF A GROWING PROGRAM

SCC was founded through the Syracuse University School of Music preparatory division, which handled all the financial matters. Between 1981 and 1987, the chorus carefully planned its growth from one choir to three choirs. As the chorus grew, the time requirements of the university staff for handling the increased amount of administrative work for the children's chorus also grew. It became apparent that the chorus needed to establish its own 501(c)(3) nonprofit corporation, thus removing this extra burden of work for the university staff members. With the encouragement and full support of the university, a board of directors was formed by the chorus, and nonprofit status was applied for and received in 1988. SCC has remained in residence at the university for over thirty years. By 2003, the university music education program added an elective course, Practicum in Children's Choirs. University music education and music industry students, respectively, became conducting interns and completed semester-long internships with the children's chorus.

EARLY COMMITMENT OF THE NEA FOR CHILDREN'S CHOIRS

In 1995, SCC had the privilege of being the only children's choir to participate in the two-year National Endowment for the Arts (NEA) Advancement Program, which ran from 1980 to 1996. The Advancement Program was established to provide assistance in strategic planning for arts organizations. It guided organizations in articulating their hopes and dreams for the future by creating a formal plan to achieve stated goals. The Chicago Children's Choir and the San Francisco Girls Chorus were the only children's choirs that had participated in this program prior to that time. Only a few children's choirs had received NEA support. Although the Advancement Program no longer exists in its original format, the NEA's support for the work of children's choirs increased in the years to come as children's choirs grew in number throughout the country and became instruments of artistic excellence.

Phase I of the NEA advancement process provided two types of assistance to developing arts organizations—*planning assistance* and *technical assistance*. The goal of planning assistance was to "optimize their organization's future while better realizing their artistic vision" by strengthening the organization's identity and developing a multi-year plan to accomplish this.[10] Technical assistance included enhancing operational skills in program development, staffing board/volunteer development, marketing, fundraising, and financial and facilities management, among other topics unique to each organization.[11]

Participation in the Advancement Program activated the process of gathering data about our organization. All our subsequent strategic planning discussions were based on knowledge drawn from the gathered data, rather than by perception and anecdotal information. The Organizational Self-Assessment Checklist, still available on the NEA website, provides arts organizations with an effective and detailed tool for self-analysis.[12] The Self-Assessment Checklist includes the following categories: organizational purpose, programs, governance, staff, marketing, public/community relations, fundraising, financial management, facilities, planning, communication/decision-making, external environment, and space for final comments.

Phase II of the NEA Advancement Program was devoted to taking the data gathered in Phase I and developing a strategic plan for the organization that would shape a strong future for solid growth and stability. With the supervision of the NEA and a consultant, the advancement process allowed SCC to formalize and refine much of what it was already doing. The process helped the board and staff look at the organization, gather data, and make informed choices about the future based on knowledge and guidance from a professional consultant. It provided an opportunity to develop goals for growth and stability on the administrative side of the organization to support the ongoing artistic work.

The NEA advancement process influenced how SCC strategically planned the future of the chorus for many years. The critical data gathered at any time during the life of a choir informs choices for the future. Knowing the data about one's choir, often with surprises and unexpected knowledge, informs the choices one makes as the chorus moves into the future.

ALTERNATE WAYS OF STARTING A CHOIR

Not every choir begins with the goal of founding a new organization. Sometimes a choir grows organically from a special project. A children's choir may be formed to participate with an adult chorus for the performance of a major orchestral work such as Orff's *Carmina Burana*, Mahler's Symphony No. 3 or Symphony No. 8, or Britten's *War Requiem*, each of which requires a boys' or children's choir. Many children's choirs have been formed for such a purpose and become a permanent ensemble following the event.

Often a district-wide select children's choir begins in a public school district where a director forms an after-school children's choir consisting of talented singers auditioned from the elementary and middle schools. These choirs often attend festivals in and out of state and tour, depending on the financial resources of the school district, parents, and community. Other school choirs invite guest conductors for special concerts, district festivals, or anniversary events.

Church children's choir festivals are often held, combining several choirs for a special service or hymn-sing event. Ecumenical choral festivals are also held. Children's choirs may be formed for a one-time special event, such as singing for the Olympic Games opening and closing ceremonies. Home-schooled students often gather to form a choir of exclusively home-schooled students. These typically are divided into elementary, middle school, and high school choirs, and often grow to include band or orchestra components. Colleges and universities across the country also provide a home for children's choirs. Some choirs exist "in cooperation with" a university, and others are formally part of a music department, school, preparatory division, outreach program, or community music school.

Syracuse University was one of the first universities in the country to found a children's choir. Other universities with children's choirs in residence include University of Cincinnati College-Conservatory of Music (Ohio), Peabody Conservatory (Maryland), Stetson University (Florida), Florida State University, Belmont University (Tennessee), Temple University (Pennsylvania), Indiana University, Michigan State University, Duquesne University (Pennsylvania), Meredith College (North Carolina), University of Hartford (Connecticut), Eastern Mennonite University (Virginia), Clayton State University (Georgia), and Butler University (Indiana). These names represent some of the many children's choirs in residence at colleges and universities across the country.

PLAN, PLAN, PLAN

Initially, it is important to have a well-articulated statement about the kind of choir you wish to start. There must be a strong reason for the choir to exist. Comprehensive data should be gathered before plans are formalized. The following questions need to be addressed:

- What are the resources you have to assist with the formation of the choir?
- What will be your competition within your community?
- What geographic location will the singers come from?
- Will the choir be advertised on the web, in social media, or in local papers?
- Will there be a website and, if so, what is the timeline for launching the website? Who will design the webpage?
- What will be the age range of the choir?
- Will there be one, two, or more choirs with varying abilities and age levels?
- Will a program for children aged five to seven be included?
- Will the number of singers be limited?
- Will the choir start with young singers only, and will the age limit be raised as the singers mature?
- Will the choir include only unchanged (treble) voices?
- How many singers will be needed to have "enough" to start?

Well-thought-out answers to these questions will assist when you articulate to others (e.g., administrators, parents, music teachers, community members, potential funders) why your choir will exist. The ability to speak clearly about the type of choir and its goals will be the beginning of a mission statement. (Mission statements are discussed in detail in chapter 3.) Once you have answered these questions, a new set of questions begins to emerge.

THE REHEARSAL FACILITIES

The topic of rehearsal location generates its own set of important questions:

- What are possible rehearsal locations: church, school, community center, local area Y (formerly YMCA), local college, or university?
- Will there be adequate heat and air conditioning?
- Is the space clean?
- Is the space adequately lighted?
- Are there enough chairs or bench seats? If chairs are to be used, do they encourage correct singing posture?

- Is there a piano? Is it tuned regularly?
- Are there music stands available?
- Is there a blackboard, whiteboard, or media screen available to use for instructional purposes?
- Are there additional rooms for sectional rehearsals, if needed?
- Is there a drinking fountain nearby, and are restrooms adequate and convenient to the rehearsal space?
- Are arrival and dismissal easy and safe for the students?
- Is the outdoor area adequately lighted if rehearsals are to be held at night?

When dealing with a children's choir, these questions are important. The kind of rehearsal space, the lighting, the ventilation, the chairs, the acoustics, and the quality of the piano and its tuning have much to do with the learning environment and success of each rehearsal.

SCC rehearses in the Rose, Jules R. and Stanford S. Setnor Auditorium in Crouse College at Syracuse University. The building was built in 1889 and is the home of the first College of Fine Arts in the United States. Choristers sit on folding chairs on the stage of the 735-seat Romanesque auditorium with stained-glass windows and an elaborate, carved hardwood interior. The stage has two Steinway concert grand pianos and a historic Holtcamp organ console with 3,823 visible pipes as a backdrop.[13] Stairs to the stage are located on either side. Surrounded by a carved woodwork interior and a seventy-foot-tall ceiling, the hall's bright acoustics provide a resonant and inspiring space in which to sing.

The challenges of the space include the following: There is no clock, no whiteboard or blackboard, and no air-conditioning; folding chairs must be set up and taken down for every rehearsal; and stairs must be accessed to get to the stage. (Historic buildings are not always wheelchair-accessible. A handicapped entrance, elevator, and lift for stage access have since been made available.)

No rehearsal space is perfect. Finding a space that adequately suits the choir's needs is important. Possible rehearsal venues might be a church basement or choir room, a school gym (sometimes with very good acoustics), a school cafeteria or rehearsal room, a recreation center, or a choral rehearsal room designed specifically for choirs with chairs on risers and vacant floor space to facilitate movement or rehearsing in circles. Some of the finest choirs in the world rehearse in the least elegant settings. What matters most are the conductor, the choir, and the strong commitment to making music.

QUESTIONS ABOUT FINANCIAL MATTERS

Financial planning should be part of the initial process at the time of formation of a new choir. Some of the questions to be answered include:

- How will the choir be funded the first year? Tuition? Ticket sales?

- Will the choir be eligible for start-up funding, grants, gifts, or in-kind donations?
- What will the choir expenses be?
- Will the director have a stipend, honorarium, or salary?
- Will the choir have an administrator or volunteer to assist the founder?
- Will the music director do all the start-up work?
- Who will accompany the choir? How will the accompanist be paid? Will the accompanist be a student, professional accompanist, or volunteer?
- How will the choir fund the purchase of music?
- How will ads and mailings (stationery, postage, and printing) be funded?
- How will the webpage be funded?
- What will be donated, and what will be actual costs?
- Will there be money designated for scholarships if tuition is charged?
- What is the cost of the rehearsal space?
- Will there be a designated phone line or cell phone for the choir?
- Will the choir have a logo? Who will design the logo? Will it be done pro bono, or will the choir have to pay for the cost of design?

In the first year of SCC, the choir began with one ensemble of fifty singers and a budget of $5,000, which was raised as tuition fees. Rehearsal space, stationery, postage, and an accompanist were provided in kind by the university's preparatory division. The director's honorarium and music came from tuition income. A former art teacher colleague donated the design of the new choir's logo. The local Kiwanis Club provided T-shirts (with the new logo) that were presented to the choristers at the first rehearsal. Volunteer parents secured donors to help with the cost of fabric for concert dress skirts, ties for the boys, and ribbon for the girls' shirt collars. A local fabric store assisted with the purchase of fabric at cost, parent volunteers made the concert dress skirts for the girls, and shirts were ordered by parents directly from a readily available department store catalog.

The choir grew over time to four levels with three full-time staff (two administrative and one artistic), two part-time directors, three accompanists, and a significantly higher budget. The growth of the choir was carefully planned and intentional. With the organization's growth, the budget also grew steadily each year. (Chapter 5 discusses financial matters in depth.)

A TIMELINE—PUTTING THE DREAM ON PAPER

Timelines are invaluable for any major undertaking. Before beginning the formation of the new choir, set a tentative timeline for the events. Begin with daily, weekly, monthly, three-month, six-month, eighteen-month, and two-year goals. Life is not always predictable, of course, and there will always be events that cause the timeline to be adjusted. However, maintaining a strong commitment to staying on track can go a long way to allowing an organization to go from an idea to reality. A timeline allows for awareness of upcoming deadlines, advance planning, and staying on top of details to avoid last-minute panic.

SURROUND YOURSELF WITH COMPETENCE

It is easy to personally assume responsibility for every detail of a new choir. If you are the founder of a community-based children's or youth choir, it is your vision that creates the new organization, and your passion for the project inspires others to become involved. As the organization grows, others may assume responsibility for many of the organizational details. Work may initially be done by volunteers or, when appropriate, paid staff. Learn to delegate. Surround yourself with competent people. Effective staff members enable an artistic director to concentrate on artistic matters.

Administrators collaborate and support the work of the music director, giving the director the freedom to be creative and do the important work of score study, rehearsal preparation, research, and visionary and artistic work. Board members collaboratively support the work of the artistic and administrative staff to allow them to thrive. The more competent the administrative staff and board members are, the stronger the organizational support will be for the choir. The choir will be the beneficiary of a positive atmosphere surrounding its work.

COLLABORATION

A strong mission statement and set of beliefs, values, and goals should be created by the board, artistic staff, and administrative staff. These inform all decisions the organization makes. A choir is strongest when the collaborative spirit pervades every aspect of it. A clear understanding of the organization's mission and responsibilities, coupled with an organized and systematic approach to every detail, will provide a strong framework to allow the choir to thrive. Is this idealistic? Absolutely. Can it happen? The answer is a resounding YES. (More information about mission statements, values, and beliefs is presented in chapter 3.)

THE FIVE-YEAR RULE

The same colleague who approved, supported, and announced the formation of SCC at Syracuse University advised me that it would take five years to establish the chorus. For one who was young and eager, this was disappointing to hear. In reality, this advice was correct. It takes five years for a choir to establish itself and settle into its true identity. The years that follow the founding are about possibilities and sustainability.

CONCLUSION

A well-thought-out plan based on research and carefully articulated goals can bring a choir from dream to reality. This may occur in a school, church, or community context. Having a vision of who the singers will be, where and what they will sing, and a concept of the ideal choral sound will begin the successful journey. Knowing why the choir exists, planning how to sustain it, and striving for excellence are important. Excitement about a new children's choir must be contagious. Others must become excited about what is going to happen and understand that they will be joining in the creation of something wonderful and new. There are many questions that will emerge. A systematic plan has everything to do with how well the choir will succeed. Progress happens one day, one event, and one conversation at a time.

Starting or expanding an existing choral program is a collaborative effort. Singing in a choir is the essence of collaboration. One singer cannot do it without others. The staff, parents, board, and community are also part of the collaboration. The purity, innocence, and ringing tones of a children's choir are unlike any other sound in the world of musical performance. What a joyful thing it is to spend time with bright and talented young artists in the creation of beauty and pursuit of excellence. It is worth every challenge one encounters.

The ultimate test is right action.
—PETER F. DRUCKER

2

ORGANIZATIONAL STRUCTURE

A FRIEND ONCE told a story about loading horses onto trailers. Frequently, horses are reluctant to step onto the trailer ramps. Each horse has its own way of getting up the ramp. One is encouraged by the reward of a carrot. Another needs to walk in a circle twice before walking up the ramp. Another needs to be dragged by the reins. Another has to be pushed from the rear. Another has to be walked around the entire trailer before walking up the ramp. Others need blinders.

People are often like horses. They have different ages, personalities, backgrounds, and ways of thinking. An organization's leader has the responsibility to get all the people who make up the organization focused on the goal (i.e., to get all the horses loaded onto the trailer so that it can proceed to its destination). How well this is accomplished matters.

Since the early 1980s, we have seen the number of community-based children's choirs grow by staggering numbers. Currently, children's choirs exist throughout the country from small communities to major metropolitan areas. These choirs must have strong structures to support the important work of education, musicianship, and artistry in school, church, or community contexts. Throughout the existence of the chorus, it is important to get people on board and keep everyone focused on the organization's mission. Choral music education for our children is a direct link to cultural understanding and appreciation of diversity. As we enter a time in our country's history of unsurpassed access to world cultures, world music, and social media, we witness the power of music to bring cultures together. Our schools reflect the cultural diversity of our population, and singing unites children in a unique way.

In an era when music education programs in the schools are once again threatened by budget cuts and downsizing of program offerings, as in the 1970s, the sustainability of these choirs is extremely important for providing choral music education opportunities for *all* children. We must emphatically encourage the preservation of our cultural heritage, experience the music of other cultures, and educate our children in the broad liberal arts. Choirs must have the support of strong organizational structures to maintain their work in schools, churches, and communities.

From Chorus America's 2009 *Chorus Impact Study*, there are data to support the case for children's choirs in school, church, and community contexts. We know that, of a conservatively estimated 42.6 million people who regularly sing in choruses, 10.1 million are children. There are at least 41,000 school choruses.[1] From this study, we also know the following:

- Children who sing in choruses have academic success and valuable life skills.
- Children who sing in choruses get significantly better grades.
- Parents of children sing who in choirs are significantly more likely to report that their children have many other qualities conducive to learning and development. These include good memory, good practice and homework habits, and high levels of creativity.
- Parents of children who sing in choirs are significantly and consistently more likely to report that their children are better team players and have more advanced social skills than those who have never sung in a choir.
- Educators are emphatic about the positive role that choirs play in childhood development and education.
- Most educators believe that choirs help schools and communities in a variety of other ways, including keeping some students engaged in school who might otherwise be lost.[2]

Although there is much more to be learned, the study gives us an idea of how many people sing, the importance of singing in our culture, and the critical importance of maintaining strong choral programs for children in schools, churches, and communities across the United States. More children should have the opportunity to experience singing. Regardless of the type of children's choir, choral programs must be sustained. How they are organized matters.

For many choirs, music was what the founder, music educator, church musician, or artistic director studied in college. Music performance, church music, or music education degrees rarely include instruction about organizational management, promotion, revenue streams, ticketing, media, and boards of directors. Music industry and a growing number of arts management programs at universities across the country now graduate musicians trained in the business management of nonprofit and for-profit music organizations.

For the performer, educator, or church musician, management matters must be understood in order to be an effective leader in a community-based nonprofit organization. Out of necessity to sustain our choirs and our art, we become entrepreneurs. The more we understand how nonprofit organizations function, the stronger we become in leading our organizations collaboratively. The models presented here are primarily from one choir; they are not the only way of structuring an organization. What works in the context of a community-based choir may or may not work in a church choir or school context. For example, fundraising may not be necessary for a school choir or a choir under the auspices of a community center or church.

This chapter will include discussion of incorporation, nonprofit designation, bylaws, the structure of a board of directors, agendas, committees, and other management topics.

INCORPORATION

For a community-based children's or youth choir, there are advantages to incorporating. As a nonprofit organization with its own governing board, an organization may chart its own future. It does not have to rely on those outside the choir to make decisions about its program. The choir has the freedom and opportunity to expand the program offerings if it so chooses. The choir is free to apply for grants and seek funding and support from others without asking permission to do so from the umbrella organization. If structured properly, the stability of the nonprofit organization provides a strong framework for the choir. Choirs are not required to incorporate, but it is wise to do so.

Some children's choirs may choose not to incorporate. The choir may fall under the auspices of an existing nonprofit organization, such as an adult volunteer choir, community choir, or professional choir. Other choirs may be part of a school, government-sponsored community center, nonprofit organization, or church. Some choirs will not fall under the auspices of an organization and determine not to incorporate. The founder will determine the best course of action in consultation with others.

If incorporation is the chosen path, the founder and new choir's board of directors will make decisions about how to proceed. Each state has its own laws regarding incorporation. When applying to establish a nonprofit organization, it is wise to work with an attorney familiar with state corporation law. An attorney may be hired, or these services may be donated by an attorney who is supportive of the new choir. For incorporation, articles of incorporation, bylaws, officers, and a statement of purpose for the new organization will be required. Many attorneys will have a booklet or kit of materials to assist with the process. Resources are also available online.

A viable mission statement or statement of purpose is a necessary component of the organization's articles of incorporation (for state filing) and for the tax-exemption application process (for both federal and state purposes). Great care should be taken to ensure that the organization's operations are consistent with the mission statement as reported to these governmental agencies. The organization's tax-exempt status can be jeopardized if actual operations are different from what is reported to the Internal Revenue Service or state agency. The mission may be modified, and goals and activities may be altered to accommodate changing times and conditions. Should this occur, the authorizing governmental agencies must be informed of any changes. This is usually done when the organization's annual tax return is submitted.

At the time of incorporation, it will be necessary to have written bylaws that will be approved by the state.

BYLAWS

It is common for a choir to begin with four officers—president, vice president, secretary, and treasurer. Basic bylaws may be written with the guidance of an attorney. Appropriate papers are filed with the government as required by state law. The four officers are named and sign the original papers of incorporation. Once the nonprofit status is approved, the chorus is officially founded.

Bylaws should specify term limits, officers, annual meeting dates, monthly board meeting dates, how communications will be handled, committee structure, voting (what constitutes a quorum), fiscal policies, amendments, and the date when the bylaws were approved and became effective. They may also state that use of the term "he" is gender-neutral throughout.

The original bylaws for a choir should be broad and not overly detailed. They should contain enough detail to give structure to the beginning organization, but should be broad enough to allow for the growth of the choir without the necessity of frequent changes to them. (See appendix 2.1 for a sample set of bylaws.)

Bylaws should be periodically reviewed and revised. Any revision to the bylaws should be taken very seriously. It may be advisable to make the bylaws difficult to change, to keep them short, to keep them broad so they will last, and to be flexible enough to allow for growth. There are many websites and professional organizations that offer information about how to construct bylaws. Chorus America also offers valuable assistance. Looking at several choral organizations' bylaws before writing your own is also helpful.

Once the incorporation application process is completed and approved, an Employer Identification Number (EIN) will be issued by the Internal Revenue Service. A separate tax ID number may also be assigned to the organization by the state. The choir is officially founded. The next step is to apply for the choir's federal tax-exempt status, as defined under Section 501(c)(3) of the Internal Revenue Code. When this is completed, the choir may apply for the state tax-exempt status, sometimes called charities registration.

Next, application should be made for state sales tax exemption and unemployment insurance. If proper legal procedures are followed, and nonprofit status is applied for and granted, the organization must continue to follow its mission statement, or intended purpose, as stated in its incorporation papers. Once the nonprofit incorporation is established, the appointment of a full board of directors follows.

STRUCTURE OF THE BOARD OF DIRECTORS

The selection of capable working members of the board is very important. The board of directors will look for people who are supportive of the mission of the chorus and its activities.

Serving on a board most often requires a financial commitment to the organization. Board members must attend meetings, serve on committees, work on special projects, attend concerts, and contribute financially. Board members must understand the chorus well and have a consistent message to share in each encounter with prospective donors, funders, and potential audience members. It is important that prospective board members understand these responsibilities before accepting the invitation to serve.

One of the committees of the board of directors will be the nominating committee, sometimes called the governance committee. It is the committee that is responsible for making recommendations of new members to the board of directors. When a member of the board of directors brings the recommendation for a potential new board member to the nominating committee, the process of getting to know the candidate begins. Questions to be asked include the following:

- Will the candidate be a good fit with the other board members?
- What skills, expertise, and community connections will the candidate provide?
- Will the candidate bring expertise that does not already exist on the board of directors?
- Does the candidate agree with the mission of the choir?
- Does the candidate understand the time commitment required?
- Does the candidate understand the financial commitment required?

Often the president of the board and the board member who recommended the candidate will invite the candidate out for lunch to get better acquainted and to explain the work of the chorus and the requirements of board service. The candidate may also be invited to be the guest of a board member at an upcoming concert. In the case of a candidate who is well known to several board members, he or she might be invited to attend a board meeting as a guest. As many board members as possible should get to know the candidate. Once the candidate has become familiar to the board and the nominating committee feels the candidate would be a good fit with the organization, the candidate's name is presented by the nominating committee to the full board of directors for approval. Once approved, the candidate is formally invited to join the board.

Candidates who are not willing to assume board responsibilities should not commit to the board. The appointment is not just a line on a résumé, but rather a strong commitment to the important work of the organization.

TYPES OF BOARD MEMBERS

There are three basic categories of board members: the board of directors, honorary board members, and advisory board members. Initially, a choir may begin with a small number of members of the board of directors who will be charged with overseeing the fiduciary responsibilities of the chorus.[3] Once incorporated, regular board meetings will be held, and the board of directors will begin to expand. Gradually, the number may increase to ten members or more and eventually will settle at the optimal size for the choral organization. Board members are not usually paid, and the number of board members may vary depending on the size and growth of the organization.

Advisory board members are those individuals who can be called upon from time to time to give advice to the organization, or to provide a special service. Advisory board members may include former board members, arts consultants, businesspeople, and community members of varying professions who willingly offer their support to the chorus. These people may offer special skills that are not needed on a regular basis, but who are willing to advise the choir occasionally. Advisory board members may or may not reside in the immediate vicinity of the chorus and do not attend regular board meetings or have any fiduciary responsibilities.

Later, when the chorus becomes more established, honorary board members may be appointed. Honorary board members are individuals who are recognized in the field of music at the national or international level and who graciously lend their names in support of the artistic work of the chorus (on the chorus's stationery and in concert programs, for example). These individuals may also be locally well-recognized individuals who support the work of the chorus. Honorary board members may include composers, educators, symphony orchestra conductors, professional singers, or other well-known individuals. They do not attend regular board meetings or have any fiduciary responsibilities.

All board members should be able to speak passionately about the choir regarding its artistic and educational work. With strong commitment, passion, and steadfast focus on the mission of the organization, these individuals will carry its name forward and provide support in many ways for the choir.

BOARD EXPERTISE

The professional background of each member should be considered. Although the board of directors' responsibility is primarily fiduciary, the occupations of board members may assist the nonprofit organization in many ways. In addition, a board member with prior board experience may be an asset to the organization.

Board members of a nonprofit organization have fiduciary responsibility for the organization and are not personally liable. Liability insurance coverage is available for directors and officers. Most board members will require this insurance coverage to be in place before they agree to serve on a board of directors. (See the section on insurance matters found later in this chapter.)

It is advisable to have the board of directors include people with varied professional backgrounds. The board may include attorneys, insurance professionals, accountants, professional musicians, bankers, educators, media specialists, sales and marketing professionals, advertising executives, and others. In some choirs, the board is intentionally not made up of a majority of parents or musicians. Parents cannot be expected to always be objective if their own children are in the choir. A board that includes a significant number of musicians is not as likely to bring the varied business expertise and breadth of community connections in the for-profit sector that a chorus might find helpful.

The board size will vary depending on the size of the choral organization. Ideally, members of the board should bring a wealth of business experience and financial support. They also may have connections to people who can support the chorus. Board member duties are varied. For example, board members may approach businesses to become season sponsors, concert sponsors, or donors of services. They may open doors for board officers or staff to contact foundations that might be interested in funding the chorus. They may assist with advice on insurance matters, legal matters, financial matters, and arrange for special fundraising events. They may assist in finding vendors who will provide services pro bono or at a reduced cost. A loyal board member with a passion for children's singing and a willingness to serve can be a true asset to the choral organization.

As any volunteer board member knows, serving as a volunteer is often difficult work, and it may be time-consuming and sometimes challenging. That said, it is also very rewarding. Satisfaction can come to a board member when he or she attends a concert and is moved by the music-making or sees the smiling faces of the choristers who inspire the audience. A board member's gift of service to the chorus benefits everyone involved, and the satisfaction of volunteer work is often returned tenfold to those who give their time and talents.

INVITING A NEW BOARD MEMBER

The committee targeted with overseeing the appointment of members of the board of directors may be called the governance or nominating committee. Each year, this committee reviews the list of current members, determines how many new members will be added, and solicits possible recommendations from other board members.

The committee should seek people whose skills, connections, and abilities fill a specific need on the board. For example, if the nominating committee determines that the chorus needs a successful for-profit business owner who has connections to other local businesses and is a supporter of the arts, the chair may ask the full board for recommendations.

Initial contact of a prospective member is done by a board member or the board president. A conversation about possible interest in the organization ensues. An invitation may be extended to the candidate to attend a concert as the guest of a board member. A follow-up luncheon with the candidate, board president, or other board member may occur. A new board member questionnaire may be completed by the candidate, or a résumé may be requested if the person is not well known to members of the board. Following a get-acquainted period, if there is consensus among the nominating committee, the candidate's name is put before the full board of directors for discussion and approval.

This process may take several attempts. The timing may not be right at first for a prospective member. Commitments to other boards may preclude participation, or lack of time to make a definite commitment may be a consideration. Care of aging parents, a growing family, or increased work responsibilities may preclude service to the organization.

Sometimes a person will be appointed to a committee of the board as a non-board committee member. An example might be to work on an auction fundraiser for the choir or a special dinner event. Serving on a committee in this introductory capacity allows board members to get to know the person prior to their being considered for nomination to the full board.

The proposed board member must be a good match for the organization. Appointing the right person will facilitate smoother work of the board of directors. Getting to know a candidate well before appointment and mentoring a new member after appointment can serve the organization well. Each candidate will bring new expectations and abilities to the organization. A new person should understand what is expected before committing to serve on the board of directors.

MENTORING A NEW BOARD MEMBER

Once the candidate's appointment has been approved by the board of directors, the president should send a letter of welcome and invite the new member to attend the next scheduled full board meeting. A complete schedule of board meeting dates and concert dates should be included in this letter. At the first board meeting, the new member should be introduced and welcomed, and given a board handbook. The introduction will be appreciated by other board members who may not have met the new person prior to board affiliation. Board members should introduce themselves individually and briefly describe their work affiliations, and roles or years of service on the board. This allows the new member to become acquainted with the other colleagues.

CHORISTER REPRESENTATIVE TO THE BOARD

A unique ex-officio (nonvoting) member appointed to the SCC board of directors was a current chorister. The artistic director selected a bright, articulate, highly motivated chorister from the most advanced choir to attend the full board meeting each month to give a brief report. The chorister was appointed for one year (September to May) and was called the chorister representative.

Each month, the chorister representative attended the board meeting and read a brief report that gave the board insights into his or her experiences and those of fellow choristers. (See sample chorister reports in appendix 2.2.)

Board members could see and hear a child speak about the essence of his or her choral singing experiences: what is loved most about the choir, excitement about concerts, a favorite song, a fun rehearsal moment, new concert attire, speculation about an upcoming tour location, or the experience of working with the symphony orchestra or a guest composer-in-residence. It reminded the adult board members why they work so passionately for the organization. The visible smiles and nodding heads as the report was read each month confirmed the need for this important voice to have a brief and direct presence with the board. This experience increased the board's understanding, energy, and commitment. At the board's request, the one-year trial chorister appointment became permanent.

SELECTION OF THE CHORISTER REPRESENTATIVE

Each year, this appointment was offered to a chorister who had been in the choir for a minimum of four years and was a senior member in the most advanced choir. Criteria used to select the chorister representative included demonstrated commitment, motivation, artistry, responsibility, and leadership. After the summer chorister camp was held in August and once September rehearsals were well underway, the appointment was made in October each year. The decision about which chorister to select was made by the director of the most advanced choir in consultation with the full-time staff members who knew the choristers well. (More information about chorister camp is presented in chapter 6.)

One year, it was not clear who should assume the responsibility of chorister representative. There were several equally qualified and outstanding choristers, and it was a very difficult decision. The choristers were asked to write a brief statement about why they wanted the position. The chorister was selected based on this essay, as well as the previously stated criteria. Once it was determined who the representative would be, the chorister's parents were contacted to invite their child to assume this responsibility. Parent questions included the following:

- What would the time commitment be?
- What did this appointment involve?
- What was the scheduled time of meetings?
- If there was a test at school the day of a scheduled meeting, could the chorister miss a meeting?

After parents agreed to the meeting schedule and to provide transportation, the chorister representative was confirmed. Guidance about what kinds of topics the chorister might want to write about initially came from the director of the ensemble. Once the first report was given, the chorister representative was more familiar with the process and thereafter determined the topics for presentation at future meetings.

Occasionally, there were two chorister representatives appointed in the same year who would alternate months to accommodate rigorous school schedules. Each month, the board looked forward to hearing what it was like to be a singer in the chorus. An unexpected outcome was that board members could speak to community members and possible supporters about firsthand comments from a child who benefited directly from the choir experience. This process proved to be tremendously important. The strong message was coming directly from a participant.

Another unexpected outcome of this appointment came from the choir itself. It became an acknowledged honor within the choir each year for the chorister selected for the appointment. Choristers started setting a goal of being named to this position when they had achieved seniority. For those who served in this position, it was a strong leadership and volunteer credential for college applications.

When confidential matters were to be discussed at a board meeting, the chorister representatives would be asked to leave the meeting early. This would include such topics as confidential search committee reports, need-based scholarship discussions, and staff appointments for the coming year. Often the school schedule precipitated the chorister's leaving the meeting early. Choristers were present for agenda items such as the opening remarks, introductions of new board members, approval of the minutes, financial reports, and other select items depending on how long the chorister could remain. The chorister representative was learning not only about community service, but also about parliamentary procedure. A comment heard from a chorister representative following her first board of directors meeting was, "I had no idea there was so much to running the chorus that we never see."

WHEN A CHORISTER RETURNS AS A FULL BOARD MEMBER

The experience of serving as a chorister representative laid the foundation for future community service and leadership. Several years after the choir began appointing a chorister representative to the board of directors, one of the earliest appointees, now a college graduate and pharmaceuticals representative, was invited back to the choir to become a board member. The perspective and understanding she brought to the monthly meetings was invaluable because she understood the organization thoroughly.

Many skills learned in a children's choir serve the singers well in the future. The poised alumna of the choir who became a board member was asked to present a session for a very large group of people at a work-related conference. When her supervisor asked if she would be too nervous to do a presentation for such a large gathering of two-hundred people, she replied, "I sang in a solo group of ten with a choir of 2,000 in Vancouver, British Columbia, when I was young, so I think I'm okay talking to two-hundred."

REMOVAL OF AN INEFFECTIVE BOARD MEMBER

Removing a member from the board involuntarily is never an easy task. An example of one such case was that of a colleague of a board member who was looking for a community service opportunity required by his place of employment in banking. After attending a concert, he enthusiastically accepted the invitation to become a board member. At the beginning of his tenure, he appeared to be very excited about the organization. He and his wife were to have their first child soon after accepting the appointment. At the end of his first year on the board, he had attended only two board meetings, no concerts, and had not contributed financially or with volunteer time. Every time the board member assigned to mentor him called, he gave excuses for his lack of participation. His wife had unexpectedly given birth to twins. His mentor on the board of directors suggested that perhaps this was not the right time for him to make a commitment and perhaps serving at a future time would be better. The overwhelmed new father agreed to resign.

TERMS OF OFFICE

When establishing the first board of directors, it is important to define staggered terms of office so that all directors do not rotate off the board at the same time. By having one-third of the new board members appointed for a two-year term, one-third appointed for a three-year term, and one-third appointed for a four-year term at the time of incorporation, the natural rotation of the board will be established, thus preserving its stability.

TERM LIMITS

Establishing term limits in the bylaws is one way of guaranteeing the rotation of board members. By staggering the terms, you also encourage those with institutional knowledge and history to serve with newer members who bring fresh ideas and energy. For example, an organization may establish a three-year term for each person on the board of directors. This term might be renewed twice, for a maximum of nine consecutive years of service. At the end of each three-year term, the nominating committee reviews the commitment of each board member, discusses the person's willingness to continue, and invites his or her return, unless it determines he or she is not fulfilling the commitment and subsequently recommends the appointment not be renewed.

What happens when someone leaves the board before his or her tenure is completed? The procedure to handle an early departure should be detailed in the bylaws. The board of directors may invite a new person to fill a shorter appointment caused by the vacancy. The new board member would then be eligible to begin a full-term appointment with two possible additional terms. If this type of term limit is established, the bylaws should clearly state that no member of the board of directors may serve more than ten consecutive years. Each organization must decide what length of term is most appropriate. Not all organizations designate a three-year term for directors.

What happens when the board of directors wishes to retain a competent board member but that person's tenure is completed? In this case, a board member may take one year off, perhaps serving as an advisory member or assigned to a committee, and then may be invited back to the board of directors to begin a new tenure.

THE BOARD HANDBOOK

A board handbook is a very helpful tool for all current and new board members. The handbook may be in binder format with tabbed sections and may include the following:

- Contact information for all board members
- Contact information for staff members
- Schedule of meeting dates for the year
- Copy of the mission, beliefs, and values
- List of committees and their personnel
- List of board member terms of office and rotation
- Copy of the bylaws
- Minutes
- Agendas
- Financial statements
- The organizational chart
- A copy of the organization's strategic plan

Additional items might include a season concert brochure and a copy of the chorister handbook. The binder encourages members to keep their chorus materials well-organized and readily available.

CONFLICT-OF-INTEREST POLICY

All nonprofit organizations must have a conflict-of-interest policy as required by the Internal Revenue Service. Annually, each member of the board of directors of a nonprofit organization should receive a copy of the conflict-of-interest policy and sign a statement acknowledging that he or she has read, understands, and agrees with the terms and conditions outlined in it. The purpose of the conflict-of-interest policy is to protect the nonprofit organization's interest when it is contemplating entering into a transaction or arrangement that might benefit the private interest of an officer or director of the organization. (See appendix 2.3 for a copy of the Chorus America conflict-of-interest policy and statement.)

In addition to the conflict-of-interest policy, some states may require nonprofit organizations to have a whistleblower policy to provide a process for employees to resolve workplace concerns and disputes, including complaints of discrimination or harassment. (See appendix 2.4 for a copy of the Chorus America whistleblower policy.)

INSURANCE MATTERS

Once the organization has been established, discussion about insurance coverage will quickly ensue. The insurance committee of the board will review what various kinds of insurance will be necessary for the newly formed organization. Types of insurance may include the following:

- Liability for general operations
- Property coverage for office contents, supplies, equipment, wardrobe, and music library
- Personal injury
- Special coverage for travel and accident
- Officers' and directors' liability insurance
- Employee theft and dishonesty insurance
- Group medical insurance
- Workers compensation
- Unemployment insurance
- A life insurance policy for the director or other key staff members
- Health and dental insurance for staff

An organization may wish to seek the advice of an insurance professional who understands the industry well. This person will be able to advise the organization about appropriate coverage for the specific needs of the choir. An insurance professional will also be able to advise what is necessary or unnecessary, and when it is appropriate to add certain coverage as the organization grows.

If a choir is formed under the auspices of an existing program, such as a nonprofit adult volunteer or professional choir, symphony orchestra, parks and recreation program, school, or church, some insurance coverage may be available through the umbrella organization of the choir. It is important to be aware of the legal responsibilities and seek good counsel from experts.

BOARD MEETINGS AND AGENDAS

Board meetings typically occur once a month. They may be held early in the morning, in the afternoon, or in the evening. Early morning meetings that end by 9:00 A.M. allow members to depart for work or daily activities. Board members unable to attend because of out-of-town commitments may use conference calling via speaker phone, Skype, or videoconferencing, if available, to allow for full participation in meetings. In advance of the monthly meeting, agendas and copies of the minutes from the prior meeting are distributed by e-mail or first-class mail. This allows the members to prepare in advance for informed discussions of important matters. The agenda provides a systematic listing of topics to be discussed. (See appendix 2.5 for a sample board meeting agenda.)

Every committee does not need to give a report at each meeting. In this case, the chair of the committee (or appointed spokesperson for the committee if the chair is not present) indicates this.

For an organization with a small staff and a collaborative model, it may be advisable to have the full-time staff attend the board meetings. They may be asked to attend other committee meetings as needed, such as the development committee. The administrative staff members are the experts in the day-to-day work of the choir and answer to the managing artistic director or to the board of directors, depending on the organizational structure. With both artistic and management personnel present, the board has quick access to accurate data to supplement the written reports from the staff, if needed, during meetings. The staff is requested to leave when the board goes into executive session for matters that are inappropriate for them to hear or discuss. Examples of this might be discussions about personnel, salaries, performance reviews, or artistic director transitions. The collaborative practice of having the full staff present for board meetings may serve the organization well.

The daily work of the choral organization is executed through a strong collaborative model between artistic and administrative staff and board. All staff must work together toward the same goal with the choristers' best interests at the center of the decision-making. Allowing the full-time staff to attend the board meetings reinforces the collaborative relationship of the chorus at all levels. When a choir rehearses in a circle, the singers learn everyone is equal in creating a focused choral sound. Rehearsals are a collaborative process among singers, accompanist, and conductor. Similarly, the staff works collaboratively with the artistic director. For small organizations, the staff has a strong involvement with the organization and ideally is committed to helping the organization strive for excellence in all musical and nonmusical matters.

The collaborative nature of an organization further reinforces a transparent organization, where everyone has a voice, and carries a responsibility to honor the chorus's beliefs and values. All participants work together to accomplish the articulated goals.

A collaborative model shows how strong leadership coupled with a collaborative management style works. It allows staff members to make commitments to the organization that go beyond having an ordinary job. It allows them to be given responsibilities for their own successes by challenging and demonstrating their creative abilities. Collaborative models exist in many exemplary organizations throughout the country in school, church, and community children's choirs.

COMMITTEES AND AGENDAS

Various committees, each with a different focus, will be established by the board of directors. The committees should be defined in the bylaws. Ad-hoc committees may be added as needed. Larger boards of directors may have an active executive committee. Having an executive committee, and how often it will meet, is usually determined by the president of the board or defined in the bylaws. The executive committee meets in advance of full board meetings to make recommendations about various ongoing matters and to set the agenda for the upcoming meeting.

The finance committee regularly reviews the budget and financial statements, and oversees preparation of the budget for each new fiscal year. The treasurer's report often complements the finance committee report, as the treasurer should be well-versed on the status of the budget and financial reports. The treasurer will often make recommendations to the finance committee for its consideration. Such advice might pertain to cash-flow analysis, purchasing versus renting a copier, or oversight of a quarterly tax report being submitted to the IRS. After discussing any issues, the finance committee will make recommendations to the full board.

The personnel committee oversees all matters pertaining to the paid staff. This includes making recommendations for salaries, making sure all staff positions are filled, reviewing benefits, assisting when vacancies occur, and any other issues that may arise.

The development committee oversees the fundraising efforts of the board with the assistance of the chorus staff, who provide support materials as requested. Financial goals and timelines are set by this committee and the board each year, and the creative planning to accomplish these fundraising goals comes from this committee also.

Committees may include board members and non-board members. A non-board member may have a particular skill or wish to become involved with a particular project as a volunteer. Sometimes this is the beginning of a demonstrated relationship with the organization that indicates a strong commitment to its mission. This commitment may lead to an invitation to become a full board member in the future.

The founding director may or may not initially be a member of the board of directors at the time of incorporation. As the organization begins formal operations, the founding music director should quickly transition away from being a board member to his or her assigned position within the organization, as managing artistic director or artistic director. Once the board of directors expands, an executive committee may become operational.

APPRECIATION FOR BOARD SERVICE

The work of the board members should be acknowledged. Often a quick thank-you phone call from the board president for a special effort, a compliment in passing at a meeting, or a handwritten thank-you note, sent on a postcard or stationery, will be most appreciated by the recipient. Efforts beyond the gesture of a quick e-mail are noticed.

BOARD RESOURCES

Many resources are available to assist nonprofit children's or youth choirs in working with boards of directors. Chorus America provides strong organizational support specific to children's and youth choirs through their research, publications, annual national conferences, and extensive member services. Their publications "Leading the Successful Chorus: A Guide for Management, Board Members, and Music Directors" and "The Chorus Leadership Guide" are important resources for beginning choirs, as well as for those that are restructuring, expanding, or re-energizing their choirs.

An important non-choral resource is Board Source, which provides workshops, conferences, online webinars, training, assessment tools, print resources, and information about current and best practices for all types of nonprofit organizations.[4] Two of the many resources available from Board Source are "The Nonprofit Board Answer Book" and "The Handbook of Nonprofit Governance." The Carver Center and ASAE-The Center for Association Leadership are two additional resources for governance matters.

CONCLUSION

Gathering a community of people to collaborate in the formation of a new choir is only the beginning. A conductor-teacher may choose to found an independent nonprofit organization that will provide enrichment for those already participating in school programs where they exist, or for those who have no music education programs in school. In all instances, establishing a nonprofit organization requires great dedication and a willingness to oversee the many details involved in creating a musical structure that will thrive. The next chapter continues the discussion of nonprofit organizational structure and support.

> *We cannot predict the future. But we can create it.*
> —JIM COLLINS AND MORTEN T. HANSEN

3

BEYOND THE BOARD

WHETHER A NEW choir will be successful and able to sustain its music-making over many years is an unknown, just as predicting what will happen tomorrow is not possible. How well a choir creates its future will be based on how it negotiates one day, one board meeting, one rehearsal, or one concert at a time.

The previous chapter dealt with creating the framework for the organization. This includes matters of incorporation, establishing the choral organization's structure as set forth in its bylaws, and appointing a board of directors. Once established, the strength of the new choir and its sustainability will be based on its artistry and how it will create the future through strong organizational planning. This chapter is an overview of matters beyond the initial framework. Topics include creating a mission statement, beliefs, and values; the challenges of a growing program; staffing; strategic planning; and other organizational matters. As with striving for excellence in musical matters, striving for excellence in organizational matters is equally important at every stage of development, whether the chorus is a newly formed or a growing organization.

THE ORGANIZATIONAL CHART

Clear lines of communication and a defined understanding of duties, responsibilities, and authorities for each staff member are important to the success of the newly formed choral organization. An organizational chart provides a quick and visual understanding of the various components of the organization and how the lines of responsibility and communication flow. With graphic presentation, the boxes or circles delineate who is responsible to whom. Ultimately, of course, someone has to be responsible for final decisions in all matters.

Key elements of an organizational chart may include the board of directors, the artistic director (or managing artistic director), assistant directors, administrative staff members, accompanist(s), and the choir. The chart may also include volunteers, an advisory committee, or a parent organization. Not all choirs will have each of these categories, depending on the size of the organization and how extensive the program offerings are. (Sample organizational charts may be found in appendix 3.1.)

A choir may have several versions of the organizational chart as the choir expands from one choir to include several choirs of various ages or levels, and as the staff number increases. Eventually, the organization may grow to include several staff members, both artistic and administrative. With each growth phase, the organizational chart will change.

MISSION, BELIEFS, VALUES, AND GOALS

Organizational structure provides a framework for the choir. Developing a mission statement, a set of beliefs, values, and specific goals for the choir is tremendously important to define the organization to the world, to guide all aspects of the program, to guide decisions about the choristers, and to give parents a broad understanding of the organization in which their children participate. Again, you must know who you are, why you exist, and what you do best. A viable mission statement is also a legal necessity for nonprofit organizations, as required by both the state and federal governments. Nonprofit organizations must reflect their mission statements in their actions and report to the government what they actually do.

Keeping the mission statement conspicuous is important. Post it in the chorus office. Read it at board meetings. Print it in programs, on the website, in newsletters, and on the chorus stationery. Revisit the mission statement periodically to see if it still well serves the organization.

Preparing value and beliefs statements provides an opportunity to focus on the *who*, the *what*, and the *why*. Preparing these statements is a difficult task but essential to the core mission of the organization. This work defines to the public how you will function, and what motivates the decisions made by those who lead the organization. The process is initiated by gathering key personnel to formulate a statement about the organization. It is a document that shapes the organization in very important ways. Everyone should understand all aspects of the organization. A consultant can assist greatly when preparing the mission statement, set of beliefs, values, and developing a strategic plan for the future of organization.

STRATEGIC PLANNING: CREATING THE MISSION, BELIEFS, AND VALUES

> *The future is not some place we are going to, but one we are creating. The paths to it are not found but created, and the activity of making them changes both the maker and the destination.*
>
> —JOHN H. SCHAAR

Strategic plans help an organization focus on short-term and long-term goals: the big picture. With the numerous layers of activity in a children's choir, there are few moments when you have an opportunity to reflect on what your goals are for the next five years. It is easy to be involved with the day-to-day events, next concert, next rehearsal, next tour, next season's planning, or next fundraiser, and sideline the long-term goals. Strategic planning affords the luxury of looking at all aspects of the organization, assessing the current status, and envisioning the future with a detailed plan and timetable for specific goals to be achieved.

Strategic planning further allows the organization to examine what it does from the inside out. Gathering data from an audience survey may provide useful information about how patrons view ease of access and preferred concert venues, parking, or ticket purchase. Choristers and parents may be asked about what they like best about participation in the choir. By collecting data, the choir may discover that its assumptions about what people think about the organization differ from what they actually perceive. Sometimes there are surprises that help inform decisions for future planning in important ways.

By establishing a realistic plan for specific projects and targeted goals, you are reminded often to document progress, monitor work toward stated goals, and move the organization forward in a systematic, well-planned manner. Some organizations may create a one-year plan, two-year plan, or five-year plan, depending on the size of the organization or level of activity. Others may create an eighteen-month plan with three-month, six-month, and twelve-month benchmarks to assess progress. Regardless of the size of the organization, it is important to keep the big picture in mind. In addition, your organization should always strive to remain vital, current, and aware of trends in society and the marketplace. Management expert Jim Collins states: "Enduring great companies preserve their core values and purpose while their business strategies and operating practices endlessly adapt to a changing world. This is the magical combination of 'preserve the core and stimulate the progress.'"[1]

A STRATEGIC PLANNING RETREAT

Strategic planning can be accomplished during a weekend retreat or during several consecutive weekly sessions. Hiring a professional consultant is advised. Experts who work with arts organizations regularly contribute a wealth of knowledge, resources, current trends, and data that can assist your organization in the process of preparing an effective strategic plan. The professional consultant is an outside voice with no strings attached to the organization, and he or she can be an objective sounding board. By learning about the organization from materials requested in advance and interviewing staff and board members before a scheduled retreat, the professional comes to the process with a strong background about the organization. A strategic planning retreat may accomplish the following:

- Create or revise the mission statement.
- Create a list of what the organization values.
- Create a list of what the organization believes.
- Create a list of specific goals for a specified time (six months, twelve months, twenty-four months, etc.).

Sample questions to ask might include the following:

- What do we do well?
- What can we do better?
- Where do we want to be six months from now?
- Where do we want to be one year, two years, or five years from now?
- Whom do we serve?
- Do we want to change whom we serve?
- Is there an interest and talent pool that is sufficient enough for us to exist and grow?
- What do we want to change? And how will we do it?
- What impact will changes have on our organization?
- Who are our competitors?

The list of potential questions will come from within the organization. Participants may be asked to suspend their beliefs and disbeliefs for the duration of the retreat. Participants should be encouraged to listen with an open and creative mind. The atmosphere should be one of trust and openness, where ideas may be presented freely and candidly. Sometimes, issues are difficult to initiate or discuss, but they should be addressed. Ideas should be considered and evaluated in the context of what is important to the organization.

Retreats are often difficult work. Sometimes, not all the work is accomplished within the allotted time, and follow-up meetings may be needed. There may be homework assignments for specific individuals. Thoroughly evaluating an organization and envisioning its future requires the work of an honest and dedicated group of people. Some ideas will be kept, and some will be discarded.

The creation of well-articulated and specific goals for the organization gives everyone focus and a sense of purpose. Instead of always reacting, board and staff become proactive while working toward agreed-upon goals. Progress can be measured periodically. Successful accomplishment of specified goals makes people realize that they have achieved something important.

DEVELOPING THE MISSION STATEMENT

A mission statement should be short, concise, and articulate. It should reflect who you are as an organization and give the essence of what you do and why you do it. Creating a concise mission statement is a challenge. It must specify the salient points that you want people to know. There are many printed and online resources that can assist. For some, working with a consultant proves to be the most focused and efficient approach.

It could take years for everyone to agree. By working first to agree on the essence of what the organization is, you can begin to put thoughts into a well-articulated, concise statement. Many children's choir mission statements may be found online. At the time of writing, this was the mission statement for SCC:

> The Syracuse Children's Chorus creates collaborative experiences in which young people share their joy of singing, develop their sense of beauty, and deepen their commitment to excellence through choral music education and performance.

The first mission statement was several sentences long. This was not effective in a short conversation. No one could remember it. In an era of short video clips and sound bites, the essence of what is important about your organization should be very brief and direct. You should be able to say your mission statement in the time you get on an elevator on the fourth floor and exit it on the first floor. If it is any longer than that, you should rethink it. Our first mission statement would have been appropriate for an elevator in the Empire State Building.

BELIEFS

The beliefs statement is what the staff and board believe about your children's choir. The task of creating a list of beliefs about your organization can be daunting. It can also be exciting and creative work. Choral music participation for children can be the place where a lifetime love of music begins. We believe many things about children that inform our decisions as musicians, educators, and parents. These beliefs encourage us to make good decisions about what is best for the choristers and for the organization. Artistic staff, administrative staff, and members of the board of directors may work intensely to create a list of beliefs about the organization. A facilitator will keep the discussions focused and productive. The resulting beliefs, values, and vision statements will provide insights into the organization. Periodic revisions at subsequent strategic planning sessions will be made as the organization continues to grow or change over time. Parents appreciate articulate statements that inform them about the organization, and how it thinks about choral music education, artistry, and excellence for their children. (See appendix 3.2 for the statement of beliefs for the Syracuse Children's Chorus.)

CORE VALUES

For some choirs, a weekend retreat or meetings over several weeks or months will provide an opportunity to create the mission statement, beliefs, values, goals, and strategic plan. For this author's choir, the participants wished to distill the essence of the children's choir into three core values that captured what the organization valued. Following much discussion, the following three emerged:

- We value excellence.
- We value collaboration.
- We value artistry.

For other choirs, the list may be longer.

Core Value I: Pursuit of Excellence

The English dramatist and novelist W. Somerset Maugham said, "It's a funny thing about life; if you refuse to accept anything but the best, you very often get it." The pursuit of excellence is a goal for this choir. In considering excellence in the context of a children's choir, some questions emerged:

- How do you create a children's choir that will be exemplary?
- What will excellence look like?
- Will you know it when you have achieved it?
- How will you develop or expand existing skills to become excellent?
- How will you teach talented young singers to sing with proper vocal technique and read musical scores?
- How will you shape the sound of your choir?
- Where will you find music of fine quality?
- What criteria will you use to define "quality" music?
- How will you develop effective programming?
- How much will you challenge your singers?

Excellence is a choice that educators and conductors make in each class and each rehearsal. Striving for excellence may be a goal for every rehearsal, every meeting, and every day in the life of the choir. The process of striving for excellence is a lifetime journey, a way of being. Each minute of life is precious and should not be wasted by settling for mediocrity. There are many average singers, but it takes commitment and work to be excellent. Each opportunity to create beauty through choral singing is a gift to be cherished and should never be taken for granted. In the words of a chorister, "You demanded hard work, and expected nothing less than excellence, and I loved that." Jamie, an alumnus said,

> I have found music on all kinds of instruments to be emotionally provoking at times, but no instrument is as compelling as the voice. If I had never sung and developed my voice, I never would have come to this conclusion. Thanks for giving me, and the rest of us, the gift of singing, communicating, and connecting in this way.

Erin, a chorister alumna serving as a Foreign Service Officer in Kabul, Afghanistan, wrote,

> Traveling in China with choirs from Guangzhou, Israel, and Sweden in 1998 opened my eyes to the world beyond upstate New York. It was the first time I really understood and experienced music as a world language, uniting people from across the globe who on first glance seemed to have little else in common. Speaking with the choristers, I quickly learned that Chinese children and Swedish children were not at all that different from my neighbors down the street, despite the fact that a week before we left on tour, I could not imagine anywhere more foreign than China.
>
> Now, working in Afghanistan with civil society groups and women's activities, I am regularly reminded of the lesson I first learned in China: As foreign as a culture might seem, people across the world share the same human values.... I joined the foreign service to work on people-to-people exchanges and connect the United States with foreign countries through cultural means, all thanks to the experience I had as a fourteen-year-old chorister.

Another alumna chorister, Carrie, now a singer-songwriter and former Broadway lead, wrote,

> I learned to honor music, and my voice; to treat sound and song with respect; to have integrity with the craft and the discipline to get better. I learned that beauty can be found in music in the most unconventional places, and how you approach a song makes all the difference in the world.

Holding the organization to standards of excellence in all matters makes a difference. You never know when your choristers are learning big ideas.

Core Value II: Collaboration

The word *collaboration* is defined as "the action of working with someone to produce or create something."[2] Collaboration is the essence of a choir. Without choristers, boards of directors, parents, staff, mentors, teachers, funders, visionaries, professional musicians, composers, and the community, the choir would not exist. As the cultural anthropologist Margaret Mead said, "Never doubt that a small group of thoughtful, committed citizens can change the world. Indeed it is the only thing that ever has." Choral organizations, specifically children's choirs, are changing our world one day at a time across the country and beyond. The presence of a choir changes the community and all those who are touched by its artistry.

The choir's beliefs about respect, dignity, care, compassion, diversity, and inclusion are part of collaboration. Learning the behavioral norms of "how to be" in the choir goes far beyond the musical skills. Learning to work with others toward a common musical goal not only educates and challenges children, but also teaches them about ways of being that are essential life skills.

Musical collaborations are one of the most opportune ways to create multigenerational music-making with a children's choir. Following our first experience in premiering a new song in 1983, we established a commitment to new music that was to become a signature of the choir. Each year, creative programming and premiering new works stretched and challenged the ensemble in new directions. These collaborations led to premiers of new music with orchestras, string quartets, woodwind ensembles, brass ensembles, international choirs, public school choirs, professional singers, ballet companies, adult volunteer choirs, jazz trios, children's authors, professional choirs, a puppet theater, and more.

Choral singing changes lives. Choral singing inspires. Choral singing with multiple generations is a powerful art form. (Musical collaborations and commissioning are discussed in chapters 10 and 11.)

Core Value III: Artistry

Artistry pervades everything the choir does. Striving for excellence in artistry is the focus of each rehearsal with the children. Creating a safe, nurturing environment is of utmost importance. Artistry will thrive in organizations where creativity and striving for excellence prevail.

"Apollinaire said, 'Come to the edge.' 'It's too high.' 'Come to the edge.' 'We might fall.' 'Come to the edge.' And they came. And he pushed them. And they flew."[3] When envisioning the dream of starting a children's choir, excellence and artistry were part of it from the very beginning. It takes courage to take risks, but soaring is worth it.

VISION STATEMENTS

An organization's vision statements should be idealistic, but also realistic, concepts that the organization strives to achieve. They may be lofty goals for the future. Vision statements are several short sentences and are unique to each choir. Each statement begins with the phrase, "We envision...." (See appendix 3.2 for the SCC vision statement.)

WHEN THE DIRECTOR IS OVERWHELMED

In a growing organization, it is possible for a founder, or a sole director of a choir with little or no staff, to become overwhelmed by the workload of musical and administrative tasks. As the chorus expands, the number of concerts and invitations to perform increase, and touring can begin. Often there is one full- or part-time music director and possibly a part-time volunteer or staff member to accomplish all the tasks. As long as the work is getting done, everything appears to be running smoothly, and everyone is happy. The board assumes there is no need to add the expense of more staff.

Often, boards of directors are not aware of the work schedule that is unique to a community-based children's or youth choir. The all-consuming workload can extend far beyond an ordinary workday. Rehearsals are held after school, evenings, or on weekends. Concerts generally occur on weekends. Contacts with people in the business world happen during regular business hours. If the choir tours, a large amount of time must be devoted to planning the tour in addition to maintaining daily operations and rehearsal schedules.

Some founding artistic directors have full-time or part-time teaching positions or church music positions when they begin the new choir. Often, the growing clerical or administrative demands of an expanding community-based choral organization require more time than is possible for the director to give. When a director is overloaded with the increasing burden of nonmusical matters in a growing program, it can become overwhelming. The director must ask for help. Sometimes, the board of directors is unaware of the personal toll on the director. It often takes the voice of an outside consultant to meet with the board of directors and staff to increase awareness of the untenable situation and recommend a solution. This scenario has occurred frequently in children's choirs across the country. If a strategy is not in place to relieve the extreme workload, it can disrupt one's personal life, lead to health issues for the director, or even more serious problems for the health of the choir.

Hiring an outside consultant to assess the situation objectively is a wise step for an organization. A consultant is a non-stakeholder in the organization who can assist by presenting objective data gathered by interviews with key personnel. A consultant may facilitate sessions with staff and board members that lead to practical and achievable solutions for all. It may be worth the expense to the organization to work with the consultant to create a strategy and timetable that will bring relief to the music director. Nonmusical matters may be delegated to capable volunteers; or an additional part-time or full-time paid staff member may be hired to assume these responsibilities. Bringing in an outside voice to assess the inner workings of the organization and suggest possible change is a common step for an organization that is growing.

STAFF MATTERS

A growing program may periodically need to add both music and administrative staff. This may begin with adding volunteer, part-time, or full-time administrative staff to assume some of the clerical and administrative responsibilities. Part-time music directors may be added as additional choir levels or satellite locations are added. The goal for staffing an organization should be to hire extremely competent staff members. A staff member in a small organization can make or break it. Consider how many staff members will be needed, what their duties will include, and whether each position will be full-time, part-time, or volunteer. Hiring chorister parents may not be recommended.

Job descriptions should be prepared for advertising available administrative positions. They should enumerate specific responsibilities and needed skills (e.g., writing skills, accounting skills, marketing skills, knowledge of website management, Excel, Word, Peachtree or Quickbooks, Windows Publisher, or others).

Position openings may be announced both locally and nationally. The Internet also provides many possibilities for listings. Examine postings from other organizations to serve as models for your listings. The personality and work ethic of the new hire should be compatible with all members of the organization. (See appendix 3.3 for sample job descriptions and web listings.)

THE INTERVIEW PROCESS

Interviewing a staff candidate for the first time can be a daunting task. Asking for assistance from board members or advisory board members who have experience hiring people can be a good idea. They may be skilled at interviewing and can provide valuable information, or they may even be willing to assist with the interview process. Numerous management books and online resources on this topic exist and will provide additional information.

Applicants may be asked to apply in writing or online. Specific requests, such as attaching a current résumé or list of references, may be included. Acknowledge receipt of an application promptly and indicate that the organization will be in contact if an interview is requested.

The more a person interviews candidates, the more expertise that person will develop. Discuss the candidate's prior work experiences and how they may relate to the job. Prepare questions to ask the interviewee based on actual situations that occur in your organization. The candidate might be given a scenario of an awkward situation with a parent or concert attendee and asked how he or she would react. If the new hire is going to be writing newsletters, grants, press releases, text for the website, or weekly memos, ask for a writing sample. This will provide input about the candidate's accuracy, language skills, and creativity.

The organization may require a background check to be completed before the prospective employee is hired. Once approved, an employment contract should be issued. The employment contract, signed by the new employee and the appropriate chorus administrator or board president, will be placed in the employee's personnel file. There will be additional forms required to be completed at the time of employment that will be retained in the new employee's personnel file. Required forms may vary from state to state. (See appendix 3.4 for a list of required personnel forms.)

CONTRACTS

A nonprofit organization sets the dates of its fiscal year, which may begin the first day of January, June, or August. Some organizations use the calendar year for financial reporting, regardless of the fiscal year dates. Staff contracts may be prepared and issued annually at the beginning of the organization's fiscal year. For new employees, a contract is issued at the time of employment and reissued at the start of each new fiscal year. Paychecks may be issued weekly or twice a month. Part-time assistant directors may be paid following the academic calendar or based on the choir's season. Each organization determines what is best.

Accompanists for each choir are often independent contractors, meaning that they are not employees of the organization. As outside contractors, they are responsible for declaring their income from the organization on their personal state and federal income tax statements. Depending on how much income they receive for their services, certain tax forms may need to be prepared and issued by the organization (usually, an annual 1099 form reporting the contractor's total earnings for the year). An accountant will be able to offer advice about current laws regarding this. Organizations do not provide benefits for outside contractors.

Musicians who are hired for a concert, such as a harpist, flutist, string quartet, etc., are also outside contractors. Written agreements are sent in advance of a performance detailing the repertoire, rehearsal times and locations, amount to be paid, declaration that he or she is an independent contractor, and notification of when payment will be made. The written agreement formalizes the relationship in a professional manner and avoids any errors or misunderstandings.

When the chorus is invited to perform with a professional orchestra, opera company, or for a performing arts series, the contract will come from the outside organization. The chorus is typically paid a fee for each performance. This will vary from city to city and depend on the number of minutes of music and the number of performances. Again, the concert date(s), repertoire, fee to be paid, date when payment will be made, contact person with complete contact information, and other expectations are listed in the contract. In the case of orchestral engagements, often both the executive director of the orchestra and the managing artistic director (or executive director) of the chorus sign the contract agreement, with copies retained by both parties. Cancellation policies are usually included in such contracts.

STAFF EVALUATIONS

Some organizations evaluate staff annually. This provides an opportunity for the evaluator to review the work of a staff member. Benefits of an annual performance review include providing an opportunity to articulate a staff member's strengths, highlighting particular occasions when the person excelled during the past year, and keeping a written document of objectives for the coming year. It also gives an opportunity to discuss strategies and set realistic goals for improving areas of weakness. Two copies are typically made, one for the staff member, and one to be kept in the personnel file that also contains a copy of the employment contract and any other necessary or required information. (See appendix 3.5 for sample staff evaluations.)

Current thinking suggests that this is not necessarily the most effective way to review performance. UCLA faculty member Samuel A. Culbert suggests that year-end performance reviews often cause tension and stress for employees and do not necessarily inspire teamwork, leadership, and collaboration.[4] For some, doing staff evaluations is a difficult task. In the collaborative model, staff members are nurtured, given opportunities to gain greater skills, and encouraged to do good work and continually improve. Feedback is frequent and immediate throughout the year, not reserved for a formal, annual review. Formal staff evaluations sometimes seem counterproductive to the collaborative atmosphere of the organization. Ideally, staff members bring individual expertise to the organization and grow with the experience each year. Immediate feedback is far more relevant as collaborators work through events together and solve challenges as they arise.

Some organizations have the employee complete a self-evaluation form while the organization's evaluator completes one as well. Then, both meet and discuss the evaluations. The collaborative process of discussing strengths and weaknesses should result in a unified plan for the next year. Dialogue about best practices in managing employees continues. This is something each organization must decide how to handle for itself.

STAFF RECOGNITION

Recognition of a staff member for outstanding work may be given spontaneously. Often, board members will have unused tickets to a theater production, concert, or sports event that may be passed along to a staff member. It is helpful to know staff members' preferences should an opportunity arise for acknowledgment of extra effort. (See appendix 3.6 for a staff recognition survey.)

ALUMNI AND PARENT COMMITTEES

A parent and/or alumni chorister committee may be formed to support the work of the chorus. For some choirs, these committees may become part of the organizational structure, either formally or informally. Parents may become involved informally in a booster club to support a fundraising effort or serve on a parent advisory committee. Some choirs have a formal parent organization that is governed by its own set of bylaws, including officers and committees. Alumni of the chorus may form a committee to organize a special project or participate in a concert or chorus event. There are many ways in which parents and alumni may become involved in supporting the chorus.

Some organizations choose not to have parent organizations or committees. Each choir makes decisions about what is best for its own organization based on its needs and what is doable.

LICENSING AGENCIES

It is important for a choir to be aware of its obligation to obtain performance rights for concerts and recordings. ASCAP, the American Society of Composers, Authors and Publishers, licenses and distributes royalties for the non-dramatic public performances of its members' copyrighted works.[5] Other licensing agencies include BMI (Broadcast Music, Inc.), SESAC (Society of European Stage Authors and Composers), and ACEMLA (La Asociación de Compositores y Editores de Música Latinoamericana).[6] As part of their regular duties, the staff members will maintain records and submit reports, programs, and fees to the appropriate licensing organizations as required.

CONCLUSION

Founding a choir begins with a vision for what the choir will become. The journey of bringing the choir and the community together follows. There will be anticipated and unanticipated challenges. Is it worth it? YES! Children who have a chance to sing with others who have similar interests and abilities will ideally thrive.

Children who have opportunities to sing with others will also thrive in life. Learning new songs to share with friends or parents, singing with professional orchestras and soloists, singing music of world cultures, and working with living composers will give choristers a different view of the world. Such experiences will stretch and challenge young singers.

The structure of the chorus is critical to supporting the artistry and sustaining the choir. The board, parents, choristers, staff, students, foundations, granting agencies, contributors, sponsors, and community all have a stake in the organization. Staying true to its mission and striving for excellence in all aspects of the organization, from the board structure to the music sung at each rehearsal, encourage sustainability.

"Hope" is the thing with feathers–
That perches in the soul–
And sings the tune without the words–
And never stops–at all–[1]
—EMILY DICKINSON

4

LEADERSHIP TRANSITION

WHEN A FOUNDER leaves a choir following a long tenure, there is often much emotion attached to the separation for both choir and founder. The founder's emotions may range from reflection to joy, sadness, anticipation, frustration, impatience, and hope. It is also a stressful time for all those who are associated with the organization. There is much anticipation about who will succeed the founder. Will the choir find the right person? *How* will the choir find the right person? Who will it be? What are the available resources to assist with the costs of conducting a search? What will the new reality be like? Will the choir continue to be a stable organization? Will the choristers like the new person? How will the organization change? Will the staff choose to stay or leave? How will the board of directors handle the transition? Or will the decision be made to end the organization?

Assuming the decision is made to seek a new artistic leader, there are many stakeholders in the choral organization who will be affected by the change in leadership. These may include the board of directors, artistic staff, administrative staff, choristers, parents, contacts at the host rehearsal facility, funders, donors, volunteers, season subscribers, alumni choristers, partner organizations, and community members. Like a drop of water splashing into a still pond, the ripples emanating from the founder's (or the long-time director's) announcement of departure will cause a reaction throughout the community of people connected to the chorus.

At the beginning of the U.S. children's choir movement in the 1980s, few resources related to organizational structure existed for beginning children's choirs. During the ensuing years, children's and youth choirs matured and increased in record numbers across the United States. With time, they learned more about organizational structure and management. Thirty years later, an additional need arose—how to successfully negotiate the transition from founder-led organizations to those with new artistic leadership.

In a 2010 publication, Tom Adams speaks about nonprofit organizations:

> ... [W]e are at the beginning of a major leadership turnover. Though nonprofit sector experts argue over the numbers involved, leader transitions are as certain as death and taxes, and they have the potential to have significant impact on organizational effectiveness. It makes sense for leaders and organizations to enthusiastically embrace practices that reduce the risks of failed or poor transition and increase the odds of organizational progress and in some cases organizational transformation.[2]

Author William Bridges defines *transition* as a psychological "process that people go through as they internalize and come to terms with the details of the new situation that the change brings about."[3] Although resources exist to aid in transitions in general, few resources exist that address the matter of transition and succession specifically for community children's and youth choirs. Awareness of the increasing need for such information has generated new resources within the choral profession.[4] Successful navigation of transition and succession is necessary to maintain the many fine children's choirs that historically have contributed to the quality of the arts and education in communities and cities across the nation.

TIMING OF THE FOUNDER'S DEPARTURE

If a nonprofit community-based children's choir chooses to seek new artistic leadership when the founder announces his or her departure, thorough planning should begin, or a previously established plan should be implemented. The length of time the board of directors has to develop a plan for succession may depend on how far in advance the founder announces his or her departure. For some, the planning period may be very compressed, as in the case of an emergency event that forces the choir to seek new artistic leadership quickly. Others may have the luxury of ample time to carefully plan for succession as the result of a departure date announced well in advance; and others may have a succession plan delineated in the bylaws before any such need arises. Regardless of the circumstances causing the change in leadership, the plan will include procedures for the formation of a search committee, announcement of the position, interviews of candidates, and hiring of the next artistic leader. Or the decision may be made to close the organization permanently.

Current best practice suggests that, regardless of when a transition occurs, there should be a succession plan articulated in the bylaws of the organization long before the plan needs to be implemented. This plan will facilitate timely implementation of a well-thought-out strategy, thus relieving some of the board's immediate stress about procedures for transition and succession. Some organizations have a plan for transition of artistic leadership in place, but most do not.

The founder of SCC announced her departure to the board of directors a year and a half in advance. Two years before this announcement was made, she took a one-month grant-supported sabbatical to study transitions of founder-led organizations. The subject of transition and succession was one that had rarely been discussed by the board, and it was the "elephant in the room." That is, everyone wondered when she might leave, but no one wanted to bring up the subject. Because departure would be inevitable, her goal was to study how to develop a comprehensive succession plan well in advance, or at least know how to start the process and find the resources that would be most helpful when the time arrived.

At the time of the founder's sabbatical, no departure date had been determined, but it was expected to occur within five years. The sabbatical allowed time to examine case studies from other organizations that had undertaken successful transitions, and time to consider how these examples could inform the choir's search for new artistic leadership when needed. The study also showed the estimated time that would be necessary to properly plan for succession and how to prepare a tentative timeline for it. The study topic grew from the direct need within the choir and a growing awareness that this reflected what was simultaneously occurring in numerous children's choirs across the country.

By 2010, some of the founders of children's choirs who began their work in the 1980s were beginning to transition from their choirs to downsized workloads, other positions, or retirement. Other children's choirs have had transitions sooner or more frequently. How would these organizations transition to new leadership under the next generation of inspired conductor-teachers? Perhaps lessons could be learned from other choral organizations that had already successfully negotiated the transition and succession. Two years after completing the sabbatical, she announced her departure date for a year and a half later—thirty years after founding the choir.

WHERE TO BEGIN

Once the founder (or music director) announces a departure date, a timeline should be established to allow for the ongoing work of the choir to continue without interruption through and beyond the hiring of the new artistic leader. For a public school district, the advertising of a position opening will follow a well-defined procedure determined by the school board and administration. For a church music director's position, the opening can be announced to the community through church resources, such as church worship bulletins, websites, newsletters, verbal announcements, or by advertising with professional organizations, such as the Choristers Guild, the American Choral Directors Association, and the American Guild of Organists.

For a nonprofit choral organization, the board of directors will conduct the search for a new music director, managing artistic director, or artistic director—however the board defines the position. The board will oversee the transition from one leader to the next. Once the board has been notified about the founder's departure, a transition plan should be initiated, or the pre-determined plan as articulated in the bylaws should be implemented.

PREPARATION OF THE BOARD OF DIRECTORS

Confronted with a music director transition, the board of directors will address many issues and meet many challenges. This may seem like a daunting task when faced with losing a founder or long-time director on whom they have relied to guide the organization. The transition may provide an opportunity to shape the choir with new vision, energy, and direction. Or the board of directors may wish to maintain the organization with little change. Or the board may determine that closing the organization is the best decision. There are many possible scenarios, and each choir's path will be unique.

Chorus America has created a comprehensive resource to assist with artistic leadership transitions and successions. It is a self-paced guide for choral organizations that are about to undertake the transition process. Titled *Navigating a Music Director Transition,* this online seminar is an instructive tool for member organizations that face this challenge.[5] Thorough discussion of every aspect of negotiating a transition is presented in the seminar. The attachment download section includes worksheets, questionnaires, self-assessment questionnaires, sample budgets, readiness quizzes, timelines, music director evaluations, and other helpful documents. These resources allow board members to gain insight into the many matters for consideration when hiring a new music director. Respected leaders in professional, volunteer, symphonic, and children's/youth choirs speak about their experiences negotiating transitions in their own organizations.

After a founder's departure announcement is made confidentially to the board of directors, all members of the board should be encouraged to complete the Chorus America online seminar that will lay a foundation for accomplishing the task of finding a new director. It may be wise to keep the founder's departure confidential until the board has time to carefully plan the timeline of events for announcing the impending change in artistic leadership.

The board of directors may apply for a grant to assist with the cost of conducting a local, regional, national, or international search. The anticipated search costs may include fees for hiring a consultant to assist the board with the process, funds for advertising the position, travel expenses (airfare, hotel, per diem) for hosting two or three final candidates for on-site auditions, and interview, hospitality, and miscellaneous search committee expenses.

INTERVIEWING AND HIRING A CONSULTANT

For an organization that has never undertaken a transition in artistic leadership, hiring a consultant may be a wise choice. Ideally, the consultant is from outside the organization and does not have any history with it, any bias or hidden agenda, or any direct stake in what happens. The consultant is a neutral voice who can listen to all parties, guide diverse opinions toward consensus, and be a resource or sounding board throughout the search process. He or she may be hired locally or may be from outside the local area or state. Recommendations for a consultant may come from choirs who have worked with one, or from professional choral organizations that are familiar with consultants who actively work within the choral profession.

Once recommendations have been obtained, the board of directors may wish to conduct phone interviews with possible consultants. A list of questions prepared in advance of the phone interview will provide an opportunity for comparison of responses from each candidate, giving the board a sense of who might be the best fit for the organization.

Once consensus has been reached about which consultant to hire, verbal or written notification should be made to the consultant. A contract should subsequently be prepared stating the responsibilities of the consultant, fees to be paid, and a schedule for the work to be completed. The contract may include a statement of specific services, the terms of agreement, fee (hourly or daily rate), travel expenses to be covered by the organization, location where services are to be rendered, time to be devoted by the consultant, payment schedule, discussion of independent contractor tax matters, and the date and signatures of both the consultant and chorus board president. Other components may be included as necessary.

The choir should prepare a packet of informational materials about the choir to assist the consultant in familiarizing herself or himself with the organization. These materials might include the mission statement, vision statement, strategic plan, season brochure, programs, newsletters, and financial statements. It is important to include all names and occupations of board members, names of all staff members and their positions, job descriptions for all staff members, and the organizational chart.

COMMITMENT OF THE BOARD OF DIRECTORS

The board of directors must be committed to the process of transition. The work will involve many hours beyond the regular board meetings and normal responsibilities of board involvement. Board members should be candid, receptive to change, sensitive, and collaborative. They should be willing to invest time and thought in a process that might take a few months or more than a year to complete. The journey will be different for each organization, but understanding the basic components of a search will help facilitate the process. All board members should be present when matters from the search committee are presented and board input is requested. They should be present for interactions with candidates (interviewing, transporting, hosting), and they should be part of the final board vote on the search committee's recommendation about whom to hire.

SEARCH COMMITTEE

The board of directors should appoint a committee that will be officially charged with the task of conducting a search for a new music director. The search committee members, who are not necessarily all board members, should include a qualified group of people to review all applicants, select a final pool of candidates, and oversee the interview and selection process. The expertise of the committee members should be considered. Should an educator be included? Should a conductor be on the search committee? Which board members will be the most skilled for undertaking this task? The committee should be small enough for meeting easily throughout the search process. Prior to accepting the invitation to serve on the search committee, all participants should understand what the anticipated time commitment will be. The search committee members will make the final recommendation to the board of directors about whom to hire. The board of directors is not obligated to follow the recommendation of the search committee, but it most likely will seriously consider the recommendation of the skilled committee members entrusted with the task.

The outgoing artistic director should *not* be a member of the search committee. Although it may be emotionally difficult for the outgoing director not to serve on the search committee, particularly for a founding director, it is in the best interests of the organization. For the outgoing director, this is part of the process of letting go. For some, departure may be a challenge. Some will go gracefully, and others may not.

The search committee may or may not ask the outgoing director for assistance. One such request might be for suggestions about where to advertise the position. The committee may also request the outgoing director's assistance in networking with choral colleagues to increase awareness of the upcoming vacancy.

JOB DESCRIPTION

When the consultant initially meets with the full board of directors and staff, the consultant may be asked to assist in fleshing out the important criteria for the job description. There are certain questions to be answered:

- What kind of a person is the organization looking for?
- What kind of traits or characteristics are important?
- What kind of skills must this person have?
- What kind of experience is the board looking for in the new director?
- What are the educational requirements for the new director?
- What will the salary range and benefits be?

Building consensus about the kind of person the board of directors is looking for is critical to the process. Each board member should have an opportunity to speak about what is important and what the ideal candidate might bring to the organization.

Creating the job description is no small task. If the choir has carefully maintained accurate job descriptions for all positions, the creation of the job description will be easier. It should reflect current practice and any changes that will be made for the new hire. The organization must have a clear idea of what the ideal candidate for the position should be, and how the organization will define the position to the outside world. What kind of expertise will the candidate need? What will the criteria be for the candidate? Working together with a consultant to develop a clear list of criteria is important, and there should be consensus about the ideal candidate.

Examining job descriptions from other organizations is helpful in gathering possible ideas. Many examples may be found online. Looking at how other organizations of similar type and size advertise their job openings may assist in the initial stages of creating the description. Again, each organization will be unique and have its own criteria. (See appendix 4.1 for a sample job description for the position of artistic director.)

Once the criteria are determined, the board hopes to find the right person. Sometimes the right person is found in the first round of auditions and interviews, and sometimes not. The scenarios are many. The pool of applicants may not be large enough to generate any viable candidates. Additional solicitation of candidates may need to be undertaken. The first candidate interviewed may be hired. A viable candidate may withdraw his or her name from the search well into the process. A candidate may be offered the position, and the board might withdraw the offer during negotiations. A candidate may be offered the position, and he or she may choose to withdraw during the negotiation phase. A candidate may be ready to accept an offer, but an unforeseen life event may occur that forces the person to decline the offer. In short, there are many places where the process can stall. Agreeing about the procedure to accomplish the task of finding the right person is foremost. And the process always involves hope—hope that the right person will be found.

TIMELINES

Early in the process, the board should develop a timeline based on the incumbent's announced departure date and the length of time necessary to conduct a proper search. If the window between announcement and departure is brief, an interim director may need to be appointed to allow the board to have enough time to prepare for a proper search. Once the date of departure is established and the board commits to conducting a search, a timeline assists in keeping everyone focused on accomplishing the task. Time passes quickly, and if the search is to be thorough and well-run, adhering as closely as possible to the timeline will be important for stability in the organization and the ongoing work of the choir. Given the luxury of time to plan a proper search, a timeline might look something like this:

- January 2014
    - Founder announces planned departure date of June 2015 (eighteen months in advance).
- March 2014
    - Grant application is submitted for funding to support cost of transition.

- June/July 2014
  - Board president secures consultant.
  - Determine the appropriate time to tell the chorus staff about the departure of the founder.
  - Board of directors formally approves the selected search committee members and their charge to conduct a search.
  - Board members and search committee members are asked to complete the Chorus America online transition seminar.
  - Set date and secure location for August board retreat.
- August 2014
  - Board retreat with consultant (includes administrative staff, board members, search committee members).
  - Finalize job description.
  - Determine where to advertise position opening.
  - Make plans for paid ads in publications or online.
- September 2014
  - Board approves job description and announcement.
  - Announce founder's departure to choristers and their families at first rehearsal.
  - Coordinate audition dates for candidates with artistic staff.
- October 2014
  - Formally announce search.
  - Place ads in predetermined locations (websites, journals, chorus's fall newsletter).
- February 2015
  - Application deadline.
  - Review of all applicant materials by search committee (one week to complete).
  - Search committee conducts phone interviews with top 4–6 candidates (one week to complete).
  - Based on recommendations from the search committee, the board approves top 2–3 candidates to be invited for in-person audition and interviews.
- March 2015
  - Audition and interview top 2–3 candidates.
  - Search committee makes recommendation to the board of directors (one candidate or ranked list).
  - Board makes final decision and board president (or delegated person) makes offer to selected candidate.
  - Negotiation period (if needed) and deadline given for candidate response.
  - If candidate # 1 does not take the position, candidate #2 (if also approved by the search committee and board of directors) may be offered the position.

- Signed contract completed.
- Possible end scenarios: Conclude search with new hire; appoint an interim director and reopen search with revised timetable at a later date; or choose to terminate the choir.
- April 2015
  - Assuming the search is successful, announce new director.
- May 2015
  - Welcoming event for new director.
  - Introduction of new director to the choirs.
- June 2015
  - Start date for new artistic leader.

The title given to the new hire will reflect his or her responsibilities: music director, artistic director, managing artistic director, or other as deemed appropriate by the organization.

Is this timetable realistic? Yes. Are there likely to be delays along the way? Yes. Many unforeseen events may occur that change the timing of other events. What actually happens cannot be predicted. A timeline will serve as a guide, and adjustments may be necessary depending on the circumstances. There are births, deaths, illnesses, weather, flight delays, chorus events, procrastination, fundraisers, and many possible unforeseen occurrences that can cause delays in the process. Keeping a keen eye on the departure date of the founder and realizing that things sometimes take longer than anticipated will assist in moving the process forward. In some cases, the first year of a search may not result in hiring anyone. In this instance, a contingency plan may be put into place, and the board of directors may determine to repeat the process the following year. An alternate scenario is that a newly hired music director may realize that he or she is not a good fit with the organization and depart after a short stay. The organization must be prepared for whatever happens.

The search for a new artistic director may be formally announced after a search committee has been appointed, the consultant has been hired, the first board and staff retreat has been held, the job description has been written and approved, and the announcement of the founder's intended departure has been made to the choir.

ANNOUNCING THE FOUNDER'S DEPARTURE TO THE CHORUS

The children's or youth choir members and their families should be told about the founder's departure before the public announcement is made. The timing of this announcement must be carefully planned, with both consideration for the young singers and optimum results for the search. Immediately after the choristers and their families are told about the upcoming transition, the announcement should be made public. The timing of the announcement of the founder's departure may seem sudden no matter when it occurs, or how far in advance it is of the actual departure. Knowing that the organization is working diligently to plan a careful transition will be comforting for the choir members, their families, and the community during the uncertain time that will follow. The words used to speak about the founder's departure will have much to do with how people react. If the organization leaders are nervous, this will be conveyed to staff, parents, and the community. If the board is optimistic and hopeful, confidence will pervade the organization.

The procedure for applying to the position opening can be posted on the choir's website as soon as the announcement has been made to the choir. The geographic limits of the search (local, statewide, national, or international) will determine where the opening will be advertised. Local newspapers, local music educators' organizations, the state music educators' organization, and national sites, such as Chorus America, Choralnet, the American Choral Directors Association, the Association of Canadian Choral Conductors, Musical America, and others, may be contacted to post the position opening. Careful timing and strategically placed paid advertisements may also be procured with the goal of targeting the people who will most likely apply. Care should be taken to be thorough enough to generate the maximum number of candidates for your organization. Networking with colleagues, friends, chorus alumni, and former students can also assist in generating possible candidates.

REVIEW OF APPLICANTS

The search committee will be directed to review all applicant materials once the deadline for applying has been reached. Confidentiality in the committee's work is of the utmost importance. Candidates may be applying for positions confidentially without their current employers' awareness. Required materials for applicants may include a résumé, names of references or letters from references, and a rehearsal and concert video. Some organizations require a packet sent by mail; others may want materials submitted online and a DVD separately mailed. If submitted online, a password-protected and secure section of the chorus's website may be set up for search committee members and the board of directors to view all applicants' materials.

After the application materials have been reviewed, the search committee will convene to discuss all the applicants and determine which ones are worthy of follow-up phone calls to their references. Approximately six to eight applicants may be selected for follow-up. Search committee members will each be assigned one or two candidates for phone references contact. Information gleaned from references is then disseminated to the committee. The committee then determines which applicants are to be interviewed via conference phone calls. Phone interviews should be arranged with possible candidates at a time when a minimum of three search committee members are able to be present. A set of questions may be prepared in advance for any phone interview based on specific criteria required for the position, including the candidate's background, skills, and expertise, and the needs of the choir. This serves as a verbal getting-acquainted opportunity before making a decision about which two or three candidates seem to be a good fit for the organization and worthy of an on-site interview and audition with the choir.

CANDIDATE INTERVIEWS AND AUDITIONS

The search committee chair will report the findings to the board of directors. The report will include a recommendation of whom to invite for on-site interviews and auditions. The board will review all the information, discuss, and make a determination about how to proceed. Once the board has determined which of the top candidates to approve for on-site interviews and auditions, arrangements will be made to bring the candidate to the chorus, including flight reservations (or driving directions), hotel reservations, and a finalized itinerary.

As much information as possible should be given to each candidate to assist in preparing for the chorus audition. Rehearsal scores should be provided. Guidelines about what music the candidate will be expected to conduct should be provided. Notes about the current status of work on each piece from the choir's current director will be helpful (i.e., this piece is new; this piece is close to being ready for performance; this piece is memorized, etc.). Topics for consideration in planning the audition may include the following:

- Will the candidate warm up the choir?
- Will the candidate conduct an entire rehearsal or only part of a rehearsal?
- Will the candidate teach a completely new song selected by the choir, or will he or she bring a new song to teach?
- Will the candidate be given different styles of music to conduct?
- Will the candidate be asked to teach something by rote?
- What is the duration of the candidate's rehearsal?
- Will the candidate conduct more than one choir (beginning, intermediate, or advanced)?
- Will the candidate be evaluated by the choristers?
- Will the board members have an evaluation form to complete?

A detailed itinerary including flight arrival and departure information, names of hosts for each event, locations of hotel and meals (names of restaurants), rehearsal schedule, a meeting with administrative staff, a meeting with artistic staff, and a packet of music with notes should be sent to the candidate in advance of her or his arrival. A specific number of days should be determined for the candidate's preparation, and the packet of materials should be sent to all candidates with the same length of preparation time. (See appendix 4.2 for a sample candidate itinerary.)

During the candidate's visit, both a morning and an afternoon interview with board members may be scheduled to accommodate board members' work schedules and availability. Rehearsals may be scheduled for one or more choirs over one or two days, including the actual choir she or he will be conducting if hired, and one with contrasting age levels if the candidate will conduct more than one choir. One or two board members typically host lunches and dinners with the candidate throughout her or his stay and transport the candidate to the location of the next event on the schedule. A tour of the area may also be included to give the candidate a sense of the community where she or he may be moving.

EVALUATION OF CANDIDATES

Each organization seeking to hire a new music director will determine how to evaluate candidates. A rating scale should be used based on observable criteria determined in advance by the search committee and board of directors. The choristers may or may not be asked to evaluate the candidates. For the chorus search, the board, the search committee, the music staff, the university student conducting interns (using different criteria than the board for instructional and course discussion purposes only), and only the most advanced choir members (using a form specifically developed for their use) may evaluate the candidates.

Anonymous chorister information may be compiled and shared confidentially with the board. Choristers may be included in the process because they are major stakeholders in the organization and, as with the chorister representative, the chorister's input is valued. At no time should the candidates be discussed with the choristers. The choirs should not be given any indication before the candidate's audition that they will be evaluating the candidate. Once the candidate has left the room at the conclusion of the audition rehearsal, the choristers may be given five minutes to silently write answers to the questions on the brief evaluation form. They should immediately be collected and later compiled for the search committee and board members. (See appendix 4.3 for sample chorister candidate evaluation form.)

The board of directors and search committee may choose to develop an evaluation form that will be used for each candidate. This may include a ranking (on a scale of 1 to 5) for each criterion deemed important to the board and search committee, or criteria may be listed with points totaling 100. For each organization, the criteria will differ based on ideal candidate considerations and what the organization is looking for in a new artistic leader.

OFFERING THE POSITION

After the evaluations have been gathered and compiled, the search committee will convene to review the findings, discuss the candidates, and prepare their recommendation for the board of directors' consideration. A decision will be made to recommend a candidate, not recommend a candidate, rank the candidates, or close the search without offering the position to anyone. Once a decision is made and there is consensus by the search committee members, their recommendation is presented to the full board of directors. Discussion will ensue, and a decision from the board of directors will be forthcoming. Based on the chosen course of action, the board president (or other member of the board) may be delegated the task of offering the position and negotiating with the selected candidate.

WHAT IF YOU DON'T FIND THE RIGHT PERSON?

If no candidate is hired, the board must have a contingency plan. Possible scenarios include hiring an interim director and reopening the search at a later date, or closing the organization permanently.

HIRING AN INTERIM

Hiring an interim director gives the board time to evaluate lessons learned from the search process and consider what could have been done differently. Was the pool of applicants what they had expected? Could it have been larger? Did the search generate applicants with the skill set they were looking for? Was the job description consistent with realistic skills of applicants? Was the compensation package (salary, health insurance, vacation time, stipend for professional development, etc.) consistent with the job description? Were expectations too high? Was the timing correct? Was there unity among committee members or not? There are many reasons for the search process to stall along the way. In the end, you hope that "who you choose, chooses you."[6]

LESSONS LEARNED: SECOND TIME AROUND

Each artistic director will bring his or her own skill set, personality, and expectations to the position. At the time a search is undertaken, the organization must move forward regardless of the outcome. Not hiring someone at the conclusion of a search is not necessarily a negative, nor should it be seen as a failure on the part of anyone involved in the search process, particularly if everyone views the search procedure as successful. Rather, it allows the organization to continue, reevaluate the search process for lessons learned, consider reopening the search, and proceed with greater knowledge and possible changes. And a year later, any new hire would be less in the shadow of the founder or prior director, perhaps allowing more freedom for change.

ANNOUNCING THE NEW ARTISTIC DIRECTOR

Once the employment contract is signed by the new director, a decision must be made about the date to formally announce the appointment. This must be carefully coordinated with the new director, as his or her current employer may not have been notified. When a date has mutually been determined, the chorus can make the announcement. The chorister families should be notified first at a gathering or by simultaneous e-mail to all levels of the chorus. Once announced to the chorus, public announcement may be made on the chorus website and press releases may be sent to local newspapers, national websites such as Choralnet, or other places the board and staff deem appropriate. The press release might include a quote from the board president, a quote from the new director, and a brief bio about the new director with accompanying press photograph.

There are many ways of welcoming a new director. If the hiring is completed before the season has ended, and there is time to bring the new director back for a visit, a social event may be planned during a concert weekend to introduce him or her. An evening reception and dinner event might serve as both a welcome to the new hire and a fundraiser for the chorus. Formal invitations may be extended to friends of the chorus, supporters, and others. After dinner, a formal welcome may be extended to the new director, followed by a performance (string quartet, harp, small choral ensemble, etc.) or another appropriate activity. Because the focus should be on the new director, honoring the outgoing director should be done at a different time. During the chorus concert that weekend, the new director may be briefly introduced to all those in attendance.

AN EXIT AGREEMENT FOR THE DEPARTING DIRECTOR

The board of directors may wish to prepare an exit agreement for the departing director that states the agreed-upon date of departure and other matters. In the case of a founding director, the exit letter may state the title to be given to the founder after departure, such as *founder and director emeritus,* and request permission to use the founder's name in future publications and chorus materials. The exit agreement may include any privileges granted to the departing director, such as continued access to the music library or complimentary tickets to future performances. Each organization will shape this document based on what is best for it.

TIMETABLE FOR ARRIVAL OF THE NEW DIRECTOR

The arrival of the new director should be planned to accommodate both the needs of the chorus and the individual. The new director may need to move from another state, across the country, or from a nearby area to assume the new position, and must have adequate time for giving proper notice to a current employer. In addition, time may be needed to secure a place to live and make all relocation plans. Chorus board members may be helpful in familiarizing the director with the new area or recommending a realtor.

WHAT HAPPENS WHEN THE STAFF NEEDS ANSWERS?

One of the challenges of transition is maintaining smoothly running daily operations of the chorus. Activities do not cease while a search is in progress. Auditions are held, rehearsals continue, concerts are given, grants are written, and fundraising continues. Planning a season and preparing for auditions and more do not cease while a search is conducted and a new person is being hired. The commitment of the staff to the process cannot be underestimated. Dedicated staff members often find themselves working with additional responsibilities during this time. And when planning must be done for the following season, and a new artistic director has not yet been hired, adjustments need to be made. The staff will have to make decisions that provide a broad framework for the new director, who will then make important decisions about future programming, concerts, touring, and more. Ideally, this will be done carefully to allow the new artistic director freedom to complete the important planning when he or she arrives.

One such example of advance planning may include touring. If a choir typically tours, plans will need to be made well in advance. If an artistic director has not been hired, who will make this decision? Will there be a tour, or will it be postponed a year? Where will the tour be? Sometimes these decisions can be delayed until the new director is in place, and sometimes they cannot. The new director could potentially be making decisions for the chorus even before arriving and officially beginning work. There should be sensitivity to the enormous workload and possible emotional stress the new director may experience during this interim time. The staff will be eager for decisions from the new director so it can move forward with planning. Everyone must be sensitive to the situation and not place unnecessary demands on the new director. Technically, the work of the new artistic director begins when the contract begins.

WELCOME AND ORIENTATION FOR THE NEW DIRECTOR

The board of directors is responsible for the new music director's orientation. The exact procedure for this will be determined by the board president in collaboration with board members and staff, and should occur when the new director arrives. Orientation will occur gradually over time as the new artistic director learns the organization's culture. The learning curve will be vertical for the first year as the new director learns about the organization, staff, choirs, board, and community. Orientation should include introductions to all key personnel at rehearsal locations and concert venues, and to important funders and supporters of the choir.

Once the artistic director is settled, a welcoming event, hosted by the board of directors, may be scheduled. Invitations may be extended to funders, supporters, volunteers, media people, grant agencies, other choral conductors, and other appropriate individuals who will be part of the collaborative relationships with the choir. This will allow the community to establish a firsthand relationship with the new director and facilitate continuity for the organization.

Sensitivity to the new director's emotions is also important beyond the first few weeks in the position. The new hire may have been in her or his previous position for a short period of time or for several years. If the director has moved from a different state or region of the country, friendships may have changed or been lost. There may be moments at particular times of the year when memories of past events and successes or emotional connections to the prior position may surface. Reassuring and supporting the new director throughout the first year may be important.

CLARIFYING THE ROLE OF THE DEPARTING FOUNDER OR MUSIC DIRECTOR

The author T. S. Eliot stated, "To make an end is to make a beginning."[7] Lessons learned from other organizations indicate that the founder should step away from the choir on the date of his or her announced departure, and not look back. For some founders, this is a tremendous challenge. The founder has developed the choir over several or many years. A founder has often invested her or his heart and soul into growing the choir from an idea into a full-fledged nonprofit organization. He or she has been part of the musical development of the choir, major and minor events and decisions, strategic plans, and its shared history. Even though the founder may feel the need to advise the choir and have strong input based on his or her self-perceived expertise, the new director must have the freedom to artistically lead the organization into the future, free from encumbrances. The founder should move on as Eliot suggests, looking ahead, not back.

SAY THANK YOU

There will be many who will want to say thank you to the departing founder or director. Finding an appropriate way of honoring the work of the founder will be unique to each organization. This may be a special event or concert, a concert prepared by alumni choristers, or a reception or dinner event. A scholarship or endowment fund may be established and named in honor of the founder. Each organization will find its own way to show its appreciation. This will help the departing director with closure.

The founder will also want to say thank you to others at the end of her or his tenure. A farewell message may be included in the chorus newsletter. Personal notes of thanks may be written to the board members, search committee members, funders, supporters, volunteers, teachers, and others who have been important to the founder and the choir.

CONCLUSION

On the occasion of the founder's last concert with SCC, a collaborative grant project was undertaken with partial funding from the National Endowment for the Arts, a Syracuse University faculty grant from Imagining America, and an initiative grant funded by the Ewing Marion Kauffman Foundation. The chorus presented a collaborative project involving members of the community, local music educators and musicians, and university students in music education, music industry, and composition. A commissioned work by the distinguished American composer Stephen Paulus, and weekend events surrounding the concert premiere, brought these forces together.

Ending the thirty-year journey with the choir was not cause for sadness. An air of completeness and satisfaction abounded knowing there had been many successful accomplishments made possible by a community of people who demonstrated extensive support. This was a time for looking to the future with anticipation, excitement, and hope as the journey for the choir continued in a different way under new artistic leadership.

For the founder's final concert premiere, Mr. Paulus selected a combination of texts from two distinguished women poets, Emily Brontë and Emily Dickinson, and created a work scored for treble choir, harp, and flute. The verse by Emily Dickinson that opened this chapter captured the essence of what the founder wished to express in her final concert. The work was titled "Hope Is the Thing."

Excellence requires commonsense leadership.
—LEE COCKERELL

5

FINANCES

FOR SOME, THE thought of balance sheets, revenue streams, grant writing, audits, and preparing an annual budget may be daunting. A frequently heard comment is "Help! I don't know about accounting. What exactly *is* a balance sheet?" This chapter attempts to demystify the daunting technical terms and suggest ways of successfully navigating the financial world for the new nonprofit children's or youth choir organization. It also has implications for school and church children's choirs.

CHORAL CONDUCTOR AS ENTREPRENEUR

In the case of an independent community-based children's or youth choir, the founder is often the person who has the responsibility for developing the preliminary budget. The founding director knows what the vision will be for the choir and will likely have a good understanding of what specific resources will be needed. It is not uncommon for a choral director to lack experience in preparing an organizational budget and establishing a nonprofit enterprise. Many founders of choirs are musicians, conductors, and educators; they are not always experts in the entrepreneurial endeavor of running a newly formed nonprofit or start-up choral organization.

The word *entrepreneur* is defined as "a person who organizes and operates a business or businesses, taking on greater than normal financial risks in order to do so."[1] How many music directors who founded an independent chorus think of themselves first as an entrepreneur? More often the roles mentioned are musician, conductor, educator, founder, wife, husband, partner, parent, daughter, son, or volunteer—rarely entrepreneur. And yet, by virtue of what a founding director experiences in establishing a nonprofit community-based choir, she or he fulfills the definition of what it is to be an entrepreneur.

Responsible financial planning should accompany artistic planning when a new choir is established. The artistic vision for the choir will become a reality if the necessary funding is in place to support it. To sustain the music-making over a long period, a solid financial structure is necessary. By creating a realistic budget for the new choir, a financial framework will be established. Making informed decisions about what is best for the organization is at the core of the process.

The first budget of a newly formed organization shows the projected sources of revenue (income) and projected costs (expenses) for the first year. Depending on the context of the nonprofit chorus and extent of the program, start-up costs may include but are not limited to director's salary, accompanist costs, purchase of music, printing costs (program, posters, and concert brochures), office equipment and furnishings, office space, and rehearsal and concert space rental. There are many more potential expenses, depending on how large the choir will be, the extent of the programming, whether or not rehearsal and concert spaces are donated, if a website will be set up, if instrumentalists will be hired for performances, and so on. Exact expenses will vary based on the size and type of the choir. All the financial planning is part of a start-up business and is entrepreneurial by nature. And there is definitely financial risk.

In a newly formed community-based children's or youth choir that is sponsored by an existing adult community or professional choir, budgets may be overseen by the parent organization. The parent organization may provide seed money to fund the new choir during the initial start-up phase, or permanently fund it as part of the professional or community choir's extended programming.[2] Additional grants and contributions may be sought to assist with the founding and developing needs of the new choir.[3]

What are the definitions of terms such as *financial statement, budget, audit, balance sheet, year to date, net income,* and *depreciation*? For the novice whose financial planning has been limited to a household budget and balancing a checkbook, these terms may be new. For a first budget, it is not necessary to understand all of these terms. As the organization grows, more complex financial information will be required, and an understanding of these terms will become necessary. Once the initial decisions about the kind of choir, size, location, mission, and basic overview of the ensemble have been determined, financial planning follows.

THE FIRST BUDGET

The basics of a first-year budget include income and expenses. The following two questions must be answered:

- What will the expenses be for the new choir?
- Where will the money come from to pay for these anticipated expenses?

Depending on where and how the chorus begins, the budget will vary from a very simple list of income and expenses to a more extensive list. In the case of SCC, the group was founded within the existing structure of the preparatory division of the School of

Music. The accounting was very simple the first year. The basic components of the first budget were as follows:

- Income
  - Tuition (50 singers × $100 = $5,000)
- Expenses
  - Director's salary
  - Music
  - Concert dress (ties for the boys, skirts and ribbons for the girls)
  - Design and print costs for a brochure to announce the choir's formation

The expenses of rehearsal space, concert venue, accompanist, postage, stationery, and concert programs were all covered by the preparatory division of the university. Thirty years later, as a mature arts organization and an independent 501(c)(3) nonprofit organization, the budget looked very different. The chorus had grown to include three full-time staff members (one managing artistic director and two administrative staff members), two additional part-time conductor-teachers, four choirs, rented office space, and a more extensive concert and touring schedule. The total budget amount grew steadily each year throughout the organization's history based on careful thought and planning. Always at the core of the decision-making process were the questions: "What is right and best for the young singers and the program?" and "Are these expenses and program goals in line with our mission statement, beliefs, and values, and are these expenses part of the choir's strategic plan?"

SETUP OF THE NEW ORGANIZATION'S BUDGET

A budget is defined as an estimate of income and expenditure for a set period of time.[4]

A budget for a new organization will begin with a very simple document stating the expected sources of income and the anticipated expenses. As there will be no prior history of income and expenses, the document will be quite basic. The preparation of a first-time budget may begin with a simple document set up with the following column headings and sample details (one example each of income and expense is shown below):

Account Description	Account Type (Income or Expense)	Proposed Budget Amount
Tuition	Income	$5,000
Total Revenues		**$5,000**
Brochure	Expense	$1,100
Music	Expense	$2,000

Account Description	Account Type (Income or Expense)	Proposed Budget Amount
Concert dress materials	Expense	$ 800
Miscellaneous supplies	Expense	$ 100
Salary	Expense	$1,000
Total Expenses		**$5,000**
NET INCOME		**$0**

All types of income would be listed in rows at the top of the table, with a summary total for all revenue at the end of the income items. All expense items would follow, showing a summary total for all expenses. The net income at the bottom shows the total amount of revenue minus the total amount of expenses. This number will show a balanced budget or surplus (positive number) if there is money left unspent. Or it will show a negative number (deficit budget) if more is spent than the revenue taken in. (A deficit number is usually shown inside parentheses or after a minus sign.) Many online resources and computer programs are available to assist with setting up a basic budget. As the needs of the organization increase and the accounting becomes more complex, a carefully chosen accounting program should accommodate the organization's growing needs.

Once data are entered, a computerized accounting program can provide reports and immediate information about the status of revenues and expenses. Accurate data entry results in accurate reports. When the organization formally begins operation and monthly statements and balance sheets are needed, these reports can easily be generated by the accounting software and printed for review by board members at monthly meetings. Accounting programs such as Quicken, QuickBooks, and Peachtree, to name a few, are available. Online research and advice sought from a certified public accountant can provide valuable assistance in selecting a computer software program that best fits the needs of the new choir.

COFFEE-CAN ECONOMICS—NEVER SPEND MORE THAN YOU HAVE

At the twentieth anniversary concert of the children's chorus, a board member told the story of how the chorus began: with a phone, a kitchen table, a coffee can, and a dream. The coffee can was a reference to the founder's "coffee-can economics," which was the founder's simplistic budget approach: If the money wasn't in the coffee can, there would be no money spent. There usually was enough money in the coffee can to do what was reasonable for the chorus to undertake throughout the year, and at the end of the year, some funds would remain to begin the next year. Coffee-can economics served the chorus well for many years, as did the many cups of actual coffee consumed by the staff, accountant, and finance committee throughout the process.

ONGOING BUDGETS

In an ongoing organization, one year's financial report at year end will serve as a strong indication of what the next year's budget might look like. Some organizations increase the budget using a percentage increase across all income and expense lines to reflect inflation or a cost-of-living increase for staff compensation. A typical across-the-board increase for the budget might be 3 to 5 percent. Other organizations review each expense and income item line by line to carefully assess the change over the past year and the anticipated activity for the next year. Rarely, if ever, do costs decrease for phone, postage, rent and concert hall rental (if using the same spaces). Decisions about budgets should be made based on what is in line with the choir's mission and core values. From year to year, new initiatives may be added and other activities may be modified or discarded.

In times of economic challenge, organizations often seek ways to reduce costs by soliciting more in-kind services, such as the donation of printing. Ways of increasing revenue may be sought by holding more fundraising events, increasing the number of donors, or implementing strategies to increase audience attendance at concerts. One such example of a way to cut expenses for advertising is exchanging ads with other arts organizations. For example, a children's choir might exchange program ads with another arts organization, such as a professional theater company, at no cost to either organization. No monies are exchanged, and the ads benefit both organizations by reaching a different audience of several hundred potential patrons.

There are many creative ways that arts organizations have sought to maintain their missions while implementing cost reductions. Typically, choirs are frugal, and income and expenses are carefully matched. Funding for the arts is a challenge, and choral organizations ideally should develop the necessary skills to accomplish the task of balancing the budget each year.

For an existing organization, the current year's budget will inform preparation of the upcoming year's budget. For the example below, assume that the fiscal year begins June 1, 2013, and ends May 31, 2014. In preparation for the 2014–2015 fiscal year budget (the upcoming season), the budget preparation working document might be expanded from the first year's budget to look something like this example. (Note that only one line item is shown for income, and only one line item is shown for expense.)

Account ID	Account Description	Account Type	Annual Budget 2013–2014	Year to Date Actual	Proposed Budget 2014–2015
4010U01	Contributions—Individual, unrestricted	Income	$1,500	$1,700	$2,000
7130U01	Music, permanent library	Expense	$1,000	$1,100	$1,250

Below each heading will be the list of line items included in the budget, first sequentially listing all income line items, followed by sequentially listing all expense line items. The Account ID is the number in the accounting system that represents that specific item. For example, an Account ID number might be 4010U01. The Account Description would be "Contributions—Individual, unrestricted" (meaning that a person has donated to the choir and not requested the gift be used for a special purpose such as a scholarship or endowment). The Account Type would be "Income."

The next column would list the Annual Budget amount designated in the above example for the contributions (individual and unrestricted) for the current budget year. The Year to Date column in this example would contain the exact dollar amount contributed in this category as of the exact end date covered by the report. The Proposed Budget column would list the unchanged or new number if changed (up or down from the current year's budget) for the upcoming fiscal year 2014–2015. The number represents the best estimate of what that revenue or expense item will be for the upcoming fiscal year.

For an organization with a June 1 to May 31 fiscal year, budget work would likely need to begin in March and April to be prepared to start the new fiscal year on June 1. Once the complete budget has been prepared by the staff with the finance committee, and approved by the finance committee, the budget is brought to the full board of directors for approval. Those who prepared the budget should be able to provide thorough information to support the numbers included in it and be able to justify any revenue assumptions or expenses that are called into question.

For purposes of this discussion, the vote on the new budget might occur at the monthly board meeting in April or May. Once approved, the new budget would be in place for the June 1 start of the new fiscal year and would become the guideline for the next fiscal year for all financial matters. Will it always follow the exact numbers for expenses and income? No. But it is the organization's best guess as to how the year will proceed. There are always surprises, both bad and good. At the end of the year, the goal is to have balanced the budget and achieved all the educational and programming goals of the organization.

SOURCES OF REVENUE FOR A CHOIR

Revenue to support a choir comes from many places. Revenue for a school choir may come from a line on the school district's budget for the music department and be distributed to each school in the district by the music supervisor. Funding may come from a school building's budget and be distributed by the building principal to the choral program. A parent support group or booster club may provide supplemental funds to the school music program. The school's parent-teacher association may fund special projects of the school choir when the school's music educator submits a request. Fees from concerts or fundraising events sponsored by the school may supplement the existing choral music education budget. For some, there may be no funding available, and fundraisers must be held to provide the much-needed basic materials for the school choral music program. Other districts may have significant funds that provide for part-time voice teachers, purchases for the music library, accompanists, hiring professional musicians for concerts, commissioning of composers, and so on.

The needs of a children's/youth choir in the church context may be funded directly by the church music program. Sometimes the choir has its own line on the budget. Specific fundraising events may be undertaken for special projects on an as-needed basis. For each context of school, church, or community children's and youth choirs, funding needs will vary.

There are basic budget categories common to many children's and youth choirs. Although the following list of revenue line items is not a complete one, it is an overview of some of the components an organization might choose to include:

- Contributions—Individual restricted
  - Income from an individual that is restricted to a specific use
- Contributions—Individual unrestricted
  - Income from an individual that is placed in the operating budget of the organization
- Contributions—Board
  - Income from individual board members
- Contributions—Corporations restricted
  - Income from a corporation that is restricted to a specific use
- Contributions—Corporations unrestricted
  - Income from a corporation that is placed in the operating budget of the organization
- Contributions—Foundation restricted
  - Income from a foundation that is restricted to a specific use
- Contributions—Foundation unrestricted
  - Income from a foundation that is placed in the operating budget of the organization
- Contributions—Other restricted
  - Income from other sources that does not fit into categories above and is restricted for a specific purpose
- Contributions—Other unrestricted
  - Income from other sources that does not fit into categories above and is placed in the operating budget of the organization
- Contributions—Scholarship Fund
- Contributions—Endowment Fund
- Project Grants—Federal
- Project Grants—State
- Project Grants—Local
- Project Grants—Corporation
- Project Grants—Foundations

- Interest and Dividend Income
- Tuition
- Audition Fees
- Contracted Performances
- Ticket sales
- Sales—Promotional merchandise
- Sales—CDs
- Chorister Camp Income
- Annual Fundraiser

The above categories represent a sample list of income sources for a children's choir. Some choirs may have more extensive types of income, and others may have a far simpler list based on the size of the organization, amount of activity, and the type of programming.

For children's or youth choirs sponsored by an adult professional choir or volunteer choir, funds may be given by the parent organization toward salaries, accompanists, promotional materials, music, and more. A tuition fee may be charged to participating choristers that defrays some of the expenses. Each choir will develop its own budget strategy within the contexts of its own organization and what is doable.

EXPENSES

Expenses will vary from choir to choir. The following list cites some of the basic budget line items for a community-based children's or youth choir:

- Staff Salaries
- Payroll Taxes
- Insurance (liability, director and officers, health, travel, etc.)
- Performance Cost—Major Event
- Performance Cost—Minor Event
- ASCAP Fees
- Accompanist(s)
- Bank Service Fees
- Outside Contracted Musicians
- Concert Venue Rental
- Rehearsal Space Rental
- Newsletters
- Postage/Shipping
- Concert Recording Fee
- Audition Expenses
- Camp Expenses
- Music—Permanent Library

- Music—Commissioned Work
- Grant Expense
- Accounting Service Fees
- CPA Audit Fees (if necessary)
- Printing
- Rent (office and equipment)
- Wardrobe
- Office Supplies
- Copier Maintenance and Supplies
- Phone, Computer, Internet
- Transportation for Choral Events (e.g., motor coach, airfare)
- Professional Development and Continuing Education
- Mileage Reimbursements
- Board Expense
- Annual Fundraiser Event Expenses
- End of Year Awards

The sample list of expenses will reflect the initiatives for each year of the organization. The number of choirs, number of staff members, and extent of the programming will determine what is appropriate for each organization. The budget will vary from organization to organization and year to year. (A sample budget worksheet may be found in *appendix 5.1*.)

FINANCIAL REPORTS: THE BALANCE SHEET, THE BUDGET, AND THE INCOME STATEMENT

The three parts of a financial report are:

- the balance sheet
- the budget
- the income statement

The *balance sheet* is a short overview or summary of the current financial status of the organization. It summarizes the assets (things owned by the choir—cash, property, facilities, music, and equipment) and liabilities (monies the choir owes). The difference between the two (assets minus liabilities) is called the *equity balance* and is equal to the organization's "net worth." (See *appendix 5.2* for a sample balance sheet.) The *budget* is the list of projected sources of income for the year and the anticipated expenses for the year. The budget answers the following questions: "What expenses do we expect to have?" and "What income will be generated that will cover these expenses?" The *income statement* reports the actual revenue and expenses and the net income that is derived from these totals; it articulates the actual revenue earned and expenses for the year to date; and it might also include the annual budget numbers so it is possible to track how close the income and expenses compare to the projected budget numbers for the year. The *fiscal year* for a choir may be one calendar year from January 1 to December 31, or it may be set following a different sequence of dates established by the board of directors in the bylaws of the organization, such as July 1 to June 30.

For the musician not trained in business matters, learning how to create a budget and read a financial report will serve the organization well. Typically, the administrator of the choir (or founder who is initially doing the setup work) prepares the budget. This may be done in consultation with an accountant or in consultation with the finance committee of the board of directors or overseeing body, if one exists. In the simplest form, the founder might require music, an accompanist, funds for a salary, print and postage costs, and a rehearsal location. Later, funds for additional expenses, such as concert attire or scholarships for the choristers, may be added. The artistic staff will have ideas for programming that may include the purchase of music; commissioning a new work; hiring a string orchestra, chamber ensemble, or additional instrumentalists; purchasing props or costumes for a staged production such as an opera or theater piece; or other requirements that will affect line items on the budget. If an organization has administrative staff, discussions should occur collaboratively between artistic staff and administrative staff to determine what financial resources are needed and what sources of revenue might be available to support these expenses. These numbers are included in the budget if deemed appropriate.

Artistic programming might include outside performances that may generate income for the choir, such as singing with a local symphony orchestra for a classics series or family concert, or singing for an event such as a large convention or civic function where an honorarium may be given to the choir.

All revenues and expenses will be included in the first budget of a new choir or, in the case of an existing choir, in the upcoming year's budget. It is not always possible to anticipate all of the income and expenses that will occur. A budget is your most informed statement about what you expect the coming year to look like financially, but it may be adjusted as the year unfolds. It is not absolute. There are always surprises.

One such surprise might be the unanticipated need to find office space for the choir midyear, and the additional expense of rent that will be incurred. Another example might be a special invitation to a festival or performance out of town or out of the country that arrives after the budget was prepared. The significant costs for such a tour must somehow be covered without affecting the chorus's annual operating budget. Another unanticipated event might be the gentleman who walks into the chorus office and hands the staff a check for $1,000 two weeks before Christmas because he enjoys giving outstanding local organizations a surprise at holiday time. One never knows what will happen on any given day.

The unanticipated expenses and revenues must be dealt with on a case-by-case basis. Certain questions should be asked:

- Is it feasible to take on the project, event, or financial challenge being considered?
- What are the pros, cons, or alternatives?
- Where will revenue be found to cover this unanticipated expense?
- How will we be good stewards of this unanticipated gift of funds?

Board members and staff members should make informed decisions about what is realistic for the organization to undertake. A carefully laid-out plan to cover unanticipated expenses should be developed. At other times, taking on an unplanned activity may require a leap of faith based on an understanding of the community and resources that potentially could be available to cover it.

FINANCIAL STATEMENTS FOR BOARD MEETINGS

The board of directors, charged with fiduciary responsibility of the nonprofit organization, will expect complete financial reports at each monthly board meeting. For example, assuming the fiscal year begins June 1, at the monthly meeting of the board of directors in September, the members would receive a financial report in the following format:

Income Statement—vs. Annual Budget. For the Three Months Ending August, 31, 2010

	Current Month Actual	Current Month Budget	Year to Date Actual	Annual Budget
Revenues				
Expenses				
Total expenses				
Net Income				

The number of horizontal rows under the headings of "Revenues" or "Expenses" will be determined by the needs of the organization. The basic reporting structure is standard and easily generated by the accounting software. The board of directors must be able to see the budget categories, what the actual expenses are to date, and what amount was budgeted for the year in each category to be able to track the progress throughout the year.

Often, the "Current Month Budget" does not accurately reflect what happens during the year. This number reflects the total line item budgeted dollar amount for the year, and in some scenarios is simply divided by twelve so that the dollar amount is evenly distributed across each month in a linear fashion. Children's choirs are not linear, meaning that the expenses and revenues are typically not evenly distributed across each month throughout the year. The linear method of calendarization is not always used. Some organizations create a more sophisticated month-to-month budget to reflect anticipated figures more accurately. The annual total budget remains the same. (See *appendix 5.3* for a sample monthly budget report.)

An example of uneven distribution of income may be from tuition. For some organizations, tuition revenue may come in mostly at the start of the academic year. Income from ticket sales will increase when season subscription orders are received, and increase again at each concert when walk-in ticket sales add revenue. At other times of the year, such as July, there may be no activity whatsoever for ticket sales. If there are four annual concerts from September to May, there will be a pattern to this income. So, too, will there be a pattern to expenses. For example, if a choir does their concert planning in the late fall of 2014 or in January of 2015 for the 2015–2016 concert season, the cost for the purchase of new music for the 2015–2016 season may occur during the summer of 2015, in preparation for the fall start-up of rehearsals. The purchase of music does not necessarily occur in an equal dollar amount each month throughout the year.

In contrast, expenses for full-time salaries, rent, and phone service *are* more linear and remain mostly the same for each month. There is a natural flow to each year. And, most often, it takes an entire year to run the complete sequence of events for a children's/youth choir. This differs from a business that has more linear income and expenses that remain steady throughout twelve months.

For the founder or managing artistic director, the work on budgets may seem daunting at first. With good advice from a certified public accountant or capable staff member who handles the accounting, working with numbers gets easier. In larger organizations where staff members are assigned the accounting responsibility, the artistic director must work in cooperation with the staff to provide reliable information about the cost consequences of his or her artistic planning. Some examples of this follow:

- The choir will stage an opera next year and need costumes, a staging director, a chamber ensemble, and music scores. This will cost *x* number of dollars.
- The choir will require a harpist for *A Ceremony of Carols* for the December concert, which will cost *x* number of dollars.
- New sight-reading books will be needed for the beginning choir for next year that will cost *x* number of dollars in addition to the choral octavos for this choir.

- The choir will need to purchase a *djembe* (drum) and an *axatse* (percussion instrument) to supplement the existing drums we own for an African singing, dancing, and drumming segment for the May concert.
- The newly commissioned work will premiere in May and will require a professional string quartet at the cost of *x* number of dollars. This may also include honorarium, hotel, travel, and per diem.

Each of these requests will require revenue to support the artistic programming. Expenses for each will need to be included in the operating budget.

Although the task of overseeing the budget for the founder, artistic director, or managing artistic director is significant work, there are many people willing to help one understand the process. Seek good counsel. With careful planning and responsible spending, and an awareness of what is possible, it is a skill that artistic directors are capable of learning.

BUDGETS FOR YEARS THAT INCLUDE A TOUR

Typically for a children's or youth choir, the budget will show a dramatic increase in a year when a tour occurs. For example, a domestic tour may cost $80,000 for choir, staff, and chaperones. This would be an $80,000 swing in the budget (i.e., the budget would reflect $80,000 more in income and a similar amount in expenses that would not be a typical yearly event). The larger or smaller the tour, the more the total budget number will vary. Tour revenues and expenses are often isolated from the operating budget for an organization, or a separate bank account is established for tours only. (See tour budget discussion later in this chapter.)

Isolating the tour expenses from the general operating budget may be set up in the computer accounting program. It is possible to set up "jobs" in the accounting system for special projects such as a tour, fundraising event, or grant-funded project. All financial matters related to a specific project/event are tagged with the same job code and may be isolated into one specific report for the event or project. Complete details for the finances (both income and expense) for the tour can be articulated in a job report and referred to often to carefully monitor progress.

TUITION AS A SOURCE OF INCOME

Members of school and church choirs rarely, if ever, are charged a fee for participation. For community-based children's choirs, though, there is often a tuition fee for participation. This cost may range from a small dollar amount, to several hundred dollars; or several thousand dollars for a year-long residential program. This will depend on the context of the organization. Scholarships may be available to financially deserving choir members to help defray the cost of tuition.

At the time of acceptance into a choir that has a tuition fee, the payment may be due in full, or a nonrefundable deposit may be required to secure the child's place in the choir for the upcoming year. Some choirs require a deposit from every child, regardless of scholarship needs, to indicate the commitment of the parent to the child's participation in the organization. Other scholarship programs fully fund a chorister's tuition. Some choirs audition once a year; some audition on a revolving schedule throughout the year; and others have a set audition time occurring at the same time each year. (More about auditions may be found in chapter 6.)

Billing for tuition may be twice a year, monthly, weekly, or in full at the start of the academic year. Each choir will establish a system that works best for its own organization. Accurate records must be kept for each chorister, indicating the amount of the payment, whether it is cash or check (with the check number), and the date of payment. Photocopies of all checks should be kept should a question about payment arise. Each choir will develop its own tuition tracking system for each child. Some choirs keep records using the organization's accounting software package, some set up an Excel spreadsheet, and others create binders or ledgers with handwritten records for each child. Regardless of the method, accurate records must be kept.

SCHOLARSHIPS

In children's and youth choirs where a tuition fee is charged for participation, there may be a need for scholarship funds to support the participation of financially deserving choristers. For scholarship applications, each choir must decide how to handle this discreetly. The utmost confidentiality is required for all involved in the decision-making process for scholarship awards. At the time of the child's acceptance to the chorus, application materials for financial assistance should be provided to the parent or guardian. Clear instructions should be included indicating how to apply, the due date of the application, and what materials will be needed to substantiate the family's financial status. (See *appendix 5.4* for a sample scholarship application form.)

The financial status of some families may change suddenly when a parent becomes unexpectedly unemployed or another dramatic event occurs. For some, the prior year's tax records (if required for submission at the time of the scholarship application) do not reflect the actual current reality of the family situation. Optional supplemental information from a parent can assist in understanding the current unique and/or changing needs of a family. For families with more than one child in the chorus, some consideration may be given to them at the time of scholarship application, in the form of a reduced tuition fee. Some choirs will choose to fund transportation costs (subway, bus) to and from rehearsals and concerts as part of the scholarship award.

In the interest of neutrality and fairness, some organizations have a person outside the choir rank the scholarship applications from most financially deserving to least. A person in the scholarship office of a local college or university who is trained in evaluating scholarship applicants would be a good resource for ranking the choir's applications.

These professionals are often very willing to assist and make a recommendation about the ranking of the applicants. A scholarship committee may be set up by the chorus board of directors to review the applications after they are ranked by an outside party. This committee can award the available scholarship funds based on the data from the outside evaluator and input from administrative staff who know the families. A staff member was often heard saying, "This is my favorite day of the year, when we get to give away the scholarship money. It always makes the families so happy."

Another gesture of kindness the choir may extend to scholarship families is to provide two complimentary tickets to each concert. This gives at least two of the family members an opportunity to attend the child's concerts without the added burden of the cost for concert tickets (if concerts are ticketed events). Again, this may be done confidentially.

PROJECT BUDGETS

As the choral organization grows, the choir may choose to take on creative projects that involve guest artists, such as a dance company, jazz combo, a professional choir, instrumentalists, a puppet theater, commissioning composers, or opera productions. A timeline project budget will need to be developed for each event that goes beyond the basic operating costs for the choir. A timeline will also be necessary to ensure that the project is doable. One such project might be to commission a new work for the chorus. (The process of commissioning a composer will be discussed in depth in chapter 9.)

Project Budget for a Commissioned Work

The project of commissioning a composer to write a new work for a choir begins with the artistic director's vision for what the project will be. The commissioned work might be presented to celebrate a special anniversary of the chorus, to honor someone, or written in memory of someone. A new piece might be composed for a festival or a tour performance in a special location. Once contact is made with the composer and the fee for commissioning the new work is determined, the next cost to be determined is the type of instrumentation that the composer will choose for the new work. The choir will determine if the composer will be funded to attend the premiere of the new work. The costs of commissioning a new work from the beginning to premiere might include the following:

- Commissioning fee for the composer
- Travel cost for composer to be in residence for the premiere (costs to include airfare and ground transportation)
- Hotel and per diem for guest artists
- Performance fees for outside contracted musicians (e.g., string quartet or woodwind quintet, assuming local musicians will be used)

- Additional guest artist: honorarium, airfare, hotel, and per diem for guest artist (e.g., an *erhu* player brought for premiere of a piece as requested by a Chinese commissioning composer)
- Print and mailing costs of promotional materials to invite area choral music educators, university composition students and faculty, and local composers to attend premiere-related events

Costs should be determined for every aspect of commissioning and presenting the new work. The total sum of these costs is then put into the annual budget. Grants might be sought to support the additional expenses. Applying for grants is discussed later in this chapter.

Tour Budget

Another frequent activity of a community-based children's or youth choir is touring. When considering a tour, detailed planning begins before the final decision is made to undertake the tour. All tour expenses must be determined as carefully as possible to determine if the tour is financially feasible. The tour budget is completed after much research into the anticipated costs of all aspects of the tour can be compiled.

Budgets for each tour will vary depending on duration of the tour, the distance of the tour (whether it is local, state, national, or international), and the type of transportation that will be used (e.g., air, bus, train). The anticipated costs of meals and hotel stays, if required, will need to be researched in addition to gathering any additional information for all cost-bearing events of the tour, such as sightseeing or admission tickets for a museum, theater, or other activity.

For a seven-day domestic tour of forty-eight choristers, seven chaperones, and five staff (one administrative, one director and spouse, and two accompanists), a list of expenses might look like the following:

- Round trip airfare for sixty people
- Ground transportation: motor coach cost for six days
- Hotel (two nights' stay) location #1 (*x* number of rooms at *x* amount of dollars)
- Hotel (two nights' stay) location #2 (*x* number of rooms at *x* amount of dollars)
  - Note: two nights will be home stays (including two breakfasts and one bag lunch)
- Hotel (two nights' stay) for chaperones and staff only (*x* number of rooms at *x* dollars)
- Meals (cost of five lunches and four dinners ×sixty people)
- Cost of sightseeing (admission for sixty people at two different locations)
- Tour T-shirts (staff and chaperones included)
- Printing costs for tour program

- Miscellaneous expenses (cabs, extra food, bottled water, rehearsal snacks, etc.)
- Administrative fee (a small percentage of tour cost) divided equally between paying participants (for administrative staff time and office expenses directly devoted to trip preparation)

The dollar amount will be determined for each expense item for the tour. Revenue for the tour should also be calculated at the beginning of the project. How will the tour be funded? Revenue sources may include but are not limited to the following:

- Per person fee to participate (will everyone pay, or will some staff be covered by all paying participants?)
- Fundraising event, such as a plant sale, where all proceeds are designated to defray tour expenses and reduce participant share of cost
- Benefit concert to raise money for tour (all proceeds go directly toward tour expenses)
- Corporate sponsorships
- Individual fundraising events that choristers may elect to participate in or not, proceeds for which directly defray part of the chorister's individual cost (e.g., cookie sale, candy sale, pie sale, etc.)

Tours may be handled as special projects that are self-supporting events.

Some performances or short tours that do not involve extensive travel may be revenue-generating events for a choir. An example of this is when a choir is invited to be the guest artist for a performing arts series in a concert located not too far from the choir's home. Costs for bus rental, program printing, and ASCAP fees may be covered by the host organization, and an honorarium may be given to the choir. This revenue would contribute toward the general operating budget of the choir and be included in the budget under the income category "Concert Revenue—Outside event."

Other Fundraising Opportunities

Other special events might generate income for the choir's operating budget. One example might be an invitation-only reception following a concert premiere. Invitations may be sent out to invited patrons to attend a reception or light supper honoring the guest composer. Expenses for this might include the following:

- Print costs for formal invitations for the dinner
- Mailing costs
- Cost of caterer
- Facility rental (if necessary)

Many of the costs for this type of event can be donated or in-kind services given by volunteers who are willing to contribute to the event. University student conducting interns or alumni choristers may be invited to volunteer to be servers for the reception, and all proceeds from the event can be given directly to the choir. If the event is held in a home, a performance by a guest artist, chorister, small ensemble, or alumni chorister might be included.

GRANTS

Another source of income for a school choir or a community-based children's/youth choir is grants. There are many granting agencies, government offices, corporations, and foundations (both public and private) that grant awards to nonprofit organizations. Finding the right place to apply takes time and research. The granting agency or foundation must be a good match for the choir's grant proposal or proposed project, and vice versa. Many published and online resources exist that offer guidelines for writing grants.[5]

A grant from a foundation signifies a partnership between the grantor and the grantee. The grantor becomes a stakeholder in the organization's event or project. Together, the organization and the funding agency can make a difference in a community through projects that are mutually compatible with both organizations' missions.

For some children's choirs, January and the summer months are optimal times to research grant funding opportunities. At these times of year, the choir may have a less intense schedule that allows for larger blocks of uninterrupted time to research grants. Once research has been done and possible grants have been identified, a grant summary sheet should be created. The summary indicates the grant agency, project to be funded, date grant application is due, amount being requested, notification date, and actual amount received (or not). Having an Excel spreadsheet or single page summary will assist in tracking the applications. Mapping out due dates for grants on a calendar may also be helpful with advance planning for preparing the grant. Some grants may be as simple to prepare as writing a letter of request, and others may take several weeks of work to complete. (See *appendix 5.5* for a sample grant timeline.)

When applying for a grant, time should be spent thoroughly fleshing out the project. The types of questions to answer might include the following:

- What will the project be?
- Why is it important?
- What resources will be needed?
- Is it in line with the choir's mission and beliefs?
- Is it in line with the grantor's mission and beliefs?
- What is the timeline for the project?
- What will the outcomes be?
- How will key personnel evaluate the successes and failures of the project?

Basic components of a grant include a project overview, the objectives, the staff or performing forces needed to accomplish the project, the project budget, how the project's success (or failure) will be assessed, and supplemental information about the organization. Once the project is well defined and developed, an opportunity to speak with a potential funder can often provide valuable information before the actual grant application is finalized and submitted.

Care should also be given to how the material is presented. All grant application materials should be prepared in a professional manner. Narratives should be articulate and succinct. Grant applications often require supplemental materials in addition to the project application and budget. These materials should be carefully compiled and checked off as each requested item is gathered. The required supplemental materials might include the following:

- Choir's mission statement
- Choir's organizational chart
- List of board of directors including names and occupations
- Sample programs from the past three years
- Season brochures from the past three years
- Concert reviews from local papers
- Sample recording (CD or DVD)
  - Note: This may include recordings from the current season or from prior seasons.
- A copy of the budget for the current year
- A copy of the audit from the prior year

Grant applications may be very specific as to how many copies of materials must be provided and how they should be bound (binder clip, notebook, single sets, etc.), and exact instructions about how to submit (via e-mail, website, certified mail, etc.) may be included. Some grant applications may be submitted online with supplemental materials sent by mail. Some grantors may request a letter of intent to apply and respond only to those that are approved to move forward in the application process. In this case, a letter of invitation to submit a full application with detailed instructions follows. Each grant application must be carefully read, understood, and followed to the letter.

When a work sample such as a CD, DVD, or MP3 is requested, utmost care should be taken to prepare the submission. Specific criteria unique to the particular grant may be requested;these may include the exact duration of music required, a request for a variety of styles, a request for an a cappella selection, and others. The work sample should be of the highest quality possible, both in terms of the recording quality and the artistic product. For some grants, the CD is the first level of criteria to be evaluated. If the musical excellence of the submission does not meet the acceptable standards of the granting agency, the application will be eliminated from consideration. For other grants, no recording may be required, and other criteria will be used to evaluate the application.

The artistic staff and the administrative staff will need to collaborate on the grant application (unless the founder is solely preparing the grant). The creative side of the grant is the project the music director wishes to undertake. The financial data for the project require the collaboration of the artistic staff and the administrative staff. The creative concept and key phrases used in the grant narrative will come from the artistic director who has the vision for the creative music project. It is up to the grant writer to convey the essence of the project and why the project is important for the grantor to fund in a way that is concise and easily understood by the reader of the application. The narrative should inspire the reader to become intrigued and interested in seeing the project move forward. For grants that do not require a creative musical component, the administrative staff may proceed without artistic input.

There are many types of grants. Some are specifically targeted to support operating costs. More often, grants are targeted to support creative programming, collaborative projects, scholarships, or equipment purchases such as computers. Some are targeted for concert season support. There are many kinds of possibilities for funding opportunities. A sample list of how grants may be used includes the following:

- To ask a local cultural resources council for funding to bring a nationally known performing artist to perform with the choir.
- To fund an educational program in the schools as an outreach project of the choir.
- To fund a workshop for area choral music educators at the elementary and middle school level.
- To support the creation of a theater piece involving a children's author, a local theater company, and the choir.
- To support the commissioning of a new work.
- To fund a composer-in-residence.
- To support a recording project of historically significant repertoire.
- To fund need-based scholarships.
- To support concert production.
- To inspire other giving through a matching funds challenge grant.
- To support hosting an international choir.
- To support a collaborative commissioning project with three choirs from diverse geographic locations.
- To fund an event involving a professional choir, high school choirs, a youth symphony orchestra, and a children's choir in a collaborative concert.
- To fund a collaborative event with university faculty, a community arts group, university students (composition and music education majors), and invited participants from the local community, including music educators.
- To purchase a portable electronic piano to facilitate concerts in nontraditional concert locations.
- To support a sabbatical leave for a founding director to study how to structure the transition of the organization to new leadership when it is time.

- To support hiring a consultant to lead a strategic planning session with board and staff.
- To hire a consultant to work with a board of directors to facilitate the hiring of a new artistic director.

The above list is a sample of the types of grants that can be written and projects that may be funded. Researching past funded projects may give insights into successful grant applications and the types of grants an agency or foundation likes to fund. It may also inspire new ideas for projects the choir could undertake.

How well the grant is written, how strong the project is, how well it matches the goals of the funder, and the availability of funds will in part determine the application's chance for success. It is not uncommon to have a grant application refused. During difficult economic times, competition for funds is elevated. Seeking information from the granting agency about why a grant was refused may give insight into how to better prepare applications in the future. There are always lessons to be learned.

Choir budgets should not be based solely on funding from grants. For fiscally sound planning, projects should be developed that can be modified should grant support not be available, or when funds are awarded at a lesser dollar amount than the full amount requested. An organization that bases the choir budget significantly on grant funding is one that puts the organization at risk. Support from grants is not real until the proposal is accepted and the dollars are awarded. One never knows for sure if a proposal will be accepted or not. Thoughtful and responsible planning is always advised.

Following confirmation of a grant being received, the funds are sent to the organization according to the timetable established by the granting agency. Some grants may be offered in installments contingent on the organization's ongoing compliance with the terms of the grant. The granting agency may require periodic reports throughout the project or one report at the conclusion. The final report may include a detailed written accounting of how the funds were used and a written narrative about the project's successes, challenges, and the grant's impact.

AUDITS

Some grants may require the organization's financial audit from the last completed fiscal year to be submitted with the completed grant application. Or, in an effort to achieve best practices of good governance and properly execute fiduciary responsibilities, an annual audit may be requested by members of the board of directors, whether or not it is needed for a grant application or required by governmental authorities. The definition of an audit is "an official inspection of an organization's accounts, typically by an independent body."[6] The procedure is for the organization to hire a certified public accountant (someone from outside the organization) to examine and test all financial documents and provide a written report to the board of directors. This document substantiates that the financial records of the organization are complete in all material aspects as presented. The auditor will provide an overview of internal office financial controls and procedures and recommend any changes that need to be made. He or she will also examine the internal checks and balances for the management of money to be sure that proper procedures are in place. The auditor will also examine whether the organization is in compliance with federal and state tax laws, as well as meeting the requirements of the organization's 501(c)(3) designation.

COMPUTER SECURITY AND STAFF DEPARTURES

To protect computer and physical records for a nonprofit choral organization, two individuals should be assigned administrative rights to all computer files and records. The assigned administrators might be a member of the board of directors and the chief executive officer (or administrator) of the chorus.

Administrative rights mean that only the administrator can grant staff members computer permissions and physical access to corporate records and documents. These permissions allow staff members to edit, change, add, or delete records on the computer, including financial records, and materials necessary to accomplish their work responsibilities.

Each new staff member will need to be assigned a unique password for access to the organization's computer. Similarly, access will need to be granted to important records kept in locked file cabinets. When a staff member ends his or her employment, the assigned administrator should immediately remove the departing employee's ability to access all records of the corporation. This is done for security purposes.

RETENTION OF FINANCIAL RECORDS

Business documents are an important history of transactions with customers, vendors, creditors, and employees. Records should be maintained and available to resolve questions that may arise. Corporate records should be maintained for as long as they are related to possible IRS proceedings or a taxpayer's claim for a tax credit or refund. Certain circumstances involving pending or potential litigation may require an extension of time for record retention. Legal counsel should be consulted prior to discarding documents that may be subject to such an extension. (See *appendix 5.6* for a list of documents and the required retention time.)

CONCLUSION

For the musician, conductor, or educator, the financial matters of a choir may seem overwhelming. However, with entrepreneurial zeal, commitment to the vision of what the choir will become, research, and good counsel from friends, colleagues, and professional advisers, financial matters become more understandable. Similar to becoming a musician, new financial skills and abilities are developed with practice. It is possible to be a founder and a managing artistic director (one who oversees both artistic and administrative matters) if necessary. Or, as an artistic director, working in collaboration with staff and the board of directors, these skills will assist in bringing the choir to fruition and secure an ongoing, strong financial structure for the organization. Is it a challenge? Yes. Is it easy? Not always, but it is possible. And it happens one day at a time.

> We are what we repeatedly do.
> Excellence, then, is not an act, but a habit.
> —ARISTOTLE

6

REHEARSALS AND PARENTS

"I WISH THEY would just read the memo. They are calling to ask about information we have already put in the last three e-mailed memos." This comment is often made by children's choir administrators. Most recently it has become, "I *know* that information was in the e-mail we sent to the parents, and it is posted on the website." Eventually it may become, "We already tweeted and texted them the information, why do they need to call us and ask?"

Structuring a children's choir for excellence, regardless of the context of the choir, happens when there is strong communication and commitment. Excellence does not happen accidentally. The open lines of communication between artistic staff, administrative staff, parents, and board matter greatly. Collaboration and communication within the organizational structure of a choir are just as important as the collaboration and communication between choir, conductor, and accompanist.

For school choirs, the building principal, secretaries, and janitorial staff must be in the communication loop with the choral music educator, as all of these people are involved when the choir presents a concert. The janitorial staff will most likely be responsible for setting up risers for the choir and chairs for the audience if the concert is to be held in a school gymnasium. Or, if concerts are held at the district high school or nearby church, coordination among all those who manage those facilities will need to be involved in the planning and preparation. The school secretarial or office staff will most likely type and make copies of the program for the concert audience. The conductor of the choirs will schedule concert dates with the approval of the school administration and possibly coordinate with the district music coordinator or fine arts coordinator if one exists. Collaboration may occur between the music teacher and classroom teachers for special projects. And possibly teachers in the areas of reading, social studies, language arts, and art may be involved in all-school projects involving classroom choirs. Other events might include volunteer parents who help make scenery and provide props or costumes for special musical productions. Conductor-teachers will need to coordinate with all those involved in special school events, such as parades, musicals, school assemblies, morning sings, field trips, or special concerts involving the choir. With all of these events, strong communication enhances the flow of information and ensures the likeliness of their success.

In the church context, children's choirs are scheduled to sing at selected times during the year, weekly, or once a month based on the overall planning of regular worship services. The children's choir may sing for special services, pageants, church holy days, or other events, such as a performance with combined adult and children's choirs, or with an orchestra. This scheduling may be done by the music director of the church, organist/choir director, or director of the choir at the request of the worship committee, minister, rabbi, priest, or worship leader.

Regardless of context, if the choir is to achieve excellence both musically and organizationally, it will depend on how well the choir is organized, how well choral rehearsals are conducted, how thoroughly information is communicated to all participants, and how thoroughly planned in advance each event is. Having choir members arrive at the correct location, at the correct time, wearing the proper clothing, and well prepared to sing has much to do with how those details are organized and communicated.

A children's choir staff member was heard saying the following at a parent orientation session held at the first rehearsal of the year: "Here's all you *really* need to know for the year: read the memo, read the memo, read the memo." Everyone chuckled. And then they heard why this is so important. Memos may be the chosen method of communication in which all important information is conveyed to parents about chorus matters. Some choirs distribute this information in printed format. Some distribute memos via e-mail and post similar information on a secure section of the chorus's website for chorister families only. The organization where the above statement was made has earned a reputation for strong communication by sending thorough advance notices to parents regarding every aspect of the choral program throughout the year. Educating parents about expectations and organizational procedures is as important as educating choristers how to enter and exit the risers for a concert. In the fast-paced lives of contemporary families, attention to detail and easy access to information are appreciated, as are additional advance reminders.

THE CHANGING WAYS OF COMMUNICATING

The twenty-first century has expedited the sharing of information at an astounding rate. Internet and cable television have given us access to information from around the world as rapidly as it occurs. Most recently, a shift in communication has been occurring with the unprecedented increase in the use of social media. *Social media* are defined as "websites and applications used for social networking."[1]

Facebook, Twitter, YouTube, and other social media platforms are rapidly increasing as means of communication. Author Erik Qualman states, ". . . if Facebook was a country, it would be the third largest in the world, only behind China and India."[2] Twitter is currently gaining increased use. The first photograph to appear of the U.S.

Airways flight that was heroically landed in the Hudson River in January 2009 was uploaded to Twitter, and relief efforts poured into Haiti following the 2009 massive earthquake there via texted donations.[3] In the less than three years from 2006 to 2009, social media became the most popular activity on the Internet. As social media use increases, there are significant implications for nonprofit organizations and how they communicate. Children's choirs will increasingly use these digital communication tools.

Implications for the future of the arts may be found in how people connect and by what means they communicate. Qualman states the following about the current use of social media:

- Social media is about people.
- 50 percent of the world's population is under the age of thirty.
- Social media are the number-one activity on the web.
- Facebook tops Google for weekly traffic in the United States.
- 95 percent of companies using social media for recruitment use LinkedIn.
- Generations Y and Z consider e-mail passé.
- 69 percent of parents are "friends" with their children on social media.
- Sales for books on eReaders have surpassed traditional book sales.
- YouTube is the largest search engine in the world.
- Every minute, twenty-four hours of video are uploaded to YouTube.
- 90 percent of people trust peer recommendations.
- 14 percent trust advertisements.
- 93 percent of marketers use social media for business.[4]

At the inaugural Social Media A Cappella Conference (SMACC), the impact of social media's impact on the arts, and specifically on the rapidly growing collegiate a cappella movement, was the focus.[5] A subculture exists unlike at any other time in our history based on electronic communication through Facebook, Twitter, and other social media platforms. College students announce a cappella concerts, and an audience fills the concert space minutes before a performance. National professional organizations are using Twitter and Facebook to communicate with members during national conferences and beyond.[6] Flash mobs have suddenly appeared singing the "Hallelujah Chorus" at shopping malls all over the country during the month of December. The Mormon Tabernacle Choir flash mob sang at Historic Williamsburg in Virginia. Social events are organized in minutes, and those who are "connected" build relationships in this way. All these ways of communicating are influencing how we organize our lives, make decisions about what activities to engage in, and with whom we choose to engage in those activities.

The children currently singing in our choirs do not remember a time without Internet, cell phones, cable television, DVDs, MP3s, and satellite radio. These choristers will be the most "connected" generation yet. And, five years from now, the technology will be more advanced, as we have seen with the recent addition of iPads, iPhones, touch-screens, and tablet computers. The rapid development of technology allows those who use social media to be instantly connected with their friends, and their friends' friends and beyond, if they choose.

These rapidly changing modes of digital communication have implications for children's choirs. The time will come when, if a children's chorus is rehearsing with a symphony orchestra and the rehearsal ends unexpectedly early, parents will be texted accordingly. Not everyone will receive the message, but the network of parents will quickly spread the word about the earlier required pick-up time for the choristers. Generating audiences may be done by sending tweets and sharing on Facebook pages. Blogs about choirs and their concerts will appear and generate enthusiasm and audiences. The possibilities are just beginning.

The choirs that flourish will take advantage of social media to communicate in potent ways. With developing strategies for organizational excellence as a goal, this chapter focuses on positioning your children's choir for excellence in its day-to-day operations.

AUDITIONS

One method of selecting choir members is by audition. Some community-based children's/youth choirs require an in-person audition before acceptance is granted for participation. Preparation for these auditions begins several months in advance. It may be helpful to develop an administrative timeline well in advance of the auditions that shows the sequence of activities from the time of the auditions announcement through completion of registration. This timeline may include dates for an introductory letter to be sent to area music teachers (if asked to submit recommendations), those on the chorus waiting list, or those who have expressed an interest in having a child audition. Audition location facilities should be confirmed, and all printed materials should be created or updated. Forms included in the teacher packet might include the recommendation packet cover letter, FAQ sheet (frequently asked questions, with answers), audition recommendation information form for teachers, and a form for teachers to request a complimentary ticket to a concert. (These may also be provided online from the chorus website.) (See appendix 6.1 for a copy of an audition timeline.)

Some choirs may require a written recommendation from the child's school music teacher prior to the student's audition. Recommendations from the teacher (or private teacher in the case of home-schooled children) may be submitted in writing or by e-mail. Once recommended, information about the chorus and an invitation to the child to audition are sent to the child's family. The chorus materials might also include the following:

- Congratulatory message about being recommended by the music teacher
- Chorus season brochure (with photographs of the choirs)

- Audition requirements
- Map with the audition location, driving directions, and parking instructions
- FAQ sheet (frequently asked questions) about the chorus
- Chorus website information where similar information is posted
- Instructions about how to schedule an audition
- Office contact information and phone numbers

The above information may be sent electronically or by mail and may be the first direct contact from the chorus to the parent. How the choir presents itself in all printed materials (letters, diagrams, season brochures, etc.) matters. The materials should offer a favorable impression of the chorus to the child and the family and generate interest in becoming part of the ensemble.

The next contact the chorus office may have with the parent will be by phone or e-mail to schedule an audition time for the student. Once the audition is scheduled, the first face-to-face contact with the chorus will happen.

The Canadian journalist Malcolm Gladwell suggests that people make a snap judgment when they enter a space or meet a new person. This "blink" moment shapes how they initially perceive the person or event. He suggests that we make "very quick judgments based on very little information."[7] As artistic excellence is the goal in singing, having an excellent experience for the parent and child at the first encounter with the administrative and artistic staff is the goal as well. The atmosphere created from the moment the child and parent enter the audition space will give them clues about the organization. Are they greeted warmly? Is the atmosphere child-friendly? Are procedures well organized and on schedule? Are current choristers present to greet the new students and help them through the process? Is there a comfortable waiting room where parents may sit while their child auditions? Are photos of the choirs visible? Is there a DVD playing that shows the choir singing or includes interviews from choristers and parents?

Some choirs audition in groups. Some allow or require parents to attend the audition. Others audition the child and hold a follow-up interview with both the parent and child. There are many ways of accepting choristers into the choir, and each organization will determine what is best. (See appendix 6.2 for an audition room setup and appendix 6.3 for a list of materials to be prepared by the staff for auditions.)

Once the audition process has concluded, the student will be notified of the results. This may occur at the time of the audition. Others send notification of acceptance, or not, by mail. Others take every child who expresses an interest without an audition. For those who audition and are not accepted into the choir, an encouraging letter suggesting ways the child can gain more experience and practice for possible future auditions is recommended. Others may have a choir of non-auditioned and/or non-accepted members to provide a nurturing environment for those with weaker skills or hesitancy about auditioning. Each organization will develop its own acceptance and notification procedures.

PARENT COMMITMENT AND TRANSPORTATION

Parent commitment to the children's choir is important for both the child and the organization. The active involvement of the parent validates the work of the child and its importance. When a child has an opportunity to participate in the practical routine of music-making and develops a consistent commitment to the focused work ethic of rehearsals, he or she will learn and grow. When a child does not have the strong support of the parent and misses rehearsals or concerts, she or he will not learn the important life lessons and richness of commitment.

For those who must rely on adult transportation to participate in a choir, the commitment of the parent (or others) to transport the child to and from rehearsals and concerts may be a requirement for the child's participation. In cities with high traffic and no mass transit system, or rural areas where children have to travel a great distance to get to choir rehearsals, a parent (or a neighbor, relative, friend, guardian, grandparent, carpool parent, or designated driver) may be the one responsible to transport the child. In large cities with mass transit systems, the child may be able to take advantage of the train, subway, or bus system to travel to and from rehearsals, and some choirs provide tokens or rail passes for their choir members.

Parents may take an active role working side by side with the choristers at a car wash or plant sale to assist with raising funds for an upcoming tour. This kind of volunteerism models important future behaviors for choristers as adults teach them about the rewards of such philanthropic work. (More about volunteering is discussed later in this chapter.)

When parents are not able to provide transportation or a mass transit system does not exist, chorus outreach programs may be possibilities. Choirs that have outreach programs in satellite locations away from the central rehearsal location increase the possibility of sharing choral music experiences with more children and reaching a more diverse population. If these locations are within a reasonable walking distance for the child, transportation is not an issue. Satellite locations may exist where children already participate in an after-school program. This may include after-school programs located at the child's school, neighborhood or community recreational facility, or church.

REGISTRATION

There are many ways to accomplish choir registration for each child. The following discussion describes one choir's procedure in depth. This is not the only way to organize registration, but is rather offered as one possible structure.

With the letter of acceptance, materials are sent to the parent or guardian prior to in-person registration. The materials include all forms for registration and may be sent approximately two weeks in advance such as in May, with registration occurring the first week in June (three weeks before the school year ends in certain parts of the country). Sending forms by mail in advance of registration allows for thorough completion of all forms before arriving at registration. The mailing may include the following materials:

- Enrollment and tuition agreement
- Chorister information form
- Wardrobe order form
- Permission to photograph and record release form
- Scholarship application form
- Parent volunteer information
- Maps of registration
    - Driving directions and geographic map for registration location
    - Floor/room diagram for in-person registration
    - Checklist for in-person registration (parents check off each station they must visit to complete registration before final check-out and payment)
- Other forms as necessary

In-person registration may be held in a large gymnasium of a church parish hall or school. Or it can be done by appointment, one family at a time, at the chorus office. By having one scheduled time for each choir to register, the registration process is condensed into one evening for up to four choirs at a central location. If held in a large, open space, numerous people will be accommodated, and parents and choristers can move from station to station to complete the various steps of the process in an organized flow of traffic. The stations may include wardrobe fittings for concert attire, T-shirt fittings, chorister photographs, purchasing chorus merchandise (CDs, water bottles, day packs, etc.), and a final check-out where all forms are reviewed for completion and the tuition payment is made. (See appendix 6.4 for a registration floor diagram, and appendices 6.5 and 6.6 for a chorister information form and a permission form to record and photograph, respectively.)

After registration, during the summer months, the artistic and administrative staff will prepare repertoire and all materials for the beginning of fall rehearsals. One such material is a list of names, addresses, and phone numbers of choir members (separate lists for each choir) that will be sent to parents in an August mailing to assist them in arranging carpools for rehearsals. Additional administrative summer tasks may include the following:

- Purchasing wardrobe for all choirs
- Purchasing music
- Preparing the concert season brochure
- Reconfirming all concert locations
- Revising or creating a chorus handbook
- Updating the chorus database

- Updating all choir lists and chorister file folders
- Preparing carpool lists (list of choristers with addresses and phone numbers to assist parents in arranging carpools where possible)
- Confirming plans for chorister summer camp
- Preparing the music packets for each chorister for distribution at summer camp for the advanced choir, and for September all other choirs
  - Pulling scores from the music library
  - Numbering and stamping (with chorus name) all new scores
- Taking inventory of wardrobe and tour items (garment backs, backpacks, extra T-shirts)

A summer tour (state, national, or international) may occur during the early summer months for the touring or most advanced choir. (More information about touring may be found in chapter 12.) Later in the summer prior to the start of the new academic year, a summer camp may be scheduled for the most advanced choir.

CHORISTER SUMMER CAMP

Summer camp provides an opportunity for eager, well-rested, and energized choristers to gather and share the joy of choral singing. In addition, they learn new skills, are challenged by music of varying levels of difficulty, experience new styles of music, share choir favorites from the past, share social time, participate in team-building activities, and participate in enrichment sessions, such as yoga, hiking, arts, and crafts, or other activities, such as African singing, dancing, and drumming. Holding the sleepover camp at a location such as a scout or church camp facility affords the opportunity to incorporate many types of activities that help the choristers bond as friends, accomplish much musically, and learn new skills.

Traditional camp activities may include a flag-raising ceremony in the morning and a flag-lowering ceremony at dusk. Choristers who are Girl Scouts or Boy Scouts are often willing to be responsible for these ceremonies. And of course, camp would not be complete without the traditional evening campfire and s'mores. Learning an a cappella selection appropriate for singing before a shared meal (something reflective and inclusive) may also become a favored camp memory for the choristers.

The camp schedule should allow for well-planned and structured time that continually engages choristers in productive activity. Camp may be spread over two days, several days, a week, or longer. A careful balance of well-planned working rehearsals, quiet activities to allow for resting of voices, physical rest (midday and at night), healthful food, and active play will keep the choristers focused, energized, rested, and ready for full participation in all chorister camp activities.

Providing a chorister packing list helps each family prepare the appropriate clothing and other items required for the chorister's stay. A detailed list of what to bring and what not to bring to camp ensures that each chorister arrives with what he or she will need for the duration of the camp experience. If choristers have to carry their backpacks any distance, practicing walking with the fully loaded backpack at home may ensure that unnecessary items are left there. The packing list is also good practice for future tours where specific clothing may be required by the chorus, and suitcase sizes and weight limits are carefully mandated by the airlines (if air travel is part of the tour). (See appendix 6.7 for a chorister packing list and appendix 6.8 for a staff packing list.)

Effective use of rehearsal time at camp cannot be overemphasized. The choristers are well rested from summer vacation, and music is often learned more quickly. Choristers are glad to be with their friends in the choir whom they may not have seen for several weeks. They are not burdened with homework or school tests, and the unique atmosphere of a camp setting may inspire them to work harder. Two days at camp can often equal over five weeks of normal rehearsal time during the school year; therefore, plans should include bringing an adequate amount of music for study and performance. When the singers return to rehearsals in September to start the new school year, they will already know much repertoire. (See appendix 6.9 for a two-day chorister camp schedule.)

Camp may be challenging for some children. If a child has never been away from home for an overnight, the first-time sleepover experience may induce feelings of homesickness. One way to ease the first-time camp experience for the younger members of the choir is by having a mix of varying ages of choristers assigned to each cabin. Older choristers may be assigned to mentor younger choristers. A buddy system during the day assists with fostering friendships. These strategies may help improve the first-time experience for younger choristers.

Another challenge at camp (and while on choir tours) is the chorister's access to a personal cell phone. This is both an asset and a potential distraction. Each chorus should determine its own policy about cell phone use.

Some camps may legally require a registered nurse to be present throughout the camp session. Should a child become injured or ill, having a professional assigned to this responsibility is a comfort to parents, staff, and chaperones. Frequently, a chorister parent who is a nurse will fill this role. If not, the camp facility may be able to provide a list of available nurses who may be hired for the duration of the camp. (See appendix 6.10 for a confidential chorister camp medical and personal information form.)

Facilities at the camp should include multiple rooms for various purposes. Having several large spaces will allow for dividing the choir into smaller groups for sectional rehearsals, or they may be used for optional music skills classes or nonmusical activities. As needed, additional portable electric keyboards can be brought to camp for sectionals, vocal skills, sight reading, or theory teaching rooms.

Staffing for camp usually includes the music staff (including directors and accompanists), the administrative staff, parent chaperones, alumni chorister counselors, and university student conducting interns. The chorus's assistant directors or other professionals may be hired for specific activities, and university student conducting interns are a valuable addition to the staff. Composers may also be invited to participate in summer camp rehearsals, particularly if a premiere is planned or a large project is being undertaken. Alumni choristers may be appointed as counselors or counselors-in-training for camp. The counselors are a tremendous resource during rehearsals, recreational and team-building activities, and in the cabins at night for assisting the chaperones. The alumni choristers are wonderful exemplars for the younger choristers, and they may be invited to sing with or for the choir. Alumni choristers who are music majors in college in music education programs build experience credentials this way. Those who are voice majors enjoy coming back to their former choir, and they may be asked to demonstrate a particular technique or to sing for the choristers. Some return to camp as music professionals who are now conductors, music educators, or professional singers. Their participation reinforces for the younger choristers that singing is a lifelong shared art.

Adult chaperones, usually parents who volunteer, are a tremendous asset at camp. Some chaperones will want to participate in the full experience. Others may need to work during the day when the choristers are actively engaged in rehearsals and activities. Additional chaperones may become available in the evening to assist in the cabins with any sleeping issues. Having extra chaperones, if possible, is recommended, in case a chaperone has to leave the group to tend to an ill child or a child who otherwise needs assistance. Having a mix of new and experienced chaperones creates strong chaperones for future events and succeeding years.

Awareness of the chorister-to-chaperone ratio is important. Each camp, tour, concert, or event will require a varying number of chaperones per choristers. And chaperones who are easy to work with, take directions well, and work fluidly with choristers are ideal for future tours and large events. Camp provides an opportunity for the staff to get to know which people will be good chaperones for the year ahead.

A younger level of the children's choir may be invited to join the advanced chorus for an afternoon or partial day at camp in rehearsals for a special project. This brief experience will help lay the foundation for the later sleepover camp experience after the chorister is accepted into the advanced choir. If a performance with the combined choirs is scheduled for the upcoming season, such as a concert with a symphony orchestra where a larger choir is required, having the younger singers join the older singers to begin learning the music at camp is an efficient use of time. It also allows the younger singers to get acquainted with the older choir members in the social contexts of meals and group activities. Assigning older choristers to mentor younger choristers for the afternoon and dinner is also a way to bring varying ages together to encourage new friendships and more collegiality at the symphony performances later in the year.

At the conclusion of the chorister camp, parents may be invited to attend the flag-lowering ceremony followed by a short concert, which may celebrate all that has been accomplished during camp. The concert might include selections learned during camp, a brief selection by the alumni chorister counselors, a skit, a favorite chorus song, and presentation of camp awards. The concert may also include discussion of some of the more humorous moments that occurred during camp. If a large-screen television is available, photos taken during camp can give parents a wonderful insight into the choristers' experiences.

DAY CAMP FOR YOUNGER CHOIRS

For the younger choirs in a community children's choir, holding a day camp may be preferable to the overnight experience. This also provides the artistic director with the luxury of an extended rehearsal, longer than the weekly after-school rehearsal. For some choirs, this extended rehearsal is held for a half-day or full day on a weekend after rehearsals have begun in the fall. For others, a day camp may be held late in the summer. Dates for required day camps for the younger choirs may be included in the complete yearlong schedule that parents receive when they register their children for participation in the chorus. Day camps may be scheduled once or twice per semester or year as determined by the needs of the choir.

Held near the beginning of the school year, day camp allows for the inclusion of get-acquainted games and activities in addition to the extended music rehearsal. The expanded rehearsal time allows more time for strong skills development, work on sight reading, learning new repertoire, and laying foundations for vocal development. Two choirs may attend a half-day camp concurrently in the same location. The schedule might include starting with the choirs combined for vocal warm-up and then separating into individual choirs for team-building activities and rehearsals. The morning session may conclude with a brief performance by each choir. Parent volunteers may be asked to assist with distribution of a healthful mid-morning snack and water or juice, and they may assist with arrival and dismissal of the larger-than-normal group of singers. (See appendix 6.11 for a sample day camp schedule.)

Holding the day camp early in the fall at a location other than the usual one also provides an opportunity to practice moving the choir from one room to the next in an orderly manner for the various activities of the day. This skill is the first step in learning how to walk on and off risers appropriately. It will also familiarize the chaperones with the procedure to be used for upcoming concerts. When a concert occurs in another, new location, both choristers and chaperones will already know how to accomplish the choir's seamless movement.

SUMMER MAILING TO PARENTS

Much anticipation precedes the first rehearsal of the new school year. Choristers are full of anticipation about what music they will sing and who the other choristers will be. Directors look forward to getting started with the new choir. Parents await the details of rehearsal and concert scheduling for the year. A comprehensive August mailing to parents will assist with advance planning for them and provide much information to prepare choristers and their families for the year. Approximately four weeks before the first rehearsal, parents may receive the following:

- Welcome-back letter
- Complete rehearsal and concert schedule for the year (including major and minor performances with all dates, times, and locations)
- Parent orientation information including date, time, and location
- Chorus Handbook
- Season concert brochure
- Season ticket order form

Held in the fall, parent orientation is an important opportunity for chorister families to meet the administrative and artistic staff of the chorus with whom they will be interacting during the year ahead. Orientation may be held at a specific date and location separate from rehearsals or at the same location and time as the first rehearsal.

PREPARING FOR FIRST REHEARSALS

After the children's choir is formed, the students have auditioned, the repertoire is selected, and the location is determined, then rehearsals begin. How rehearsals are organized is as equally important as the choices of music the chorus will sing. Procedures for arrival at rehearsal should be explained in a mailing to the parents prior to or at the first rehearsal. For school choirs, attendance is taken by the conductor-teacher in the elementary school. Or, in the case of an after-school or before-school choir rehearsal, the teacher will determine the most efficient method for taking attendance depending on the size of the choir. For middle school and high school choirs, assigned seating and a seating chart will expedite accurate taking of attendance during the school day rehearsal.

For community children's choirs, a different procedure may be used to sign in students before rehearsal. Signing in choir members may be done by a volunteer parent or chorus administrative staff member who warmly greets choristers as they enter the building where rehearsals are located. An adult volunteer or staff member may also greet the choristers as they enter the rehearsal room. How to enter the rehearsal room quietly, where to sign in, and how to get a chair set up in the correct location (if choral risers or a stationary setup are not available, or staff is not able to arrange the chairs in advance) are skills that should be taught. By keeping the procedure consistent throughout the year, rehearsals will begin smoothly and on time.

Following the sign-in for attendance purposes, the chorister may be given the weekly memo to take home to his or her parents. Materials used for sign-in may be placed on a table or music stand or chair outside the rehearsal room. (See appendix 6.12 for an attendance sign-in sheet.) A plastic milk case or portable file box with a handle can be used to hold a colorful file folder for each chorister. The folders may be labeled alphabetically by chorister name or by using only sequential numbers. An efficient and time-saving system is to assign a specific number to each chorister at the beginning of the year that will be used throughout the year for distribution of all chorus materials.

Using numbers expedites recovery of dropped or lost materials during rehearsals. Writing a name on every memo that goes to each member in multiple choirs would take many hours of staff time each week. Instead, memos can be quickly numbered sequentially for each choir, allowing for easy distribution into the chorister folders to be retrieved at the time of rehearsal sign-in. Numbers run consecutively from 1 to the highest number paralleling the alphabetical list of choir members. The numbering system should be consistent for all materials distributed to the choristers throughout the year; these may include the music they are loaned for the semester, special announcements, backpacks for tours, garment bags for tours, or any other chorus materials.

Using the numbering system for each choir is efficient. If a memo falls on the floor during rehearsal, it is easy to track whose memo it is by the number. Should a piece of music or two become accidentally switched during rehearsal, easy retrieval and redistribution to the correct chorister is possible. In addition, it is advisable to assign a different color to be used for each choir. That way, if a chorister accidentally forgets to put a memo in his or her music case and leaves rehearsal, when it is found by the next choir arriving for rehearsal, the color of the number on the memo will indicate to which choir the memo belongs, and the number will indicate exactly to which chorister the memo should be returned. For example:

Choir I   Blue folders in memo box for retrieval by chorister at sign-in, blue numbers on memos

Choir II   Green folders in memo box for retrieval by chorister at sign-in, green numbers on memos

Choir III Purple folders in memo box for retrieval by chorister at sign-in, purple numbers on memos

Choir IV   Red folders in memo box for retrieval by chorister at sign-in, red numbers on memos

Additional materials required for proper setup might include the following:

- Sign-in sheets for each choir
- Box of pens, pencils, and markers
- Emergency first-aid kit
- List of all choristers and all emergency contact information
- Medical summary in case of emergency (allergies, restricted activities, etc.)
- Cell phone for calls to parents regarding drop-offs or pick-ups
- Any materials that need to be distributed to the choristers (wardrobe, CDs, concert tickets, etc.)

Rehearsal materials should be set up at least twenty to thirty minutes before rehearsals begin to allow for a prompt start. If chairs need to be set up, extra time should be allowed before the arrival of the first chorister.

Standards of excellence in organizational matters, such as efficient distribution of memos and attendance-taking, mean more minutes of productive rehearsal time. When efficiency is the goal, more time becomes available for rehearsal.

The same is true for announcements. It is very easy to do verbal announcements that can increasingly take time away from actual rehearsal minutes. The more information that can be included in the memo, the less time will be taken up by announcements at rehearsal. Important highlights may be announced briefly and details can be given in written form or accessed on the secure chorister family page on the website that is available to choristers and their families to read at their convenience.

PARENT ORIENTATION

Parent orientation is an opportunity for the administrative staff to educate parents about procedures and other important choir information that will assist them throughout the year. A suggested agenda for parent orientation might include the following:

- Welcome by the president of the board of directors of the chorus
- Introduction of the artistic staff (including directors and accompanists)
  - Include a brief overview of the music highlights for the year
- Introduction of the administrative staff
- Overview of the chorus calendar for the year
- Overview of the Chorus Handbook and specific review of important sections where questions may arise (e.g., attendance policies)
- Time for questions and answers

Parent orientation may take place at the same time and location as the first rehearsal of the year. As an alternative, orientation for parents may take place at a separate time and location, and it may or may not involve choristers.

MUSIC DISTRIBUTION

Distribution of music typically happens twice a year. Packets are prepared by the chorus staff (or volunteers) for each chorister. Numbers assigned to each chorister will be used for music distribution. Music packets handed out at the first rehearsal (or at summer camp for the most advanced choir) will include all scores to be used for the complete fall semester. Additional music for the advanced choir to be started during the fall semester and used for a spring semester performance or following a summer tour may also be included. At the first rehearsal, each chorister will receive an envelope containing the music with an attached form to be completed by him or her and a parent. The form indicates that the chorister and parent have checked the packet to be sure it is complete and signed the statement indicating such. The signed statement also indicates that the child and parent understand their responsibility for returning all music at the end of the semester upon request. (See appendix 6.13 for a music distribution form.)

At the end of the fall semester, the envelope is given back to the chorister with a form indicating what music is to be returned at that time. Again, the parent and child will check off each title and return the envelope, music, and form on the appointed date. At the beginning of the spring semester when rehearsals resume, a new set of music will be distributed following the same procedure with a similar return procedure at the end of the year.

VOLUNTEERS

Parent volunteers, grandparent volunteers, and alumni chorister volunteers are a tremendous resource for a nonprofit community children's or youth choir. Volunteers may assist with the choirs during concerts, chaperoning tours, chaperoning special events and concerts, with fundraising activities, and in many more ways throughout the year. The following is a partial list of ways in which chorister parents or volunteers may assist the choir:

- Choir chaperones for concerts
- Dress rehearsal chaperones
- Ticket sales at concerts
- CD/merchandise sales at concerts
- Ushers at concerts
- Lobby monitors
- Priority seating monitors
- Door ushers (center, right, left, and balcony)
- Tour chaperones
- Photographer
- Videographer
- Stuffing letters
- Labeling envelopes
- Rehearsal parents (one per choir for younger choirs, to take children to restroom if needed during rehearsal)
- Rehearsal dismissal parents (assist as children get into cars to leave rehearsal)
- Greeters at beginning of rehearsal
- Volunteers to assist with fundraisers, such as plant sales, auctions, or gala events
- Carpooling to transport choristers to and from rehearsals
- Greeters at auditions for new members (includes both parent and chorister volunteers)

Each choir will find ways to involve parents and other volunteers in the necessary activities of the choir. Volunteers are invaluable to a choir and should be thanked often for their meaningful contributions. Listing the names of the volunteers in the chorus newsletters or concert programs will give them additional recognition for their service. The volunteers are a wonderful example for the choristers of "those who give back to an organization." And choristers should be encouraged to thank the chaperones and volunteers as well. (See appendix 6.14 for a parent volunteer form, appendix 6.15 for a parent volunteer assignments form, and appendix 6.16 for sample chaperone concert responsibilities.)

OPEN HOUSE FOR PARENTS

Approximately one month into rehearsals, an open house for parents, board members, and funders may be arranged for each choir. Held during a regularly scheduled rehearsal, the open house provides the invited guests with an opportunity to observe the conductor and choristers in the process of learning vocal technique, sight-reading skills, intonation and listening exercises, and the varied repertoire studied and performed each week. The conductor-teacher may narrate for the parents what is happening, why the skill-building activities are important, and what the children are experiencing and learning through the process of making decisions about the music, analyzing, listening, and singing.

For the advanced choir, parents may be invited to join their children and the choir to learn a song at the end of the open rehearsal. Often, the parents are singers and eagerly come forward to sing. For those who do not sing regularly, this invitation brings them into the learning process and provides an opportunity for them to become immersed in the sound of the expanded choir, a sometimes profound experience for the adults.

CONCLUSION

Parents appreciate a well-organized choral organization. From the initial meeting of a potential chorister and family, to the child's actual participation, there are many opportunities to educate about procedures and expectations. Through detailed planning by the staff and the distribution of important information to chorister families at precise times, the likelihood of successful concerts and events increases, and recognizable achievements occur.

So many possibilities.
—SPOKEN BY THE CHARACTER GEORGE

Sunday in the Park with George,
BROADWAY MUSICAL

7

MUSICAL MATTERS

THIS CHAPTER IS devoted to musical matters, but not vocal technique, conducting, or rehearsal strategies; rather, it focuses on ways of *organizing* the musical matters of the choir. It is a discussion of the musical requirements of an audition, how to organize a music library, the structure of rehearsals, first rehearsals, voicing the choir, the seating arrangement to maximize vocal development, and effective music planning for choristers' summer and day camps.

AUDITIONS

Auditions begin the year-long cycle of the children's choir. Whether a school, church, or community children's choir that may be auditioned or not, the formation of the new choir occurs at the beginning of each new year as children come and go in each context.

For the community choir, as stated in the previous chapter, auditions may be held once a year, twice a year, or on a rotating basis. Regardless of how or when the auditions occur, having the audition process be a positive experience for the child will maximize the possibility that he or she will sing his or her best during the audition.

To assess the skills and abilities of young singers in a limited amount of time, a series of tasks may be presented. For an elementary school with limited time spent with each class every week, listening to the individual voices twice a year will provide important information for constructing a seating arrangement for classroom music that encourages maximum skill development for each child. Seating a weak singer next to a stronger singer or seating the weak singer in front of a strong singer will surround the weaker singer with models of good singing. This will potentially increase the chances of improving the child's singing ability over time. Seating the accurate singer on the side of the weaker singer's dominant ear will also help provide a good vocal model for the weaker singer to emulate. When the enjoyment of singing and proper vocal production are the focuses of the elementary classroom beginning in kindergarten, many children with encouragement and good teaching develop the ability to sing beautifully, even if no music or singing exists in the child's home environment. As distinguished music educator and past national president of the American Choral Directors Association Colleen Kirk said about children's choirs, "At least if they are there, they can get better."[1]

For general music classes at the elementary school level, each classroom may be its own choir. By using a simple assessment rubric, artist-teachers may prepare a seating chart that shows the child's name and singing ability level. Using a system of symbols, the child's pitch matching and singing ability can be quickly assessed and recorded on the classroom seating chart.

The symbols used are as follows:

|

indicates a voice that produces a sound

L

indicates a voice that goes up and down in pitch slightly and is not singing correct pitches

⊔

indicates a voice that goes up and down and is sometimes singing correct pitches

⊔

indicates a voice that goes up and down and is mostly singing correct pitches

☐

indicates a clear voice that is singing correct pitches all the time

▨

indicates an outstanding singer

This diagram can be used on the music class seating chart to provide firsthand knowledge about each child's voice at a glance. The assessment diagram of the child's voice (one of the symbols shown above) can be recorded in the upper left corner of the seating chart box for each child. Assessed again in January of the same school year, a second diagram can then be inserted in the upper right corner of the child's box on the seating chart. The child's progress can be monitored at both the beginning of the year and midyear, and throughout the years that the child attends the school.

For very large elementary schools where the artist-teacher sees several hundred children each week, the annotated seating chart provides valuable information, both for name recognition of each child and assessment of his or her singing ability, and how it improves over time. The individual voice assessment may be done easily in one or two class periods, depending on the length of the general music class. While the conductor-teacher is doing the voice assessment, the class can be assigned a worksheet or quiet activity as each child comes to the piano, one by one, to sing for the teacher. (The teacher faces the class, and the child faces the teacher with his or her back to the class.) With older students who might be more self-conscious, this assessment, if possible, may be done just outside the classroom door using an electric keyboard placed in the hall, from where the conductor-teacher can monitor the class.[2] (See appendix 7.1 for a sample general music class seating chart with strategic placement of voices to maximize vocal development.)

MORE FORMAL AUDITIONS

For more in-depth auditions, such as for a community children's choir, more comprehensive data for each child may be required. Audition activities might include the following:

- Singing a familiar song prepared in advance of the audition and memorized (this may be a folk song, chorus song from school choir, hymn tune, art song, Broadway song, patriotic song, multicultural song, etc.). The type of song will vary depending on experience and age of the child. An accompanist may be provided by the choir, and the child may be asked to bring the music for the accompanist.
- Singing "Happy Birthday" a cappella and given only the starting note (paying particular attention to how accurately the child sings the octave leap, if the child can sing accurate pitches, and how well the tonal center is maintained).
- Echo singing four melodies that progressively range from very easy to extremely difficult (director sings a short a cappella melody and the student sings the melody back).
- Singing scales up and down to assess the range of the voice.
- Echo singing linear chords using a neutral syllable after hearing the chord played on the piano from the bottom note to the top note (e.g., after hearing the major chord, the child sings do, mi, sol pitches using a neutral syllable such as [lu]). Examples progress in various keys including major, minor, diminished, and augmented triads.
- Echo singing the three notes from top to bottom of block chords using a neutral syllable after hearing the chord played all at once on the piano (e.g., after hearing a major chord the child sings sol, mi, do using a neutral syllable such as [lu]). Examples progress in varying keys including major, minor, diminished, and augmented triads.
- Echo clapping (student echoes various rhythmic four-beat patterns starting with simple ones and progressing to more difficult examples). Progressively more difficult eight-beat patterns may be used for grades five and up (a total of four patterns only to be used to assess rhythmic ability).

- Reading a sample aloud—to assess the child's reading ability, which provides an opportunity to hear the child's speaking voice and articulation.
- Conversation—asking a question that requires more than a one-word answer. This encourages the child to talk and indicates how comfortable he or she is speaking. A question might about something he or she enjoys, such as the title of a favorite book and one of the characters, or what the child likes best about his or her favorite sport or hobby.

Author and Kodály methodologist Lois Choksy provides guidelines for a comprehensive audition, which is the source for many of the above assessment skills.[3] Additional skill assessments have been added above to the audition structure suggested by Choksy to supplement the data gathered about the child's abilities.[4]

When a child auditions for a choir, he or she is also auditioning the choir. It must be a good fit for both. (See appendix 7.2 for an example of an audition form to be used at the time of audition, based on the Choksy guidelines with additional skill assessments included.) The process of auditioning can be intimidating for some children. It is important to put a child at ease when auditioning for an unfamiliar adult in an unfamiliar location. Greeting the child with a smile and a compliment will go a long way to easing the potential fear or butterflies the child may experience at the time of the actual audition.

Some choirs require their current choristers to re-audition at the end of each year. Others do not require an annual re-audition. Those who re-audition their singers annually may do so to encourage students to strive toward certain established goals:

- Demonstrating achievement of specific skills
- Demonstrating strong commitment
- Meeting the attendance requirements
- Demonstrating motivation
- Demonstrating a strong work ethic
- Demonstrating enthusiasm for singing and a positive attitude
- Getting along well with peers

By meeting the criteria established by the choir, the chorister becomes eligible to progress to the next level of advancement in the choir. The artist-teacher is also able to hear the individual growth and development of the voice that have occurred during the year's participation and may recommend focused work for any areas of weakness. Areas of weakness may be identified for future work with the choir's vocal coaches (if available) who work with the choristers in private or group vocal coaching sessions. The re-audition is also a time to celebrate and acknowledge the growth, commitment, and beautiful singing of each child when appropriate. For boys, the annual one-on-one assessment provides a good checkpoint to evaluate range and possible onset of voice change.

CHORISTERS SINGING FOR CHORISTERS

Some choirs, whenever possible, allow each level of the choir to sit in the audience for the concert. The younger choristers become aware of the growth and progression over the years as the singers move through the various levels of the choirs. A young chorister may be inspired to work toward the goal of singing in the most advanced choir, select ensemble, or touring choir after hearing the older singers. In addition to hearing all the choirs, combining all the choirs for an opening selection or finale at a concert can be a powerful experience for both singers and audience. Many community children's choirs have expanded their programs to include a high school mixed choir or a men's ensemble to accommodate changed voices and older singers. These older students may wish to remain with the choir through their high school years. And for those who don't remain through high school, returning at the end of the year to sing an annual traditional song with the choir may be a wonderful way to keep in touch with alumni choristers.

AWARDS

Some choirs present awards to their choristers annually for excellence in various categories or specific accomplishments. Many present certificates of participation to each member at the end of the year. Special perfect attendance certificates may also be awarded. Others give a framed certificate or special pin or ribbon to choristers with five or more years of membership in the ensemble. Some choirs award pins with a bar that may be attached for each year of participation. These are often worn on the chorister's concert dress outfits. Each choir establishes its own recognition system of honors and awards for its singers and determines when it is appropriate to make these presentations.

MUSIC LIBRARY

The music library of a choir represents the musical heart and soul of the organization. It is a reflection of the artistic choices of its directors over the years and provides a resource for future performances. For a children's choir, the music is the source of learning about the choral art. The amount of physical space a music library may occupy can be quite vast. Music libraries are kept in basements, garages in directors' homes, or in offices, schools, or specially constructed spaces for music. With each year and the purchase of new repertoire, the quantity of music to be numbered, cataloged, distributed, collected, and filed increases. Some music may be stored in file folders in cabinets. Others store music in cardboard boxes or heavy-duty filing boxes (covers optional). Depending on the size of the choir, how many choirs there are in the program, and the financial resources of the choir, the library may increase in size quite rapidly. Overseeing the organization of how the scores are filed, stored, and recorded is an annual task, and one that requires complete accuracy. Octavos miscataloged or misfiled may be lost for years. Knowing how to properly record the title, the composer's name, and the voicing for the database is equally important. A volunteer or staff member who is not knowledgeable about music scores may not necessarily be an asset in this context. Seeking advice from the director is recommended when questions arise about how a selection should be cataloged. For example, Schubert's *An die Musik* is also *To Music*, not to be confused with Lowell Mason's *To Music*. A decision needs to be made about which title (English, German, or both) should be listed in the database for the Schubert work.

A music library database may include the following categories:

- Title
- Composer/arranger
- Publisher/manuscript
- Octavo number
- Voicing (Unison, SA, SSA, SSAA, SSA/SATB, etc.)
- Accompaniment (piano, any additional instruments)
- Level of difficulty
- Performance duration
- Language (if other than English)
- Number of copies in the library
- Additional notes, such as when commissioned, or lessons learned after performance

There may be additional categories included in the database depending on the needs of the choir.

Computer programs may be purchased that are specifically designed for choral music library data. An alternative to a music-specific database may be to develop a comprehensive structure suited to the particular needs of the organization, church, or school using an Excel spreadsheet. Regardless of what type of computer program is used, flexibility to search the data in various ways is most useful. A director may wish to sort the library by the title of a selection, by a specific voicing, by a specific composer, or by whether a work is a cappella or has particular instruments used for accompaniment. There may be other useful criteria. The more flexible and comprehensive the database is, the more useful it will be to the director. (See chapter 14 for a treble choir repertoire list.)

REHEARSAL ROOM SETUP

The setup for rehearsal should include chairs for the choristers, the piano placed where the accompanist and director determine is the best location, a music stand for the conductor, and proper lighting and ventilation in the rehearsal room (lights on to the correct level, windows open or closed, and heat or air-conditioning regulated). Four or more rows of chairs placed in a semicircle with aisles between sections is often the chosen setup for young choirs. This allows the director to walk among the singers and also allows for good visibility between singers and conductor. Placing taller singers toward the rear and shorter singers toward the front when standing or sitting gives each chorister clear sight lines to the director. Adequate space should be provided between chairs. The curved rows allow choristers to hear the singers from the opposite side of the choir more easily.

If possible, a large rehearsal room with extra floor space to allow the choristers to move away from the risers is desirable. Dalcroze or other movement activities are possible in these open spaces, as well as rehearsing in circles, by parts in multiple circles, or in one large circle away from the chairs and/or risers.

The piano may be placed to the right or the left of the director. The director and accompanist will determine the preferred placement for ease of visual communication. Some conductor-teachers may find that using a podium eases the sight lines to the accompanist and the choir members.

STRUCTURE OF A REHEARSAL

Using rehearsal time efficiently is an admirable goal. If the conductor-teacher is thoroughly prepared for each rehearsal and has carefully planned the amount of time to be spent on each component of the rehearsal, it will be structured for the most efficient use of time. Thorough preparation of the music includes the following:

- Structural analysis of the score including
  - Text
  - Form
  - Texture
  - Tonality
  - Meter
  - Rhythm
  - Dynamic structure
  - Key structure and modulations
  - Chord analysis
  - Themes, subjects, countersubjects
  - Thorough knowledge of each vocal part
  - Thorough knowledge of the accompaniment
- Practicing the interpretation of the score through the conducting gesture including
  - Cueing
  - Releases

- Preparatory breath
- Stylistic characteristics
- Dynamics
- Knowledge of performance practice for selected titles
- Vocal considerations including
  - Vowels (IPA)
  - Vowel modification
  - Consonants
  - Where to breathe
  - Articulation
  - Intervals
  - Tone color
  - Foreign language pronunciation
  - Foreign language translation
  - How to treat diphthongs
  - Decisions about when to precisely release the tone to the breath

Once the music has been thoroughly prepared, planning for the first rehearsal commences. A well-thought-out rehearsal plan will encourage an organized approach and efficient use of time. Components to be considered may include the following:

- Physical relaxation exercises
- Breathing exercises
- Vocal warm-ups
  - Vowel unification
  - Supported vocal tone production on the breath
  - Relaxation
  - Articulation (lips, teeth, tongue)
  - Range (high and low)
  - Energized tone
  - Resonance
  - Beauty
- Sight-reading exercises
- Selected repertoire for analysis, study, practice, and performance within each rehearsal
- Ending with a favorite or recently learned song

Ending with a familiar song, a special favorite of the choir, song with movement, or selected rehearsal piece that is beautifully sung just prior to dismissal of the choir is recommended. This provides a positive conclusion to a working rehearsal, and choristers depart with a shared sense of accomplishment.

Planning the amount of rehearsal time to be spent on each component of rehearsal in advance will help the director stay focused and accomplish the intended goals in a timely manner. It will also ensure that an adequate amount of time is spent on selected repertoire and builds in variety during the rehearsal, rather than spending too much time on one piece. By changing the pattern of the activities (i.e., mixing up the order or sequence), variety may also be built into the rehearsal from week to week. As the weeks pass and repertoire is learned, new repertoire may be added. Memorization, internalization of the music, and complete mastery become part of every rehearsal.

A sample rehearsal plan for a ninety-minute rehearsal might look something like this:

4:00   Welcome and announcements
5
4:05   Physical warm-ups (body relaxation, focusing attention, posture)
3
4:08   Breathing exercises
3
4:11   Vocal warm-ups
5
4:16   Selection #1
9
4:25   Selection #2
20
4:45   Selection #3
15
5:00   Sight reading
10
5:10   Selection #4
10
5:20   Selection #5
8
5:28   Familiar song
2
5:30   End of rehearsal

The numbers between the lines indicate at a glance exactly how many minutes are devoted to each task. During rehearsal, it is important to develop a sense of appropriate pacing and be mindful of exactly how many minutes you have to accomplish predetermined goals. The amount of time spent on each selection and the number of selections per rehearsal will vary. As repertoire is learned, less time may be required on particular pieces (if included at all), and more selections may be included in rehearsal. Other selections may require larger blocks of time depending on the challenges in the music and the skills to be taught. Is the schedule always followed to the minute? Not necessarily. Awareness of how much time is spent on each piece is important for the pacing of the rehearsal and keeping the singers engaged in the music-making.

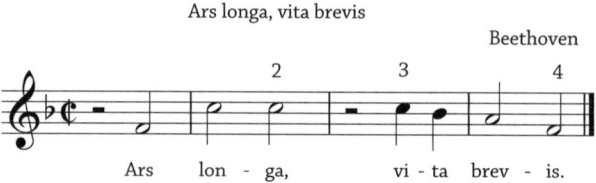

FIGURE 7.1 Translation: *Art is lasting, life is passing.*

THE FIRST REHEARSAL

After welcoming the choir and introductions of the chorus staff, the music-making begins. Beginning with an easily learned song allows choristers to share the joy of choral music participation and hear their new choir. For the director, there is curiosity about how the new choir will respond. By teaching a short canon to the chorus, the singers may learn skills that will reflect their ability to follow a conductor; adjust to dynamic changes; sing a legato line with forward motion, musical line, and shape; and sing in harmony. All this may be accomplished in a four-measure canon composed by Beethoven, "Ars longa, vita brevis." Conductor and composer Sir George Smart (England) was invited to visit Beethoven on September 16, 1825. In appreciation for the honor of the invitation and kind reception, Smart gave Beethoven a beautiful diamond pin as a remembrance. Beethoven wrote the canon in approximately two minutes as Smart stood at the door ready to depart.[5] The canon may be taught to choirs of any size very quickly by rote.

The seven-note, four-pitch melody (shown in Figure 7.1) uses the limited interval of a perfect fifth and provides an opportunity to teach choristers of all ages a short song in Latin using pure vowels, thus immediately eliminating any native accents indigenous to the geographic region where the choir resides. The pitch of the song may be moved to an appropriate key to encourage use of the head voice for young singers. The challenges of singing the perfect fifth interval in tune and maintaining centered pitches on the descending line encourage careful listening and awareness of intonation. Reminders about preparatory breath and singing with sustained sound for the duration of the phrase may also be reinforced. When the unison line has been mastered, reinforcement of the dynamic contrast of the ascending and descending line may be discovered by the singers who are asked to suggest possible dynamic shaping of the melody. Through experimentation, the choristers may determine that the rising pitches suggest a crescendo and the descending line suggests a diminuendo. Once the decisions about dynamic shape have been made, "Ars longa, vita brevis" may be sung as a canon using from two to four parts as appropriate for the age and ability of the singers. Within a very short time, the newly formed choir is singing in parts and experiencing the joy of choral music participation in the first five minutes of the first rehearsal.

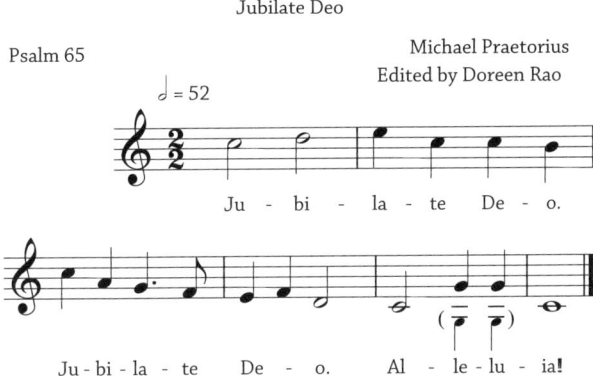

FIGURE 7.2 "Jubilate Deo" by Michael Praetorius, arr. Doreen Rao. © by Boosey & Hawkes, Inc. Reprinted with Permission.

VOICING THE CHOIR

Assigned seating for the newly formed choir should be determined soon after rehearsals begin in the fall. For the first week or two, building confidence in the singers and getting them to feel comfortable in their new choir are important. As soon as possible, assigning permanent seats (for the semester) should be accomplished. By placing the voices carefully in optimal locations, the sound of the choir can be dramatically changed from a moderate sound to a more focused, clear, ringing sound with a stronger presence.

Composer and conductor Gregg Smith for many years has voiced his professional vocal ensemble, the Gregg Smith Singers, with dramatic results.[6] With an awareness of "voicing the choir" done by others but with no opportunity to see it actually done, this author many years ago began by experimenting with where to place the young singers to achieve the optimal sound from the choir. It is a learned process. Now, years later, after experimenting with various placement of voices (and sometimes re-voicing the choir midyear or more often as voices grow and change), it is evident that this process can dramatically change how the choir sounds.

This director's preferred song for voicing the choir is Michael Praetorius's "Jubilate Deo."[7] As shown in Figure 7.2, this selection works well for young voices for several reasons: As a teaching piece, it encompasses the range of a tenth, spanning pitches from middle C to the E an octave and a third above, thus falling well in the tessitura of young singers' voices. Singing in Latin encourages the use of pure vowels. And the higher pitches provide an opportunity to hear the *ring* in the voice when listening for the overtones.

Begin by lining up the singers by height from tallest to shortest. Typically in a children's choir, there may be singers of dramatically different heights, and it is important that the taller choristers are placed toward the back and the shorter choristers toward the front to optimize sight lines. Next, determine how many rows of singers there will be. For discussion purposes, assume that there are forty-eight singers in the choir and each of four rows will have twelve singers.

Have the twelve tallest singers come forward in a straight line facing the largest space in the choral rehearsal room. Begin by having them all sing "Jubilate Deo" in unison. Then listen to them in groups of three or four at a time. Begin moving singers around at random at first to mix up the voices. As you listen to each small group, listen for the overtones and the ring to the voice, particularly when they sing the first few measures of the song. You will soon begin to hear voices that sound better when standing next to each other than they do next to other singers in different configurations. Find the optimal placement for each set of three or four voices across the row.

Voices are like fingerprints. No two fingerprints are the same, as are no two voices. By optimally placing the various sizes and colors of the voices, you can dramatically change the overall tone of the choir. Have the choristers listen carefully as the process unfolds. Ask them which placement of the voices *they* would choose. After doing this several times, the choristers will begin to hear what the director hears: the dramatic difference in sound that can occur when voices are placed next to different types of voices.

CONCLUSION

There are many layers to a children's choir. When the choir stands and sings in performance, the audience hears and sees the children singing beautiful music. Behind the polished performance are many layers of work that allow the choir to arrive at this point. Parents, volunteers, directors, staff, board, and others each have a role in bringing this choir to performance. How well the details are organized—from the director's efficient use of rehearsal time to the communication skills of the staff, to the competence of the chaperones who direct the choirs into the correct positions at the appropriate times during the concert—all have an important place in the daily life of the choir. As with singing excellence, this doesn't just happen. It happens only when there is careful thought, solid planning, strong communication, attention to detail, collaboration, and pursuit of excellence.

Know Who You Are: Wear One Hat
When organizations are clear about their values, purpose,
and goals, they find the energy and passion to do great things.
—HOWARD BEHAR, FORMER PRESIDENT OF
STARBUCKS INTERNATIONAL

8

PROMOTION AND FUNDRAISING

STARBUCKS IS NOT just about selling coffee. It is about people and creating a coffee culture in the United States. The employees know who they are and why they are there. Their mission is evident in all they do. Similarly, a chorus with a clear mission statement knows why it exists and what role it has in the cultural community that surrounds it. How clearly the mission of the choir is understood by artistic staff, board, and administrative staff will be reflected in decisions about the programming of the chorus. The mission will also shape how the organization markets itself to the public. Howard Behar states:

> When you know who you are, you will see a path or possibility literally unfold before you. You will be gently guided to follow it, or you'll create your own opportunity. Each life is filled with possibilities, but most of us miss the magical places to dig. Keep your eyes open, and you will find the treasure.[1]

Choral musicians and music educators have an inherent treasure in an art practiced every day. One of the responsibilities of a chorus, whether in a school, church, or community context, is to share the treasure of choral singing with many people. How we share the choral art with others is only as good as how well we promote and sustain the work of our choirs, thus giving others access to the experience of choral performance.

PEOPLE VALUE CHOIRS

People enjoy hearing choirs sing. If a flash mob of adults spontaneously begins singing in a mall or other public space, passersby stop to listen. They smile, take photographs with cell phones, call their friends to tell them what they are seeing, and sometimes even sing along. There is an immediate curiosity about who these people are and what they are doing. Sometimes the passersby will be interested enough to inquire when and where they might hear the choir sing again.

At a Chorus America national conference in San Francisco, the professional male vocal ensemble Chanticleer performed a free community sing on a sunny Saturday afternoon in a high school gymnasium near its rehearsal location. Community members and convention attendees were invited to join Chanticleer to become part of the music-making process. Songs were taught, the audience learned how Chanticleer rehearsed, and everyone was encouraged to sing.

At one point during the seventy-five-minute event, people in the audience were invited to greet and introduce themselves to the people sitting around them. One conference attendee learned that the young woman sitting in front of her had seen a sign on the street about the community sing while on an afternoon walk and decided to attend out of curiosity. She was a professional dance instructor and a salsa dancer. She was visibly moved when the afternoon of music-making concluded with the approximately five hundred people in attendance singing Franz Biebl's "Ave Maria." Overwhelmed by the beauty and power of the singing, she commented, "I would like to hear them [Chanticleer] again. I had no idea what this experience would be like, and I'm very glad I came. Today I sang for the first time since I was a child in school and didn't know if I would remember how."

People value singing in choirs. People who are surprised by or reminded about the experience of singing may seek opportunities to attend choral concerts or participate in choirs. The Chorus America *Choral Impact Study* stated, "Choral singing continues to be the most popular form of participation in the performing arts."[2] There are 42.6 million children and adults singing in America.[3] Why is this important? We know that people enjoy attending concerts and that so many millions of singers (both children and adults) enjoy sharing the choral art on a regular basis. Therefore, how concerts are promoted matters.

How choirs promote themselves has everything to do with the artistic vision for the choir and how it is brought to life in the artistic planning of concerts. Spreading the word about what the choir does, who sings, and what interesting programs are being presented is important for audience development and organizational sustainability. Each choir should find a way to capably market itself to offer more people the opportunity to experience the beauty of choral singing.

WHERE TO START

The word *promotion* means "activity that supports or encourages" or "to publicize."[4] Once a newly formed chorus is prepared to give concerts, generating audiences becomes a goal. For choirs that have been in existence for several years, new and creative ideas about marketing and promotion of concerts should be part of every season's planning, and maintaining an awareness of current trends should be part of the strategizing process.

A children's choir typically has a built-in audience of parents and family members who attend the concerts. Most choruses will want to expand their audiences beyond the immediate chorus families and develop a loyal following of people who come to concerts, become season ticket-holders, and eventually become annual contributors.

THE CHORUS'S WEBSITE: A MARKETING TOOL

The chorus's website gives the organization access to the world, and the world has access to the chorus at all times. The website may be the most accessible window for viewing the organization. How the organization promotes itself on the website matters. Easy navigation on a website will encourage the viewer to stay online longer and read more about the organization. Websites that are difficult to navigate create frustration and are not attractive to potential viewers. A website should provide a comprehensive overview of the choir, its activities, and its concert offerings, and should be continually updated to reflect timely information.

E-marketing (Internet marketing) is one of the fastest-growing ways for a choir to reach a wider audience. Developing a database with names, addresses, and e-mail addresses of those who attend concerts and visit the chorus's website will provide a way to keep in touch with patrons. Online e-mail marketing services, such as Constant Contact, PatronMail, and others, provide ways to add e-mail addresses to the chorus database by generating lists of people who visit the chorus website. These marketing programs also allow the chorus to track the number of e-mails opened and which links are viewed, thus enabling the chorus to monitor which initiatives are the most successful.

Through online marketing services, subscribers can be tracked, and data can be provided to the organization about ticket sales. Tracking subscribers who may have lapsed is also possible. Keeping the chorus's name upfront for patrons through e-blasts or e-mails permits more frequent contact than an occasional postal mailing. Increased awareness of the organization and participation in chorus activities, such as fundraisers, may increase ticket sales. Having patrons become "friends" of the chorus on the choir's Facebook page also links the organization regularly to patrons, and the use of Twitter increases accessibility to patrons for last-minute reminders about events.

PURCHASING TICKETS

Season brochures that include ticket order forms may be sent by postal service or e-mail to those who become part of the chorus's database. Some concertgoers order individual or season tickets using the order form and pay by check. Some choirs sell concert tickets only in person in advance, and those patrons may pay by check or cash. Other organizations have procedures for ordering tickets by credit card, mail, phone, or online through PayPal. Newer technology allows a small device called the "Square" to be attached to an iPhone, iPad, or Android device, allowing credit card purchases to be made anywhere that mobile phone service is available. Whatever method is used, the process for purchasing tickets should be effortless. With the rapid advancement of technology, purchasing tickets should only become even simpler in the future.

Chorus information should be "above the fold" on the opening page of the chorus's website, meaning that important information should be visible on the screen when you open the webpage. It is also recommended that it should take only three clicks on the chorus website to purchase a ticket.[5] An additional advantage of online ticket purchasing is that it may be done any time at the patron's convenience.

There are other ways of creating incentives to increase ticket purchases. Discounts may be offered to those who purchase season tickets or to those who order by an early, stated deadline. Deeper discounts may be offered to chorister families who order season tickets before the release of the season brochure to the public. Some choirs never offer discounted or complimentary tickets.

There is a growing trend for concertgoers to make last-minute decisions to attend events rather than purchasing tickets in advance. A well-timed e-blast or tweet reminder sent close to the day of the concert may encourage additional people to attend and purchase tickets at the door. Some choirs increase the ticket price as the time gets closer to the actual concert. Although this may seem counterintuitive, for some organizations, it is highly successful and may be more profitable in the long run. Staying informed about current practices in the field is important. Each choral organization will decide what method is appropriate.

OTHER WAYS OF MARKETING THE CHORUS

We've all heard the saying "Any press is good press." Getting the name of the organization into the media anytime creates more awareness of it. Specific marketing efforts that organizations may use to promote concerts might include the following:

- Written press releases distributed to
  - local newspapers
  - local radio stations
  - local television stations
- A short promotional video about an upcoming concert on YouTube
- A public service announcement on cable television
- Use of Facebook, Twitter, or other social media platforms to announce events
- Listing of concerts on the chorus website
- Article about upcoming concert(s) in the chorus newsletter (in print format or online)
- Interviews aired on local radio or television stations
- Google free ads
- Paid advertising
- Complimentary tickets sent to local newspaper arts editors
  - Note: Some newspapers will not review concerts involving children or only do so when they perform with another adult organization. This will vary from city to city.
- Singing at various community events where announcements can be made about upcoming events

- Newspaper interviews with guest composers, guest conductors, or invited performers
- Calendar listings on community cultural calendars (websites and newspapers)
- Announcements to the local area music teachers, church choirs, or other children's choirs in the region
- Flyers, posters, or season brochures to be distributed in many locations

Relying on only one strategy to promote concerts will not work; multiple strategies should be employed. Many organizations may have a goal of "going green" by using less printed material and taking advantage of electronic media avenues.

There should be continuous analysis of ticket sales to determine which medium is the most effective for generating them. Each organization should continually adapt to the most fiscally responsible strategy for making contact with the greatest number of people. What *is* certain is that the strategies are always changing.

VISIBILITY OF THE ARTISTIC DIRECTOR IN THE COMMUNITY

It is important for the artistic director to be visible. The artistic director's presence in the community can inspire people to become involved with the choral organization. Speaking at service club luncheons, attending other choral concerts, performing with other arts organizations, or leading a choral consortium[6] of organizations in the community are some of the ways an artistic director may choose to become more visible. Guest-conducting a school festival, all-county choral festival, or church children's choir festival are other ways of creating awareness for both parents and children.

Developing a following of friends and colleagues will increase the awareness of the chorus as news about it spreads. Creating a community of support for the chorus is all about connecting with people and sharing the passion for its work. Business cards with the chorus website, e-mail address, phone number, and Facebook link should be available when the artistic director speaks to community organizations about the chorus. Concert flyers or season brochures may be distributed at community events where the choir sings. All such print materials should list the website and encourage a visit to it for ticket purchase information.

AUDIENCE SURVEYS

For established choirs, it is important to know who their audience is, where they come from, and what their feelings are about the concert experience. Some choirs periodically conduct an audience or online survey to gather important data about the concertgoing experience and public perceptions of the choir. Information gathered about concerts may include how someone heard about the choir, his or her experience purchasing tickets, how far did he or she travel to hear the choir, the ease of parking, the ease of access to the concert venue, seating, programming, and so on. Contact information should be requested of audience members completing the survey who are not already in the database so that they may be added to the chorus's mailing and e-mail lists.

Often, children's choir concerts are general admission, and choristers are required to arrive early for the pre-concert warm-up. Audience members tend to arrive early to reserve the most desirable seats. A well-designed survey may be easily completed during this pre-concert time, thus increasing the rate of return for the survey and giving the audience something to do while waiting for the concert to begin. A brief announcement stressing the importance of the survey may be given by a board member, staff member, or volunteer. Holding a drawing to win a chorus CD or complimentary ticket for the next concert may encourage more people to respond. Any data received are good data, as they provide insight into how people perceive the choir and what they think about it; and this is information the organization might not have learned otherwise.

Online surveys provide an opportunity to gather valuable feedback. The surveys may be created by the chorus staff or through an online survey company or software, which may be free or range in price from inexpensive to more costly. Companies such as SurveyMonkey or Constant Contact may offer a variety of ways to analyze the data once they are gathered.[7] The chorus may seek professional assistance in creating a survey to help gain the most valuable information.

THE SEASON CONCERT BROCHURE

If the choir chooses to prepare a concert flyer, postcard, or season brochure, careful consideration about the design of the piece should be given. Although the current trend is moving away from elaborate brochures, if a printed brochure, postcard, or concert flyer is to be used, there are several issues to keep in mind.

A brochure provides an opportunity to generate excitement or interest for an upcoming concert or an entire season. Photographs of children singing, smiling faces, a formal choir photograph, intriguing artwork, use of colors, engaging titles for concerts, and creative designs can motivate patrons to purchase tickets. The season brochure should contain an interesting description of each concert that will spark the curiosity of the reader. It should also include the date, time, location, and any featured guest artists.

The brochure ticket order form, in print or online, should be well laid out and easy to understand. Space to include an optional contribution to the choir may be provided. The quality of the brochure should be the best the choir can afford to produce, either by purchasing the design or through the in-kind services of a marketing, advertising, public relations, or web-design firm. The brochure may be made available on the website in a downloadable PDF version if paperless communication is preferred.

Photographs of the choir may be taken by a professional photographer who is hired or by one who donates services. A chorister parent who is a fine amateur or professional photographer may donate her or his services to the chorus. Whatever approach is chosen, the quality of the photographic images is important. If there are several age-level choirs, photographs may be selected to indicate this. Photographs may be taken at various locations, including at a recent tour location. The smiling faces of the choristers, singing or not, should convey the spirit of the choir. Some photographs can be formal, and others can be candid. The photos used for a brochure may be of one child, a small group, or the entire choir. The diversity of the choir(s) can be shown in the photographs, which may include all girls, all boys, or both.

Looking at other choirs' photographs and concert brochures online and in print will provide ideas for the director or person responsible for the photo shoot and/or photograph selection. These ideas can be communicated to the graphic artist or designer of the brochure. With the advanced graphics capability of computer software, some choirs choose to prepare the brochure in house by capable staff or volunteers.

If a photo shoot is to be scheduled for the choir or choirs, careful planning should precede the event and may include the following considerations:

- Location
- Date/rain date if the shoot is outdoors
- Lighting and time of day (shadow effects)
- What the choir will wear (formal concert attire, tour outfits, school clothes)
- Who will be included in the photos
- Will the photos be taken while the choir is singing
- Will photos be staged
- Will candid photographs be taken

The written narrative in the brochure should be compelling, whether used exclusively online or in printed format. If an annual concert event has become a tradition for the organization and draws many attendees year after year, this may be included in the text. The text for the brochure should be proofread carefully for spelling and grammar, and the language should be succinct. Less is more. In the age of digital information, tweets, and soundbites, a quick summation of details will be appreciated and is more likely to be read.

The season may be formally announced to the media in the spring, and the concert brochure may be mailed in late August or early September. The timeline will vary from organization to organization. Once prepared, the online brochure may be posted immediately or according to the timeline that the choir has established for its release. For a season brochure that is mailed, postage rates will vary depending on the size of the mailing, the weight of the paper or card stock used, and the number of copies being mailed. Using bulk mailing rates, if the organization's mailing list is large enough to qualify, is the least expensive. Although bulk mail is not delivered as quickly as first-class mail, the money saved may be worth it, and advance planning can compensate for the delay in delivery.

In lieu of a season brochure, the use of "save the date" postcards is increasing. The postcards refer patrons to the choir's website for detailed concert information. This is both cost-effective and a more environmentally sound practice. Frequent electronic contact with subscribers and patrons is also found to be effective, providing savings to the choir in both printing and postage costs.

Although labor-intensive, some organizations may choose to place brochures, concert flyers, or posters in various locations around the city or town. Volunteers or staff may be able to locate strategic places where concert brochures may increase the visibility of the choir in the community.

PROMOTING THE CHORUS IN OTHER WAYS

Sometimes an opportunity to promote an upcoming choir concert occurs during a live performance presented in a train station, at a mall, on a street corner, at the zoo, at a walk-in sing, or at an outdoor community event. For a new choir, the people who support the founder's vision for the choir may help promote the concerts with friends, family, and colleagues. Chorister families will share the news about upcoming concerts and may be given incentives to sell tickets to a performance, such as a free ticket for every five tickets they sell. Initially, there will be curiosity about the new choir's events. As the reputation of the choir grows, the seasoned choir's audience should grow well beyond the immediate chorister families. The members of the choir and their families are the best advertisers or promoters of the organization. Their enthusiasm and passion for it will become contagious and encourage others to become involved.

There are many creative ways to generate an audience and encourage loyal patrons. With the use of Twitter and Facebook and other social media platforms, news about concerts may spread more rapidly. Friends trust friends. When someone speaks positively about a children's choir concert experience to someone else, an opportunity is created to generate a new audience member for a future event. Friends give others recommendations about events to attend, or share their enthusiasm for something they have enjoyed. Spreading the word and sending reminders about concerts is increasingly happening on social media platforms as the power of connectivity increases in the younger generations.

Another way of promoting concerts is through group sales to school choirs, church choirs, community centers, or senior residences. Youth groups from Ys (formerly YWCA and YMCA), boys and girls clubs, or neighborhood community centers may be encouraged to bring a group to concerts. Senior residences often take groups on outings by bus or van to attend special events. One such event could be a children's choir afternoon concert, particularly for those seniors who do not wish to go out at night.

Another way of encouraging new audience members is to offer complimentary tickets to music educators, church choir directors, or private teachers as a thank you for their recommendations of students to participate in the chorus, or to honor the work they do with their students. After a first concert, such guests may wish to return to more concerts and eventually become season patrons and contributors.

Complimentary tickets may be given by board members to prospective board members. Tickets may be offered to prospective funders, who are invited to attend a concert with a board member to learn more about the organization. Choristers may give a complimentary concert ticket to a friend, who might be encouraged at a later date to audition for the chorus. Tickets may be offered at a discount to college student alumni members of the chorus, who may wish to bring a friend who purchases a ticket at full price. Complimentary tickets may be given to funders who sponsor a specific concert. Season tickets may be given to those who sponsor the chorus's entire concert season. There are many ways of promoting the choir and increasing audience size. Using a variety of strategies and monitoring them for success will inform the choir about trends in ticket purchasing and which strategies work most effectively.

NEWSLETTERS

An annual, biannual, or quarterly newsletter may be prepared by the chorus for distribution to the constituents of the choirs. As print and postal costs increase and as society becomes more mindful about conserving natural resources, many choirs are transitioning away from mailings to online newsletters, or eliminating them altogether in favor of social media applications. Regardless of the distribution format, sharing news provides readers with insights into the many experiences and activities of the choir. Some newsletter topics may include the following:

- Details about upcoming concerts
- Quotes about the chorus from distinguished musicians
- Photographs of guest artists or choristers rehearsing
- Reports and photos from a recent tour
- Article or column by the artistic director
- Article about vocal health
- Article by a parent of a chorister
- Article by a chorister
- Article about a chorister
- Season concert dates
- List of sponsors
- List of donors
- List of volunteers
- News from alumni chorus members
- Featured article about a chorister who becomes a professional singer
- Photographs from chorister camps, tours, outreach concerts, etc.
- Interview with a staff member or volunteer

For school choirs, news on the school website might include a description of a special district choral or arts festival, school choir collaborations, news about guest conductors or guest artists, and news about all-county or all-state choir festival participants. For churches, the printed news bulletin might include dates of choir performances, special worship service music, or interdenominational choral events or services. The list is endless and should be tailored to the activities of the individual choir.

ADDITIONAL REVENUE AND VISIBILITY

Another way to increase visibility of both the choir and its supporters is by having concert sponsors. A local business may sponsor an entire concert or an entire season. By doing so, the business's name may be included in press releases, programs, newsletters, in the season brochure as a sponsor, and on the chorus website. A poster displaying the firm's name may be on display in the lobby at the time of the concert.

Another revenue-generating activity is selling advertisements for local businesses in the concert program. This gives visibility to the businesses and helps increase awareness of the chorus in the community. The ads may be full page, half page, or smaller. Additional revenue may be generated by seeking sponsors for the season brochure. Media sponsors may also be part of the promotion equation.

SEEKING DONORS

Another part of promotion for the choir is seeking annual donors who contribute to the ongoing work of the choir. Donors encourage and support choirs in many ways:

- A gift to the general operating fund
- A gift to a scholarship fund
- A gift to an endowment fund
- A gift for a special project such as education outreach or a new commission
- A gift to sponsor a fundraising event
- A gift in memory of someone
- Providing funds for a matching gift initiative
- Providing much-needed equipment (office equipment, computers, electronic keyboard, etc.)

Donors may include businesses, family endowment funds, individuals, foundations, and anyone committed to supporting the mission and work of the organization.

Asking for money is often one of the most difficult things for people to do. Having board members or others who are successful at fundraising is a necessity for a nonprofit organization's sustainability. Establishing a personal connection with prospective donors is essential: People give to people. George Bernard Shaw called fundraising "the joy of being used for a purpose recognized by all as a mighty one."[8]

Author and professional fundraiser Jerold Panas provides the following poem:

The Joy of Asking
A fundraiser stood at the heavenly gate,
His face was scarred and old.
He stood before the man of fate
For admission to the fold.
"What have you done," Saint Peter said,
"To gain admission here?"
"I've been a fundraiser, sir,
For many and many a year."
The pearly gates swung open wide,
Saint Peter rang the bell.
"Come in and choose your harp," he sighed,
"You've had your share of hell!"[9]

Anyone who has done fundraising knows that the process can be both challenging and rewarding. If the person asking for a donation believes in the choral organization and the importance of its mission, it is easy to share that enthusiasm for the choir with others. In the community choir context, the contact with donors may be done by a founder, board member, artistic director, or others designated with this responsibility. In the school context, it may be done by parents, parent-teacher organizations, booster clubs, or school administrators. This work may be supported by staff members, who provide the necessary support materials for those making calls on prospective donors.

Often, the first meeting with a potential donor is not about asking for money, but rather to become acquainted and share a conversation about the choral organization. The first meeting with a prospective donor may be to invite them to attend a concert or to thank them for attending a recent concert. The second meeting might be about "the ask." It has been said that obtaining the first gift is the most difficult. Once the first donor has given to the organization, future fundraising builds on that success by adding contributions from others—one gift at a time. Success breeds success. Continual contact with each donor will ideally nurture the relationship and lead to continued support and increased contributions.

It is easy for a potential donor to ignore a letter or not return a phone call or e-mail. It is much more difficult to say no to someone in person. Asking for a sizable donation should always be done in person. The person soliciting funds should be prepared to present materials about the choir when meeting the potential donor. A short DVD or flip video may be played on a laptop computer. It may include brief statements from a chorister, the director, and a parent about choir experiences. A CD of the choir may also be given to the prospective donor for later review. Seeing a chorister speak on a DVD about the profound effect the choir has had on his or her life may be quite captivating and moving for the prospective donor.

An important part of meeting with a potential donor is listening. Listening to those from whom you seek funding is more important than monopolizing the conversation about your organization. Any presentation should be succinct, comprehensive, and well prepared in advance. Getting to know the prospective donor and learning about the person's passion for the arts is as important as what you present about your organization. Professional fundraiser Mary Deissler said, "God gave you two ears to listen, and one mouth to talk. Therefore, listen twice as much as you talk."[10] She suggested that one of the mistakes those who solicit contributions often make is talking too much about their organization and not listening to what the potential funder cares about, or thinks about the organization. Much can be learned by listening.

Keeping in touch regularly with those who donate to the choir is important. One thank-you note with no further follow-up contact is not enough. Sharing good news about the choir or sending a progress report about a project that a donor has funded keeps the donor informed about how his or her contribution is making a difference for the organization. The update might be as simple as a short handwritten note.

Saying thank you is a must; say it promptly; say it often. A thank-you note signed by the director of the choir or chief administrator should be sent within forty-eight hours of receipt of a gift. Adding a personal note to the standard thank-you letter is a plus. An additional handwritten thank-you note may be sent from a board member, or an update on the project funded by the donor may be sent from a staff member showing appreciation for the donor's support. Handwritten notes are a refreshing change from the form letters or e-mails that are usually received.

Another impromptu handwritten note to a donor may be a surprise thank-you postcard from a chorister while attending chorister summer camp. Mailed by the staff after camp, these postcards may not be directly related to a recent gift, but are instead sent as a surprise during the summer months. The text may be as simple as "Thank you for keeping us singing" and signed with the chorister's first name.[11] There are many creative ways to send thank-you messages throughout the year.

Making periodic efforts to increase annual donors' contribution amounts should be a goal for those charged with fundraising efforts. It is appropriate to canvass all donors, whether they give small gifts or larger ones.

Sometimes the work of fundraising can be discouraging, particularly in challenging economic times, but persistence matters. If the choir is clear about its mission, and the philosophy is in line with the donor's philosophy about arts organizations, music, education, and young singers, the likelihood of success in fundraising increases. Subsequently, strong relationships are built as the chorus makes connections with the community and increases its visibility with the supportive people who respond to these requests.

OTHER FUNDRAISING OPPORTUNITIES

Not all fundraising is achieved by calling on donors. Events other than concerts may be scheduled with the sole purpose of raising funds for the children's choir in the school, church, or community context. Friends who are not regular subscribers may be invited to attend, and they may decide to purchase tickets for an upcoming concert. Some of these types of events may include the following:

- A reception and dinner party
- A dessert party
- Dinner parties held simultaneously in homes in various locations to benefit the chorus
- Invitations to a "party-less" tea party (Send a complimentary tea bag with invitation to enjoy a cup of tea compliments of the chorus and suggest a contribution be sent in lieu of attending an actual tea party event.)
- Chorus auctions (either held in person or online)
- A wine and cheese party with a guest author (for a short presentation and book signing)
- A car wash
- A pizza sale (assemble pizzas and sell fresh and ready for baking or freezing)
- A spaghetti dinner or chicken barbecue
- A "thank-a-thon" (Choristers gather at a local business with multiple phone lines to make calls to past donors to say thank you for their contributions. There is no "ask" involved. A script may be prepared for the chorister to memorize and say to the donor or left on voicemail.)
- Sell the notes in a performance piece for one dollar per note until every note of the piece has been sold. (Perform only the number of notes that have been sold by concert time. Ask the audience to help complete the piece so the choir can sing the whole selection at the next concert.)

The list of possibilities is endless, and some are more labor-intensive than others.

PROMOTION OF CHORAL MUSIC EDUCATION IN SCHOOLS

The twenty-first century has seen a significant decline in the number of schools offering music programs. During times of economic challenges, many school music programs are downsized or eliminated. A survey of music programs often reveals that they are more likely to exist only where there is sufficient funding to support them.

An important way to promote choral music education for *all* children is through advocacy for music education programs in the schools, which has never been more important. Music must be part of every child's well-rounded liberal arts education. Former Federal Reserve Chairman Alan Greenspan stated:

> Critical awareness and the abilities to hypothesize, to interpret, and to communicate are essential elements of successful innovation in a conceptual-based economy. As with many skills, such learning is most effective when it is begun at an

early age. And most educators believe that exposure to a wide range of subjects—including literature, music, art and languages—plays a considerable role in fostering the development of these skills.[12]

Advocacy should begin while music is part of the school curriculum. Once lost, school music programs are difficult or impossible to reinstate. Chorus America stated:

- More than 1 in 4 educators say there is no choral program in their schools and 1 in 5 parents say that there are no choral singing opportunities for their children.
- Of the educators who said that their school has no choir program today, 31 percent said their school used to have such a program.
- Educators told researchers that schools whose parental involvement is high are significantly more likely to have choir programs, along with several other positive effects.[13]

To facilitate advocacy and the promotion of choral music education programs in the schools, Chorus America created *Making the Case for Your School Choir: An Advocacy Guide*.[14] Available in downloadable format from the Chorus America website, the eighteen-page guide provides data and strategies for parents, school board members, music educators, and others who wish to make a case for supporting school choirs. Although it is not a one-size-fits-all document, the compendium of resources can provide creative strategies that may be adapted for each context to help restore, preserve, maintain, and increase school choral programs.

The educational theorist Sir Ken Robinson makes the case that, while governments around the world are focusing on education, they often limit the curriculum to a small number of subjects and often focus on standardized tests rather than creative decision-making by educators. He suggests, "These reforms are typically stifling the very skills and qualities that are essential to meet the challenges we face: creativity, cultural understanding, communication, collaboration and problem solving."[15] Choral music education is a synthesis of all these skills and vital to the broad education of our youth.

PROMOTING SCHOOL CHORAL EVENTS

For those schools fortunate enough to have a choral program, a built-in audience exists of parents, teachers, and school administrators. Sending an announcement home with schoolchildren, posting concert information on the school website, and encouraging students to invite friends and family members to a school concert help generate interest in the school program. When interest is piqued, there is an opportunity to speak to the audience about why choral music education is an important part of the school curriculum.

For some schools, presenting evening concerts is difficult. Some children do not have transportation to the school for an evening performance. In this situation, sometimes parents will volunteer to transport additional children to the concert. Similarly, transportation for a before-school or after-school rehearsal can be a problem. Any music-making must be accomplished during the school day only. For schools where evening performances are not a realistic goal, daytime concerts in the school for other grade levels may be the only option. Parents may be invited to the in-school concert as their only option for seeing their children sing in a choir or perform in a music production.

Parent support groups may help fund bus transportation for the chorus or other music groups who perform outside the school. An outside performance may include singing at an art museum, a mayor's inauguration, or for a school choir festival. Some school choirs sing annually for a school board meeting. Some school choirs collaborate with guest artists or commission new works. These events may be advertised and promoted in similar ways to those used by community children's choirs. These performances are often seen as a way to celebrate the outstanding work children are doing in schools. The range of activities may vary from school to school and state to state and, once again, may be tied closely to the amount of funding available in any academic year.

PROMOTING CHILDREN'S CHOIRS IN THE CHURCH CONTEXT

One challenge many church choirs face is how to attract young singers to the choir program. In a large church, the programs of the church are very visible within the church community. An inherent structure exists for spreading the news about the children's choir through church bulletins, newsletters, the church's website, and singing for worship services. An effort to make the program inviting and welcoming for children is important. Meeting parents to talk about the choir allows the director to discuss future plans and can help generate interest and excitement for the choir, particularly at the beginning of the school year. The children who are already members of the choir may also spread the word about participation to their friends.

As with any people-driven organization, the personal contact of the director with the church families is a key factor. Formal marketing may be unnecessary or less important in this context. The children's choir will be visible to the congregation if it participates in worship services regularly. The director may choose to recruit choir members by setting up a table for choir registration before, between, and after church services as a visible reminder about the singing opportunity. Others may recruit singers during Sunday School registration. The promotion of the choir within the congregation is mostly about building relationships.

With a strong network, word travels from the church family into the community. Parents from outside the church may ask how their children may become part of the church's choral program. The choir grows as others are brought into the program. Singing in the choir builds community beyond the immediate church members, and it is particularly important where no choral music education programs exist in the surrounding area.

The church choir director may visit Sunday School classes or do targeted mailings to church families with children telling them about upcoming plans for the choir. The choir activities may include more than singing for worship services. Where music programs in the schools are nonexistent or limited, the church music program may be a thriving and vital activity sought out by parents who want an expanded music experience for their children. Where there are strong music programs surrounding the church, there may be enough capable singers to form the choir, regardless of the size of the congregation. Some choirs may be as small as seven or eight members; others may number thirty, forty, or more.

Some church programs encompass several children's choirs at varying age combinations and skill levels ranging from preschool children to high school students. Some church choirs tour, present musicals, give concerts of sacred and secular music, and perform for such professional choral organizations as the American Choral Directors Association, the American Guild of Organists, and the National Association for Music Education (NAfME, formerly MENC). In churches where there are choirs of varying age levels, concerts may include each choir performing individually, the choirs combined, or the choirs combined with the adult choirs, for both worship services and separate concert events.[16] The possibilities are endless and limited only by what the director is able to create within the specific church context.

For smaller church programs, similar recruiting strategies for establishing a personal connection with families and encouraging their child's participation may be employed. Some directors in church programs may be volunteers and not trained conductors or music educators. For those with limited formal training, additional resources, such as books by Sue Ellen Page, Helen Kemp, Donald Rotermund, and Ruth Krehbiel Jacobs, and resources published by the Choristers Guild, may provide helpful information for those who work with children's choirs in the church context.

For smaller congregations, the numbers may vary from year to year. For example, a church with approximately one hundred members may have a limited number of children in the congregation. There may be only enough children for two choirs, one of younger students and one of older students. Some years, there may not be enough children to have one of the choirs. The variability of enrollment is the reality of the fluctuation of a church's population.

Shortening the time commitment of the children's choir has been found to increase the enrollment for some church choirs. For example, having weekly rehearsals from September to the end of the school year may exclude some students who have conflicts with other activities. A church choir may choose to meet from mid-October through December and resume at the end of February and continue into early May, thus avoiding the fall athletic season, the snowy months of winter (for some locations), and ending before the spring sports activities resume.[17] By being aware of the activities that compete for the children's time, slight modifications in the rehearsal schedule may result in increased enrollment.

Not all the repertoire for church choirs need be sacred. Age-appropriate concert repertoire may include ethnic singing, dancing, and drumming; presenting a musical;

singing secular music from many periods of music history and varied cultures; and commissioning a work for premiere. The choir may host a guest choir, work with guest artists, sing with the adult choir, and participate in other creative collaborations that extend the children's experiences beyond singing exclusively for worship services. Bringing choirs together in ways that are enriching and meaningful for the church worship program expands the young singers' experiences. Promoting choir activities may be accomplished in ways similar to what community choirs do. Other church events, such as a highly popular annual pageant, may not need any promotion.

CONCLUSION

Singing in a choir can change lives. It can turn a bad day into a better one. Singing can transform people. Singing can transport audiences to a place that is indescribable. Singing can bring people to tears or put smiles on their faces. As Isaac Stern said, "Music touches directly from the soul of the creative artist to the listener."[18] Knowing why a choir exists, having a focused purpose or mission, and bringing people together in support of the choir can be a profound experience for those who participate. To give this experience to as many people as possible, promotion of the choir's work is necessary.

Positioning your children's choir for excellence has much to do with how the choir promotes itself. A visible presence in the region matters, whether it is a school, church, or community children's/youth choir. Positioning the choir to be part of the cultural fabric of the community may be done through the media, on the Internet, through mailings, through personal connections, through performances, or through advocacy for choral music education for all children. If no one knows about the choir, few will have an opportunity to hear the children's singing or understand its power and beauty. To accomplish the goal of promoting, marketing, advocating, and recruiting, a well-planned strategy is required.

Promoting is about supporting, encouraging, and publicizing the choir. It is about inviting others to share in the choral experience. It is about spreading the news about the choir, being visible in the community, sharing why singing in a choir matters, and sharing the joy of music- making.

Nothing happens unless first a dream.
—CARL SANDBURG

9

CONCERTS

DREAMING ABOUT THE creation of a choir is where the journey begins. Striving to make what we dream about into a reality is the journey of the choir's life. The mature organization will develop over time and create its own identity in the city or community where it impacts the cultural life in potentially profound ways. Erkki Pohjola, founder of the Tapiola Choir of Finland, said,

> Everyone has to find their own philosopher's stone, their own way to rehearse, to choose a repertoire and create the necessary organization in cooperation with others. Certainly you can put signs along the road—for those that can read them.[1]

Once the choral organization is formed and the singers gather, how the choir develops is determined by the leadership and creativity of the artistic director or founder, and her or his ability to make the creative plans come to life in collaboration with a community of people who support the vision, philosophy, and work of the choir. Each person will bring individual strengths to the process. Lessons will be learned along the way, and the choir will find its identity in its own community and in the greater choral community at large.

The word *impresario* is defined as "the promoter, manager or conductor of an opera or concert company."[2] More important, the word has roots in the Italian word *impresa*, meaning "undertaking." The founding of a choir is a major undertaking, and the founder (or managing artistic director) of a nonprofit choral organization is indeed an impresario by virtue of what she or he does.

PLANNING FOR SUCCESS

As impresario, the founder is often the one who plans the concerts, creates the marketing strategies that initially draw interest in the choir, and sustains the music-making in the early years. When administrative staff is hired, the staff members (or volunteers if there is no staff) skilled in this area assume the marketing responsibilities in collaboration with the artistic director to create an inspiring season of programs for the audience and a comprehensive educational program for the choristers. How the details of each event are structured is important. Advance planning is the key to success. Thinking through every detail in advance will help structure the event or project for success. Unpredictable things will happen. If the pre-event planning includes thorough preparation in a timely manner, the organization has the potential to structure as much as possible to run smoothly and, when adverse unplanned events do occur, handle them easily.

The artistic director (or managing artistic director) will guide the creative process that becomes the musical events and educational plan for the year ahead. If more than one music director is employed by the chorus, the additional music director or directors may be brought into the creative planning process. The administrative staff may or may not be asked for creative ideas prior to the work of the music director(s). The collaborative planning sessions are often entertaining and stimulating. Suggesting as many creative ideas as possible is an inspiring way to begin. Out of the many ideas for themes, types of concerts, and repertoire, a shape to the season will emerge that seems appropriate, doable, and engaging. Often there are more ideas than concerts available. Ideas worth considering for future concerts should be retained for future planning sessions. Seeds for a concert season will begin to take shape. Once the artistic director refines and finalizes the concert themes, a framework exists for the details to be planned.

TIMELINE FOR CONCERT PLANNING

The process for planning a season may begin twelve to eighteen months in advance. For some community children's choirs, the season planning begins in the late fall or no later than January, nine months before the opening of the next academic year and season. Concert themes are set, potential repertoire is discussed or refined, and concert venues are determined based on the type of concert to be presented. There are many different types of concerts that a children's choir may present:

- Formal choral concert
- Collaborative concert with orchestra
- Concert hosting guest choir from out of state or an international choir
- Choir festival involving many choirs (which may include an orchestra)
- Multimedia performance involving choir, a ballet company, and large-screen video monitor to show slides
- Collaborative concert involving puppet theater company (with very tall, oversize puppets)
- Opera production
- Concert with a guest narrator

- Informal concert with audience participation
- Taping a holiday performance for television broadcast
- Outdoor concert performance
- Jazz performance involving jazz combo and guest artists (possibly cabaret style)
- Special dinner event where the choir performs for invited guests

The list reflects some of the types of concerts that are possible; there are many others.

Performance venues are also a consideration in planning a season of concerts. Venues should adequately accommodate the unique requirements of each type of concert. When planning the next season, it is important to determine if one concert facility will accommodate all the concerts planned for the year, or whether more than one type of concert facility will be required. A formal choral concert will require a stage area large enough for the required number of risers, depending on the size of the chorus. An opera production will require a stage area large enough for props, scenery, and appropriate lighting. A concert with an orchestra will require a space large enough for the chorus to be placed on risers (either standing or sitting) and enough floor space to accommodate all the orchestral players' chairs and stands. If several choirs are involved in a festival, additional warm-up space will be necessary. One concert facility may be able to handle all types of concerts scheduled during a given season. Depending on what is available, affordable, and what type of space is required for each of the concerts, more than one type of venue may be necessary.

In addition to adequate space for all choristers and instrumentalists to warm up before a concert, there are other considerations. Are there enough rooms away from the concert hall where the choir members may leave coats and do their vocal warm-ups? Will there be a visual and sound barrier between the choir warm-up location and the audience location during the pre-concert warm-up? The audience should not be able to hear or see the choirs prior to the start of the concert. All of this must be taken into consideration when touring a performance venue for possible use. There are other questions to ask when visiting a performance venue:

- What type of piano is available?
- Are there music stands available? If so, are the required number of stands available, or will they need to be brought to the concert space?
- Are chairs available for the accompanist's page turner and for instrumentalists (if necessary)?
- Is there adequate lighting for the requirements of the concert?
- Is there adequate lighting for the accompanist, or will a piano light be needed?
- Is there a table that can be used in the lobby for ticket and CD sales?
- Where are all the entrances to the performance space, and will they be open or locked from the exterior?

- What are the acoustics like?
- Is there a sound system and microphone for pre-concert announcements, if required?
- Is the venue a union hall or a nonunion hall?
- What is the fee for rental? Are there any additional costs?
- Can the choir bring its own recording engineer and videographer to record the concert for historic archival purposes?
- Is there a floor plan available, and does it include the location of electrical outlets?
- Where will the singers warm up?
- Is there a piano in the warm-up space?
- Is it possible to schedule a dress rehearsal in the concert space? And, if so, what will the rental fee be?
- Are the concert and dress rehearsal dates available?
- What is the audience capacity of the performance venue?
- Are ticket sales handled by the venue or by the chorus?
- Where are the restrooms located, and are they adequate to accommodate the audience and the expanded number of singers?

Once it has been determined that the performance venue will adequately accommodate the needs of the performance, arrangements should be confirmed in writing and contracts signed as necessary to secure the space. Ideally, all performance venues should be secured by the January or February prior to the start of the new season. By securing the concert venues early, adequate time for detailed planning is possible.

Once the concert themes and the performance venues are confirmed, the staff (or founder or volunteers) may begin to obtain grants or sponsors for the concerts. The earlier the season plans are in place, the more time the staff will have to work on special concert components that must be coordinated and to seek funding opportunities. Clear communication between the staff and the music director are important in this context. The music director may have well-defined creative ideas for the repertoire and programming, which should be clearly communicated to the staff who will be working to prepare administratively for the season ahead. The creative concert planning also has implications for the design of the season brochure.

CREATIVE PLANNING

Creative planning for a season includes the types of concerts you will present, balancing the variety of styles and languages the choir will sing, and determining the themes and titles for each concert. Creating an inspiring concert title or one that provokes thought or curiosity can encourage attendance. (Appendix 9.1 presents a list of concert titles that incorporate a broad range of subjects and can be inclusive of many styles of music, periods in music history, and different cultures.)

REPERTOIRE SELECTION

The process of repertoire selection for each level of the choir can be intensive. Considering repertoire, refining program themes, or preparing programs with a specific purpose may consume many hours of research and creative thought. Researching the historical background of the music once it is selected or as part of the selection process may also take many hours.

Criteria for the selection of repertoire may include:

- Range
- Tessitura
- Text
- Tempo
- Dynamic range
- Key
- Harmony
- Accompaniment
- Historical context
- Level of difficulty
- Style
- Form
- Voicing
- Language
- Use of additional instruments
- Meter(s)
- Key structure (major, minor, modal, pentatonic, etc.)
- Vocal color required for the style
- Composer or arranger
- Quality of the selection

The careful crafting of a concert program is a learned skill. Including varying styles of music if appropriate, exploring different moods and colors of sound, balancing various voicings from unison to multiple parts (depending on the age and skill level of the young singers), and including varying levels of difficulty are all part of the repertoire selection process.

Some repertoire should challenge the singers, and some repertoire should be readily learned and sung for enjoyment. Repertoire should be selected based on quality, inherent value, artistic impact, level of vocal skill required, appropriateness of text, variety of style, what is appropriate for the singers to learn and study, the appropriate challenges inherent in the score, and how much rehearsal time it will take to prepare. Most important, the repertoire should inspire the singers to become immersed in the music and sing with confidence and understanding. They should respond with their innermost feelings when making music and *become* the music.

Author Wayne D. Bowman says,

> Whether one is concerned with such issues as in-tune-ness and out-of-tune-ness; with the agitation or exquisite tenderness of a passage; with sing, groove, or gesture; with musical ebb and flow, tension and release; or with the piercing or smoothing features of what we call tone "quality"—one's body and one's embodied experience is paramount. Musical experience is not simply mediated by bodily experience; music experience is corporeally constructed.
>
> Why should matters like these concern educators? This brings us back to the idea of "healing power," for musical experience qualifies our beings in important ways. It lets us experience mind-body unity as no other experience does. It delivers us to a state of non-contingent, temporally fluid presence that we find nowhere else. I cannot make these claims for other arts or, for example, the way I experience a sunset. It is utterly unique to experience music.[3]

For some directors, the selection process of repertoire begins with listening (to choral CDs, MP3s, online excerpts on publisher's websites, YouTube), examining sample scores online or in hard copy, and attending professional conferences where many choirs may be heard. Compiling ideas for future repertoire and concerts is a good way to start the process of creating future seasons of concerts. Ideas may be stored in a computer file or file folder for future reference, research, and consideration. Data gathered should include the title, composer, publisher, and where a recording of the selection may be found if available. Attendance at professional conferences will provide opportunities to be exposed to new repertoire at reading sessions, workshop sessions, concerts, and by exchanging ideas with colleagues. Websites such as Choralnet provide online dialog and links to conversations about repertoire. University music libraries, music publishers, composer's websites, the Library of Congress, and international databases may also be valuable resources.

Once selections are made, shaping a program follows. These are some helpful questions to ask:

- Is there a specific shape to the program?
- Does the concert have a theme?
- Does the selected repertoire relate appropriately to the theme?
- Does the flow of music build from beginning to end, or are there peaks and valleys throughout the program?
- Does the tempo vary?
- Should the program flow chronologically?
- Does the program include more than major tonalities?
- Is the ending of the program intentionally strong or quiet?
- Are the texts appropriate for young singers?

- Is the tessitura and range of the repertoire appropriate for the singers' voices?
- What will the young singers learn from exploring this selection?
- What musical concepts will be taught through selected repertoire?
- Are there varied styles of music from various historical periods included in the season of concerts?
- What will challenge the choristers?
- Are there multiple languages included in the repertoire?
- Is the repertoire exclusively sacred or secular music, or a mix of both?
- Does this music inspire the singer, the conductor, and the audience?
- Is the repertoire inclusive of many cultures?

Hungarian composer and music educator Zoltán Kodály spoke about composers who wrote for young singers. He stated, "Nobody is too great to write for the little ones; indeed, he must do his best to be great enough for them."[4]

Studying and performing repertoire of the highest quality is quintessential to producing the best teaching and learning experiences. Repertoire selections become the music to be studied, analyzed, practiced, and performed, whether in concert, rehearsal, or in a school music classroom or church choir. The selected repertoire may inspire each rehearsal or class. Elements of form, color, interpretation, style, text, balance, vowel unity, diction, and more come directly from the music the choir is singing. An understanding of the text and how each composer sets text to music provides an opportunity to teach choristers about literature, poetry, historical context, and performance practice. As Plato observed, "[E]ducation in music is most sovereign, because more than anything else rhythm and harmony find their way into the inmost soul and take strongest hold upon it, bringing with them an imparting grace."[5]

Each conductor-educator will make decisions about the type of repertoire her or his choir will sing and the kind of programming that will be presented. Audience involvement in singing at the concert may be part of the equation. The possibilities are limitless. (Chapter 14 includes a repertoire list appropriate for children's choirs.)

SEASON ANNOUNCEMENT

Once the framework (dates, venues, concert titles) for the season is complete, announcement of the new concert season should take place. Typically, there is a particular time each year when many of the major arts organizations simultaneously announce their new seasons. This might occur in March or April. The community children's choir should be included on various cultural events calendars in the city and other worthwhile locations where visibility will be increased for the arts. (Publicity and concert promotion are discussed in chapter 8.)

HIRING INSTRUMENTALISTS AND GUEST ARTISTS

Once the repertoire is finalized for the season, instrumental requirements will be defined for the selected repertoire. The instrumentalists to be hired should be contacted well in advance of concert dates. They will need complete information, including rehearsal and concert dates, times, and locations. A discussion about their fee or honorarium should occur at the time of booking. If professional musicians from a local symphony orchestra are to be hired, their availability may be determined by the symphony orchestra's schedule. The purchased or rented music should be given to the hired player(s) in advance. A formal performance agreement should be signed by both the chorus and the instrumentalist. The chorus should have contact with the instrumentalist periodically before the rehearsals and concerts. Reminders or updates may be done by phone or e-mail to avoid any last-minute cancellations, conflicts, or missed changes in rehearsal time or location. In-demand musicians often appreciate the communication, especially if accompanied by important updates about the concerts in which they will be performing.

Other types of guest artists may be hired by the choir. These may include composers, vocal soloists, professional choirs, authors, poets, librettists, narrators, an opera company chorus, staging directors, costumers, set designers, lighting designers, producers for a recording session, someone to write program notes, or others. As with the professional musicians, a written agreement should be signed stating all the requirements of the collaboration, including a timeline for work due (as in the case of costumer, set designer, librettist, etc.) and all rehearsals and performances, including date, time, and location (if their presence is required).

DRESS REHEARSAL AND CONCERT LOGISTICS

Once the season is planned, the concert venues are secured, rehearsals are underway and concert time approaches, detailed planning for the dress rehearsal and concert follows—again, well in advance of the actual event. The planning includes the logistics for moving choirs in and out of the warm-up area, on and off the risers, and into and out of the audience seating (if the space is available) from the time of the choristers' arrival until their departure with parents at the conclusion of the concert. Logistical plans may include the following:

- A diagram and narrative of the choreographed movement of choirs from the warm-up area to the risers and/or seats in the concert hall (if available at concert time)
    - What is the order of the choirs to leave the warm-up space?
    - What exact time will the choirs begin to move into place before the concert begins? Five minutes before the concert start? Three minutes before? How

much grace time will be granted to late audience members beyond the concert's advertised start time?
- Will they move to risers in the concert hall, assigned seats in the audience, or other location?
- A written sequence of movement onto the risers and off the risers: Which row goes onto the risers first and in what order do the other rows move? Which row goes off the risers first, second, etc.?
- Planned and written logistics for the complete concert
- Planned and written logistics for a concert finale involving all choirs (if necessary)
- Diagrams for all staff and chaperones who will lead choirs while moving
- Detailed schedules for dress rehearsal and concert
- A prepared pre-concert announcement to be read by the board president, board member, or other designated person that might include
  - A reminder about turning off cell phones, beepers, or any other electronic devices that might emit sounds during the concert
  - Acknowledging concert sponsors
  - A reminder that recording devices may not be used during the concert
  - A reminder telling parents where they may greet their choristers after the concert (to eliminate congestion) or an invitation to a post-concert reception if one is being offered

If the logistics have been carefully planned and rehearsed prior to the concert, the movement of choirs will flow seamlessly during the concert, and an air of professionalism will prevail. (See appendix 9.2 for diagrams and logistics for a sample concert, and appendix 9.3 for a dress rehearsal schedule.)

CONCERT RECORDING

"Because of the expense of studio recording, more choruses are taking the live concert option."[6] This statement was made by Gayle Ober, board chair of Chorus America. Many choirs are finding ways to distribute their live performances in formats such as YouTube, their own websites, CDs, or digital downloads rather than producing only professionally recorded CDs. Others are abandoning recordings of numerous concerts in favor of a limited number of formal recording sessions.

There are monumental changes occurring in the recording industry and how music is distributed in the twenty-first century. MP3s abound, and music is more accessible on cell phones, iPads, iPods, computers, and through digital downloads than at any other time in our history.

Children's choirs often record their performances for historic archival purposes or for CDs to be sold at a later date. These CDs may be compilations of several live performances, or a single concert in its entirety. Formal recording sessions are also held to produce recordings for national distribution. Children's choirs and other types of vocal performances appear in increasing numbers on social media, including YouTube, Vimeo, blogs, Facebook, Twitter, MySpace, and the like. Live performance has been influenced by this increased access to the many recorded performances, both good and bad, currently available on these formats.

How music is distributed also has implications for recording children's choirs in the future. By using the latest technology, it may be less of a challenge to make high-quality recordings more readily available to the public. The quality of the recording of a children's choir concert is based on both the excellence of the choir and the expertise of the recording engineer. Not all audio recording engineers have excellent skills in the context of the subtleties of classical music recording in general, and for treble choirs in particular.

There are several important matters to be considered when hiring a recording engineer to record a concert. Because of the affordability and accessibility of equipment, many recording engineers have the resources to record, but not the advanced expertise of someone who has studied recording engineering techniques, microphone technology, and the computer skills for using state-of-the-art editing software. Recording classical concerts does not use the same techniques as other styles of music. When hiring a recording engineer, there are several important questions to ask:

- Where did the recording engineer study audio engineering techniques?
- What types of ensembles does the recording engineer most often record?
- Has the engineer recorded classical ensembles in the past? If so, how frequently?
- Does the engineer have any examples of his or her work that may be loaned to the artistic director for review?
- Can the engineer offer the name of someone as a reference whom he or she has recorded for within the past twelve months?
- What type of equipment will be used? How many microphones will be used and where does he or she anticipate they will they be located? (Microphone placement might influence where the conductor should place the singers.)
- Does the engineer have a predisposition toward a particular style of production, such as a minimalist, preservation approach, or more artificially affected and/or dynamically compressed sound? How does this fit with the conductor's goals?
- Does the engineer have any musical performance background? Can he or she read a choral or orchestral score? This is important at the time of editing when referring to measure numbers for editing purposes.

Each recording engineer should have knowledge about the proper placement and types of microphones to be used for a choral concert. In order to achieve a proper sound, the engineer may have requests and limitations for placement of the recording equipment during the concert. In each concert venue, there are several matters for consideration:

- Where are the electrical outlets located that will be used by the recording engineer?
- Is there a backstage area or green room where the engineer can be isolated during the concert? Or will he or she be located in the concert hall?
- If located in the concert hall, is there an open area, space at the end of an aisle, or area with no rows of seats or pews where a table may be set up for the recording engineer's equipment (if requested)?
- Are there noise issues with the heating, ventilation, and air-conditioning equipment?

Some lighting and dimmers may emit unwanted sound. Pumps or engines running outside the concert hall may also be audible. Can these be turned off during the concert?

- For some concerts, a visual reference (being able to see the performers) for the recording engineer is important. For other concerts, it may not be required.
- Will the microphones be placed so as not to obstruct sight lines for the singers or other musicians?
- Are the microphones in the way of the audience when entering or exiting? How will they be protected from being knocked or tipped over?
- If video recording is to be done, will the microphones be minimally visible or obstruct the view?
- What are the logistics for the choir? Will they move off the risers while singing?
- Will there be music performed from locations other than on stage on the risers? In the center aisle? In the corners of the audience area? From a balcony?
- Is there a procession of singers? If so, when does this occur during the concert?
- If there is movement, will there be banners or other visual items that may move near or potentially hit the microphone stands? (Moving air may cause noise if microphones are not properly protected.)
- Will the recording engineer use a live-to-two-track recording or multi-track recording?
- Are there any soloists, trios, or quartets, etc. that will be moving off the risers into another location?
- What is the instrumentation for the concert? If instruments other than piano will be used, where will they be located?
- A floor plan for the recording engineer will be helpful, or a conversation should be scheduled prior to the concert to discuss the possible logistics that may affect the recording engineer's setup.

- What will be done about coughs, inappropriate clapping, or other sounds accidentally emitted during the concert? Will they be removed if possible? What will be the cost for this additional work?
- Will there be a rehearsal in the space prior to the concert, and can a sound check be done? If so, what are the loudest and softest volumes that the choir will sing? What is the highest note to be sung? This information will assist the engineer in placing the microphones in the optimum location for recording.

Working closely with a recording engineer will result in a better recording. When the engineer understands and anticipates the flow of events, microphones can be carefully placed to accommodate the needs of the organization and maximize the quality of the recording. For formal recording sessions not involving an audience, there are other matters to consider.

PREPARING A PROFESSIONAL RECORDING

Periodically, the children's choir may wish to produce a CD for national distribution. The creative process of putting a recording together involves much advance planning and coordination, including obtaining the proper legal permissions to do so. CDs are often prepared for release annually or biennially. Other special recording projects may be undertaken over several years as in the case of recording the works of one particular composer. Some repertoire is better suited to the acoustics of a large stone cathedral. Other repertoire is better suited for a recording studio. Decisions about where and when to record are part of the decision-making process and preparation for undertaking such a project. Whatever the schedule or project, there are certain procedures that are helpful to know before beginning.

Advanced planning matters to be considered when preparing a CD for national distribution include the following:

- Selection of repertoire to be recorded
- Licensing arranged with ASCAP, Harry Fox, and BMI for permission to record and distribute
- A recording engineer to be hired to do the recording and editing
  - Working with an engineer with whom you have good rapport is important, particularly during the stressful moments of a formal recording session.
  - A good engineer/producer is critical to the success of the recording project. Hiring someone who is sensitive to the needs of singers and their energy levels is a bonus.
- A producer may be hired to produce the CD or guide the recording session(s)
- Original artwork or a graphic artist to create a cover for the CD

- Preparation of program notes for the jewel box liner
- Arrangements will need to be made with a record company to produce and possibly distribute the CD
- A venue where the recording will be made will need to be evaluated and secured
  - It may be advisable to visit the possible locations with the engineer to evaluate the acoustics. This will ensure that the space will accommodate the needs of the recording project, including stylistic considerations, logistics, and the production style of the recording.
- Dates for the recording sessions will need to be determined
- The choir will need to be educated about what is expected of them during a recording session and how it will differ from a typical rehearsal. (This topic will be discussed later in this chapter.)

There are many matters for consideration before undertaking a recording project, many of which have financial implications for the operating budget. A tentative budget should be created before starting a recording project to be sure it is financially feasible for the organization. Once the budget has been determined, the expenses should be included in the operating budget. Potential expenses may include the following:

- Cost of the music (purchased or rental) to be recorded
- Licensing fees from appropriate agencies such as ASCAP, BMI, and SESAC
- Mechanical licensing with the Harry Fox Agency (RightsFlows Limelight service and others can assist with CD, digital, and streaming rights)
- Written releases to record from musicians performing on the recording
- Cost of CD production
- Cost of artwork for CD cover
- Venue rental
- Producer fee
- Recording engineer fee
- Recording equipment/rental fees (if required for special recording projects)
- Editing fees
- Accompanist fees
- Instrumentalist fees (if required)
- Water and snacks for the recording session

There may be other expenses.

There are many rules governing the recording and distribution of music. The artistic director of the choir, in collaboration with the staff, should be well versed in what is the correct procedure for preparing a recording to sell and distribute nationally. The organization must be completely informed about the laws governing such a project.[7] Online resources may provide detailed information about copyright, licensing, and permissions. Seeking the advice of others who have undertaken such a project is also recommended. There are always lessons learned in the process, and working with trained professionals who have strong reputations is advised.

No matter how excellent the choir's performance is during the recording session, the recording can be ruined if not properly recorded. The engineer's efficiency and expertise will be worth the investment. The excellence of the choir must be matched by the excellence of the recording engineer and those who produce the final product. Remember, a recording lasts forever.

PREPARING THE CHORISTERS FOR A RECORDING SESSION

When undertaking a formal recording session, it is important to prepare the choristers in advance. The session will not be like a typical rehearsal. The mental and physical preparation of the choristers is as important as the musical preparation. The choristers should be advised to get adequate sleep on the night before a recording session, and ideally the session should be scheduled for a time of day when they will be the most rested and energized. Recording is strenuous work, and singing is an athletic activity. Clothing to be worn for a recording session should be loose and comfortable. Choristers should be encouraged to wear comfortable shoes, preferably sneakers and socks. They may be asked to remove their sneakers to eliminate any noise coming from the floor. Any jewelry that might jingle should be removed.

The choristers should be well hydrated at least two hours before beginning to record. Water is the preferred beverage. A healthy meal should be eaten prior to a recording session to sustain the body's intense work level. Any dairy products (including milk), soda, highly sugared beverages, candy, or chocolate should be avoided.

The director should allow adequate time for a thorough warm-up before the recording session begins. If a morning recording session is scheduled, more time should be devoted to the warm-up. "A warmed-up voice has a different resonance and timbre than a voice that has not been properly warmed up. The microphones will capture the difference."[8]

The choristers should not be intimidated by the microphones or recording equipment. The microphones may be located in a different setup than for a formal concert and, for certain works, may be placed in closer proximity to the singers. Choristers should be aware that any noise from breathing, footsteps, or rustling clothing will be amplified by the microphones. Complete memorization of all music to be recorded is recommended to avoid page-turning noise. Choristers should be reminded not to be stiff, but rather to have a relaxed body, maintain proper posture, and take adequate preparatory breaths before singing. They should be advised to sing properly and not change what they do just because the microphones are present.

Before each *take* (recording segment), the recording engineer will signal when he or she is ready to begin recording. This may be a visual cue followed by an aural cue called a "slate." A slate (or "slating a take") is when the engineer gives the take number verbally in the space so that the number is present on the master recording. Stating a specific number with each take avoids confusion later when editing is done. A two-second period of silence should follow before the music-making begins. The same silence should occur at the conclusion of each take. After the music has completely ceased (including any last reverberation in the hall) two full seconds of silence should conclude the take. This allows the engineer to make use of any recorded segment, including the full decay of sound.

The order of selections for the recording session will be determined by the conductor. For those who work with children, the psychology of sequencing the repertoire to be recorded is as important as what happens musically. It is advised to record something easy for the first selection. This will allow the choristers to become acclimated to the routine of full silence before and after they actually sing, doing re-takes, learning the signals from the recording engineer, and getting used to the fact they may re-record segments of varying lengths several times. The next works to be recorded should be the most challenging and demanding, working toward those that are less so. Using this method of sequencing will allow the hardest work to be accomplished when the singers are fresh and energized. The works recorded nearer the end of the session should be less demanding or challenging, or choir favorites. Depending on the length of the recording session, a break or two should be scheduled that includes giving the choristers a healthy snack, water, and some time for vocal rest. A snack of fruit juice and a cookie or cracker with some sugar will help boost sagging energy levels during a long recording session.

If instrumentalists are needed for specific works, they should be scheduled at a specific time. The sequence might be to start with the smallest number of instrumentalists and add more as required by the music, or the reverse. An adequate amount of time should be scheduled for these segments.

Choristers should be reminded that the goals for a recording session are different from the goals of a performance. What matters is what is being recorded, not what the setup looks like. Sometimes singers, soloists, or instrumentalists may be moved to a different location from where they would play or sing during a concert. For example, in a recording session of a work by J. S. Bach, the French horn overpowered the ensemble and choir. After trying various locations, the horn was finally placed at the back of the stage with the bell pointed toward a very heavy padded piano cover to achieve the correct balance between the singers and the chamber orchestra. In another recording session, a reflective surface (wooden folding table) had to be put behind the percussion instruments to create the proper balance of sound. The engineer and producer will make judgments about the balance and advise the conductor of what is needed for the proper spatial timbres. Several re-takes may be required to achieve the desired results.

Moments of levity may decrease the tension during recording sessions. One such recording session comes to mind. The choristers had been working very diligently for about two hours. A short piece, two minutes in length, was to be recorded next. The choir began, and the engineer immediately stopped them. "Stop, there is a fly," he uttered. The choristers looked all over. "He wants to be recorded and become famous," the engineer continued. The choristers quietly laughed. The fly was buzzing around the microphone, fifteen feet in the air, and sounded like a vintage B-17 airplane in the headset of the engineer. The choristers sat down and everyone waited. Once the fly left the microphone area, everyone cheered, the singers stood up, and the recording session resumed. Soon the conductor noticed that the eyes of the normally intent and focused choristers had begun to drift away from the conductor back to the microphone. The fly had returned.

THE ACCOMPANIST AS COLLABORATOR

An accompanist, according to the *Oxford English Dictionary*, is defined as "one who, or that which, accompanies; *esp.* the performer who takes the accompanying part in music."[9] The accompanist for a children's choir has a strong role in the artistry of the choir. The accompanist works in collaboration with both conductor and singers. When synergy occurs between conductor and accompanist, extraordinary musical moments may be created with the choir. The relationship between accompanist and conductor is most unique. As with great soloists and their accompanists who completely understand the singer's body language, mood, expression, style of interpretation, and innuendo, a fine accompanist may greatly contribute to the educational and musical journey of the young artists.

The conductor is the artistic guide to what is expected musically in collaboration with the singers and the accompanist. The accompanist not only supports the singers, but should interpret the music on the highest artistic level possible and should be in complete unity with the conductor's interpretation of the piece. The more competent the skills of the accompanist are, and the more *simpatico*[10] that exists between the conductor and accompanist, the more responsive the choral singing experience will be. When the accompanist and conductor are a balanced whole, rehearsals run more smoothly, and it is more likely that a meaningful and artistic performance at rehearsal and concert will occur.

In his book *The Art of Accompanying*, the former assistant conductor and chorus master of the Metropolitan Opera, Kurt Adler, speaks about this relationship with the singer when accompanying. He wrote,

> This flame of creativeness will make the accompanist feel servant and master at the same time: humble servant of the composer and faithful guardian of the work, but also master of the free interplay of personality; recreator and creator of music. In such moment, the accompanist will stand on the highest rung of the ladder that leads into the elysium of Art.[11]

In the choral context, the role of the accompanist is no different. The interplay between conductor and accompanist is a significant part of the artistry of the choir.

An accompanist can ease the process of rehearsing with a choir or be a burden. Accompanists who try to control from the keyboard, interject pitches that are not requested, or play uninvited when the conductor is speaking, do not help the rehearsal process, but rather interfere with it. An accompanist who plays wrong notes when demonstrating a passage, or plays without musical expression, hinders and diminishes the educational process for the young singers. A fine accompanist will provide strong support for the conductor-teacher and choir at every rehearsal and concert.

HIRING THE ACCOMPANIST

There are several considerations when hiring an accompanist. By interviewing, auditioning, and getting to know a prospective accompanist, the conductor will make an informed decision about whom to hire. The process should include the following:

- Gathering résumés of prospective accompanists
- Interviewing prospective accompanists
- Assessing performance skills of the prospective accompanist at the time of the interview
  - Ask candidate to sight-read a selection provided by the director
  - Ask candidate to play excerpts from two piano solos (contrasting styles) selected by the pianist
  - Ask candidate to play a choral octavo (requested by the director and given in advance) including the vocal parts or accompaniment (when no piano reduction is printed, this can help gauge the pianist's ability to play several vocal parts in "open score")
  - Ask candidate to play a vocal warm-up as instructed simulating an actual rehearsal
  - Conductor directs a piece (given to perspective accompanist in advance)
- Charles Ives's *Circus Band* works well to determine the advanced ability of the accompanist

A rigorous audition will indicate to the prospective accompanist the level of artistry and the standards of excellence expected for the position, as well as the working style of the conductor. By assessing the demonstrated skills of the prospective accompanist, the conductor will be able to determine his or her capabilities at varying tasks and gain insight into the type of working relationship that might ensue if the person is hired. Flexibility, professionalism, a sense of humor, reflective listening, awareness of issues of balance, sensitivity to what is happening at any given moment, and the ability to follow the conductor are all important skills. The more that is known about an accompanist before he or she is hired, the more likely a strong working relationship will develop.

ONCE THE ACCOMPANIST IS HIRED

Once the accompanist is hired, communication about what repertoire is to be performed, the order in which it will be presented throughout the year, and a full list of concerts and rehearsal dates should be provided. Weekly communication should occur between conductor and accompanist about specific goals for each rehearsal. A rehearsal plan may be e-mailed or given to the accompanist in advance of the rehearsal. The conductor may request a special rehearsal with the accompanist to work on specific passages. The working relationship between accompanist and conductor should be a model for the singers, as all are collaborators in the music-making process. As the conductor respects the singers, so too should the conductor and the accompanist be mutually respectful.

FROM THE ACCOMPANIST'S PERSPECTIVE

The accompanist will look for certain things from the conductor as well. A clear preparatory beat, clarity of beat throughout the selection, indication of where the music should "breathe," accurate tempi, interpretive marks or shadings, and eye contact with the conductor are all important. The longer the accompanist works with the director, the more he or she will learn about the style of the director and what he or she expects during a rehearsal for sequencing and pacing. An accompanist will learn to anticipate what the director will do next, contributing to an efficient rehearsal. A good accompanist should have his or her music well organized for efficient retrieval during rehearsal and keep a pencil handy for marking scores as directions are given to the choir by the director. The accompanist should carefully prepare his or her music in advance for challenges such as difficult page turns. If errors occur during a rehearsal, sensitivity to the accompanist or director must be given, and corrections should be made either quietly in consultation if appropriate, or after rehearsal. Everyone makes mistakes, and how they are handled is important in setting a good example for the young singers.

An accompanist will develop an artistic connection with the director. Eye contact during rehearsals and performances is important and should not occur only at the beginning and/or end of a piece. The conductor and accompanist are co-creators of the music with the choir and should be of like mind about the interpretation, as directed by the conductor. A good accompanist will know when to be serious and when to be humorous. Some have even been known to make a humorous musical comment from the keyboard at an appropriate moment during a rehearsal.

When being interviewed about her role as a professional accompanist, Alice Muzquiz stated, "It is rare to find someone who becomes your collaborative musical soul mate, but it is possible."[12] Many accompanists have the ability to establish a strong musical relationship with a conductor quickly. A fine accompanist will be able to adapt to conductors with varying styles and personalities, and each will bring his or her own artistry to the music-making. Muzquiz related the art of choral accompanying to that of an artist's canvas. The canvas is blank at the beginning. The accompanist brings a palette of colors for the keyboard as requested by the conductor. The conductor guides the process of creatively bringing the canvas to life by adding the palette of colors brought by the choir. When the aural canvas of sound is created, the picture is complete. The longer the conductor and accompanist work together, the more synergy may develop. When the "elysium of Art" that Adler refers to occurs, the choir and audience will be part of the resulting magic of live choral performance.

UNFORESEEN EVENTS

Even when the most thorough concert planning has been done, and every possible scenario has been discussed and considered, things may still not go as planned. There are always surprises; and the list is endless. Some past scenarios of such occurrences and their creative solutions include the following:

- What do you do when the composer-in-residence is stranded in an airport having completed only the first leg of his flight and can't get to the advertised open rehearsal for his presentation of a newly commissioned piece that was in the early stages of preparation?
  - The open rehearsal for invited community members, chorister parents, music educators, university faculty, and students was rescheduled for the dress rehearsal a month later when the composer would return. All were invited to attend. They also were invited to remain for the entire rehearsal, and the conductor presented an impromptu lecture about the process of commissioning a new work. All the audience remained for the full rehearsal, observed the early preparation of the work with the choir, and joined the choir at the end of the rehearsal in a song the conductor taught the audience members.
  - The dress rehearsal, a month later, included observation of the full rehearsal and was followed with an expanded question and answer session with the composer.
- What do you do when a fire marshal unexpectedly enters the concert in progress and wants it to stop because there are too many cars blocking the fire lanes?
  - The fire marshal was persuaded to wait until the performing choir completed its performance set and, before the next choir sang, an announcement was made for cars to be moved from the fire lanes. The concert was completed in its entirety.
- What do you do when the composer-in-residence calls the morning of the concert and says she is stranded on the opposite coast of the country, and

no flights will get her to your city in time for the afternoon concert? She will miss her pre-concert lecture and the introduction of her work to be premiered at the concert.
  - The conductor interviewed the composer via speaker phone and recorded the conversation on her iPod. With a microphone held up to the iPod speaker at the concert, the composer's apology and introduction of the premiere were successfully broadcast over the speakers in the concert hall for all to hear.
- What do you do the week of the symphony concert when your boy soprano who is preparing to sing Fauré's "Pie Jesu" with the symphony orchestra starts having vocal issues (related to quick onset of vocal change)?
  - A quick checkup with a pediatric otolaryngologist (who was also a singer and church choir director) was scheduled, and reassurance was given that the boy would be fine to sing the solo for the weekend performances with the symphony orchestra. Two weeks later, it would have been the understudy's solo.
- What do you do when your long-time accompanist has serious medical issues with her hand and cannot complete the season?
  - A substitute accompanist was hired to complete the season, and the long-time accompanist returned after much physical therapy on the hand.
- What do you do when a chorister's suitcase doesn't arrive in London on the first day of a ten-day tour? Or the second, third, or fourth day?
  - Choristers loaned their peer necessary items, spare concert dress pieces were put into use, a chorus administrator hemmed a parent chaperone's skirt that matched the color of the chorister required skirt, and a toothbrush and toothpaste were purchased. The chorister handled the situation graciously with smiles throughout the five days, being the center of attention. And, when the suitcase finally was delivered, the chorister was smiling even more.
- What do you do when you are in a distant foreign country and a strange food item appears on the table, and ten choristers all exclaim, "Eeeuuuwwww!," which might seem disrespectful to the hosts?
  - This was a teachable moment. The appearances and tastes of food served in a foreign country may be significantly different from what American choristers might expect.
  - The choristers were reminded that if the foreigners were in America, *our* food might look very strange to *them*. The choristers were encouraged to be sensitive to the feelings of others, sample everything, eat what they wanted, and show respect and appreciation to their hosts. At the same meal, when the hosts discovered that the American choir really liked the French fries that were served, the fries magically appeared at every breakfast, lunch, and dinner for the next week.

- What do you do when you find out a highly respected international children's choir is coming to your city in ten days and you will be hosting them for overnight home stays and a concert?
  - Following the visiting choir's tour of the city and dress rehearsal in the concert location, a meal of their native food was prepared by the local community and served at the school cafeteria located next door to the concert venue.
  - In anticipation of the upcoming concert, the chorus quickly learned a simple lullaby in the guest choir's native language. At the concert, the guest choristers were in tears as they listened to the very familiar lullaby they all knew so well. It was a strong reminder of home and a profound experience for both choirs.

No matter how well one plans, there will always be unexpected events. It is important that the unexpected events not be due to bad planning on the part of the chorus. It is also important that the unforeseen event is handled with creativity and that negatives are turned into positives. The Chinese symbol for crisis is the symbol for opportunity amid danger. There is always an opportunity to take an unforeseen event and turn it into something good. Or, as a phrase from Leonard Bernstein's "Simple Song" (from *Mass*) states, "make it up as you go along." Handling the unforeseen events with dignity, poise, and a positive attitude by making the best of an awkward situation will go a long way to lowering the level of stress for those surrounding you when the event occurs. And sometimes it reflects creativity at its best.

CONCLUSION

Planning for success happens each day. It happens one meeting at a time, one day at a time, one rehearsal at a time, and one event at a time. It happens when the organization is true to its mission, keeps the big picture in mind, and carefully plans every detail. Empowering the choir for excellence has much to do with the artistic vision, the creative planning, engaging and inspiring the choristers, and by providing a strong framework in which to function. For the community children's choir, the artistic director (or impresario) is charged with nurturing the artistic vision. The hours of creative planning, research, and preparation come to fruition in every rehearsal and concert.

It is the nature of music, unlike painting and most of literature,
that its final creation is not its original creation.
Music needs to be sounded, needs to be sung.
It needs to be heard. In this sense the composer literally
must leave his work to be finished by others.
—ROBERT SHAW

10

BUILDING COMMUNITY

CHORAL PARTICIPATION IS the essence of community. Whether singing in a virtual choir or in the physical presence of others, singing is one way of sharing the choral experience with others. This chapter addresses selected ways in which a children's choir may reach beyond its own organization to collaborate with others and build community.

This chapter will include singing with choirs of differing ages and types, joining with other children and youth choirs for festivals, collaborating with a puppet theater and a children's author, collaborating with composers to commission new works, and collaborating with folk dancers, ethnic music ensembles, and others—all of which build community beyond the immediate choir.

The world has become more connected through the Internet and the media. With this connectivity, changes in society are occurring at a faster rate than ever before. More people are spending time sitting at computers, texting, reading iPads, communicating on portable electronic devices, and listening to music on iPods. They often spend hours isolated from others. Those who are digitally "connected" have many friends in the virtual domain with whom they communicate regularly. For some, increasingly less time is spent in actual face-to-face contact with others.

The art of choral singing has entered the virtual realm bringing people from across the globe together in a shared choral experience in digital format. The first virtual choir premiered on the web on March 21, 2010, with the performance of Eric Whitacre's "Lux aurumque" ("Light and Gold"). One hundred eighty-five singers from twelve countries participated to create this choral performance.[1] A second virtual choir, the Virtual Choir 2.0, was replicated in the spring of 2011 with the performance of Whitacre's "Sleep," this time with the participation of 2,052 singers representing fifty-eight countries.[2] In 2012, Virtual Choir 3.0 made its debut singing Whitacre's "Water Night" with 3,746 videos submitted from seventy-three countries.[3] Several million people have viewed these performances on YouTube. Each singer who was selected for participation prepared an individual performance of the work while isolated in his or her own location. These were edited and combined to form the virtual choir. The experience of being part of the virtual choir was profound for many and brought them together in a shared experience that was the first of its kind. More such events are likely to occur in the future.

The shared experience of choral singing is the essence of building community. The choir may be a group of people who have never sung together before, such as those who gather for a *Messiah* or *Carmina Burana* sing-along, or it may be a group of people who formally gather to sing on a regular basis. The choir may be located in a community center where children gather to sing. The choir may be children from multiple grade levels singing in a church or school context, or it may be a self-run high school or collegiate a cappella group. The choir may be senior citizens who gather to sing as a recreational activity at the senior residence where they live, or it may be those who gather to practice multigenerational shape-note singing, one of the oldest singing traditions in America. Regardless of who gathers to sing and of what ages, each person contributes to the collective experience.

Singing is collaborative and builds community in other ways. A choir includes not only those who sing, but also the entire community of support that surrounds the choir. For a children's choir this may include the music director(s), accompanist, parents, and the organizational structure, such as the school, church, or board of directors. These choirs may exist at the local, state, regional, national, or international level. Author Matthew Sigman states, "Choral music is the hardiest of arts: [I]t thrives in all cultures, all geographies, and all economic climates. Choruses are at their very essence communal organizations."[4]

An experience rich in building community may occur when a children's choir reaches beyond the traditional concert format and collaborates with other community arts organizations for performances. Many types of collaborations that bring various types of artists together are possible. Events that encourage an opportunity for community engagement may involve authors, poets, dancers, choirs of varying ages from children to senior citizens, visual artists, actors, puppet theaters, other children's choirs, or nontraditional instrumental ensembles. Collaborative concerts may be given to benefit a health organization or other types of humanitarian organizations with a specific social purpose. Collaborations where choral music is presented in intriguing and innovative ways or with new combinations of groups often stretch both the performers and the audience in surprising ways.

Choral collaborations occur in many contexts, from professional choral organizations that bring auditioned young singers together for honors choirs, to international festivals that bring choirs from all over the world together to share their artistry. Ongoing world festivals, such as the Llangollen International Eisteddfod founded in Wales in 1947,[5] and Festival 500, founded fifty years later in 1997 in Newfoundland, are just two examples of the many festivals that bring choirs from all over the world together for a shared choral experience. Whether singing together at home or abroad, the shared experience of singing builds community.

BUILDING BRIDGES WITHIN THE REGIONAL COMMUNITY

There are many ways a children's choir can depart from traditional formal performance practice and begin to explore dynamic and creative programming. Varied programming is possible by involving other performing arts organizations located in the surrounding region. The following list of collaborative performances indicates some of the ways a choir may experience the music of various cultures:

- Performing an a cappella work in Chinese accompanied by *erhu* (traditional Chinese string instrument)
- Singing and dancing with a Brazilian drumming ensemble
- Performing a concert of Jewish music with a klezmer ensemble
- Performing *gahu* (traditional African singing, dancing, and drumming)
- Performing a concert with a dance theme that may include traditional songs, costumes, and dances of many cultures
- Performing a concert of classic jazz tunes with piano, bass, and drums and having a swing dance club join the performance
- Working with the adult members of the Lost Boys of the Sudan (orphaned boys who were victims of the second Sudanese Civil War) who now live in the local community to present a concert that tells the story of their childhood experiences through singing, narration, and large-screen projection of photographs
- Performing a concert of Celtic music including Irish step dancers and bagpipes
- Inviting a local gospel choir to collaborate for a festival of spirituals and gospel songs
- Presenting a school choir concert with repertoire from a selected culture that includes a dessert reception serving traditional food of the culture, and displaying clothing and artwork created by the students depicting the culture

The possibilities for collaboration are limitless and often easily available by looking at what ethnic populations live in the community surrounding the choir. By attending musical events and various cultural festivals, much can be learned about possible collaborations.

Working in partnership with other ensembles or organizations gives children a better understanding of various cultures and their music. These collaborative performances may celebrate the diversity of the cultural heritages of the choir members. Performances of this type provide an opportunity for developing shared understandings in a rich educational environment.

CHOIR FESTIVALS

Children's choir festivals are a more traditional type of collaboration where multiple choirs gather for study, practice, and performance, sometimes under the direction of a guest conductor. These festivals may be a one-day event, occur over a weekend, or be held over several days or longer. Festivals may be hosted by a school, church, or non-profit children's choir. Others may be sponsored by a for-profit business or touring company that brings choirs together to present festivals under the direction of guest conductors. Depending on the type of festival, the size may range from one guest choir hosted by a community choir, school, or church, to many choirs who participate in a large festival of several hundred singers.

One type of choral exchange may involve two school choirs, such as a city school and a county school. Each school's choir performs a concert in the other school during an academic year. The concert at each school may end with the choirs combining for a final selection conducted by the guest choir's director. A work by a local composer may be commissioned for such an event if funds are available.

Another festival collaboration may be that of four community-based children's choirs who gather annually from across the state for a three-day festival. A regular rotation schedule is established four years in advance, giving each choir an opportunity to host the event in the predetermined year. Following a similar schedule each year, the weekend event includes rehearsals of the combined choirs working under the direction of an invited guest conductor, eating meals together, and sharing a social activity. The final concert includes performances by each choir under its own director, and ends with the combined choirs under the direction of the invited guest conductor. Choristers who remain in their own choir for several years look forward to seeing, and possibly hosting, singers they have met in previous years at the festivals.

A church choir may host a festival with several local church choirs gathering for a day-long event that may or may not include individual performances or combined performances. This festival may be part of a larger adult festival or just a stand-alone children's event. Special events, such as a September eleventh commemorative service or Veteran's Day Memorial service, may be held at a large church or concert hall where several multigenerational choirs and those of many faiths gather to sing as individual or combined choirs.

A school choir may hire a guest conductor for a particular anniversary, such as a tenth or twentieth anniversary of the choir, or to honor a longtime director who is retiring or relocating. Alumni from the choir may be invited back to attend the event and join the school choir as soloists, to sing in a special alumni choir created for the event, or to sing with the school choir.

A community children's choir may host an annual fall concert with a different guest choir invited each year. The guest choir may be from the region or from another city. The event may take place over a weekend when the choir arrives on a Friday night, tours the area, has a social event with the host choir, shares a Saturday afternoon or evening concert, and departs on Sunday morning or later. The guest choir may be invited to stay in the homes of the hosting choir members, or the guest choir may prefer to stay at a hotel, youth camp, or area church camp facility.

Ending the shared concert with a selection sung by the combined choirs provides an opportunity for the host choristers to sing under the guest choir's conductor. If two combined-choir repertoire selections are included, both conductors will have an opportunity to lead the combined ensembles. Depending on how far in advance the concert is planned and the length of time to prepare, the combined repertoire might be as short as a simple canon or folk song easily learned by the choirs at rehearsals during the concert weekend, or a more complex repertoire that may be prepared separately in advance of the festival.

A multigenerational choral festival is another way of collaborating with other choirs in a city with many choirs of various types. In 2008, the Gregg Smith Legacy Festival, funded in part by the National Endowment for the Arts, was held in New York City celebrating American choral masterpieces.[6] Five types of choirs, including symphonic, church, professional, and volunteer from the New York City region and a children's choir from outside the city, participated in the weeklong event. Each choir individually performed a concert of American music during the week, and the festival week concluded with a concert of all five choirs singing individually and then combined under Mr. Smith's direction for the finale.

SCC similarly modeled a concert, the first of this type in Central New York, after the Gregg Smith Legacy Festival in which it participated. The year following the New York City event, seven choirs collaborated for a multigenerational concert titled A Fall Festival of Choirs. The Smith model of combining community, volunteer, children's, church, and professional choirs was maintained, and a school choir was added. When the mid-fall concert was presented, the choirs included a volunteer symphonic choir with 150 singers, a professional vocal ensemble, a local high school vocal jazz ensemble, an adult church choir, and the various levels of the children's choir. It was determined that this festival would be a "concert with a cause" to benefit a national health-related charitable foundation. A portion of each ticket sold for the October concert was donated to a chosen breast cancer foundation for research. The hour-long concert ended with the 500 singers from the participating choirs surrounding the audience to sing the finale. The singers, who ranged in age from eight to eighty, were profoundly moved by the experience, and many people, both audience and singers, requested that the event be continued. (See Appendix 10.1 for a festival-day schedule and Appendix 10.2 for logistics diagrams for seamless movement of choirs during a concert.)

The children's choir replicated the format several more times, each year with different choirs invited to participate. The successful format of professional, volunteer, school, church, community, and children's choirs was maintained. The choirs performed varied styles of repertoire and increased the audience's awareness of the many different types of choirs that perform regularly within the region, some of which were well known and others that were new to audience members. For both adults and children, an increased awareness was gained about the lifelong art of choral singing, shared artistry, and the rich diversity of choirs.

COLLABORATION WITH A COMPOSER, A LIBRETTIST, AND A DANCE COMPANY

Sometimes collaboration builds relationships in the artistic community that extend beyond the immediate geographic area. Commissioning a composer may bring artists of various types together. A composer may wish to work directly with a librettist to create a text for a new work commissioned by a children's choir. These individuals may or may not live in the same city or even the same part of the country.

The distinguished American composer Libby Larsen was contacted about writing a work for SCC for a specific concert date in 2002. After a discussion about the concert venue, date, and length of the work to be created, she began to develop a concept for a work that might be appropriate for the concert setting. Discussions ensued. The result was a unique collaboration with a librettist, composer, ballet company, harpist, and children's choir. The inspiration for Ms. Larsen's multi-movement work was selected photographs of elaborate handmade paper cut designs created by the Danish author and storyteller Hans Christian Andersen.[7] The work was scored for children's choir and harp, and Ms. Larsen envisioned that classical ballet dancers and photographs of the Andersen-created paper cuts projected on a large screen would assist the singers in telling the newly created story.

Once the concept was agreed upon, the immediate need was to secure a librettist to create the text that would become the story told through song. Ms. Larsen selected the librettist, Sally M. Gall. The chorus then made the contractual arrangements with the librettist per the composer's instructions and mutual agreement with the choir. The composer worked closely with the librettist, and several months later the finished scores for *The Ballerina and the Clown: A Hans Christian Andersen Tale*[8] were delivered. The music scores included more than just the music: they had prints of Andersen's numerous intricate black paper cuts dispersed throughout the pages.

The performance was accompanied by harp, the chorus sang from risers, and the ballet company dressed as the characters in the story. The dancers moved about the stage in front, next to, and around the chorus dramatizing the story as the choristers sang. Slides of the Hans Christian Andersen paper cuts depicting the story were projected onto a large screen as the story unfolded during the performance.[9]

Teaching strategies for the work included discussions about what a librettist is and examinations of the paper cuts and how, together with the music and text, they depicted the story. The choristers were told the background of Hans Christian Andersen and how he would visit families, gathering the children at his feet in the evening by candlelight to spin stories while creating and revealing the intricate paper cuts as the drama unfolded through his words and designs. It may be noted that Hans Christian Andersen was a fine boy soprano who had hoped for a theatrical career, but "his awkwardness inevitably doomed his stage career" and ultimately he became an author and poet.[10] The multidimensionality of the Larsen work in performance was unique for both singers and audience.

A COLLABORATION WITH A CHILDREN'S AUTHOR, A PUPPET THEATER, AND MULTIGENERATIONAL SINGERS

Another creative collaboration was undertaken that combined the talents of a children's author, a puppeteer, and the early American tradition of shape-note singing. This unique production, sponsored in part by the National Endowment for the Arts, involved the creation of a work based on shape-note singing, narration and song texts by an award-winning children's author, and a puppet theater company. Children's author Bruce Coville and master puppeteer Geoff Navius, founder of Open Hand Theater, collaborated with SCC to create a work called "The Birth, Life, Death, and Resurrection of Lake Onondaga." The concert involved all four levels of the children's choir and additional adult singers, and was based on the story of what is now known as Onondaga Lake.

The early history of the region said that the lake was a center of activity for the Native Americans indigenous to the area. As more settlers came to the area, the Native Americans gradually left. As time passed, the Erie Canal brought more activity to the area, and manufacturing began to develop. Business and commerce prospered. Much industrial waste from a soda ash plant adjacent to the lake was dumped into the lake causing contamination. The fish were killed and the water fowl were poisoned. In recent times, a rebirth has taken place. Remediation of the lake has been undertaken to restore it to its original health allowing fish and wildlife to thrive once again.

To prepare for the telling of the story of the lake, research into both the local history and shape-note singing was done to form the historical and musical foundation for the dramatic presentation. Recordings and DVDs were gathered to study the authentic practice of shape-note singing, a tone color that differs from that of traditional bel canto singing. Strong breath support and bright vowels were the foundation for the healthy tone production. Shape-note sings were attended as part of the research phase.[11]

The American tradition of shape-note singing "is separate and distinct from other musical traditions."[12] Multigenerational communities gather to sing hymns and anthems from *The Sacred Harp* songbook, a book that was originally compiled in 1844 by Benjamin Franklin White, and revised three times (1869, 1936, and 1991) with new material added. The tradition began in colonial times in the "singing schools" where itinerant singing masters traveled from town to town to teach beginners to sing by using sol-fa syllables. The music notation uses four different shaped notes that include a triangle (the syllable "fa"), the oval (the syllable "sol"), a square (the syllable "la"), and a diamond (the syllable "mi"), thus the term *shape note*.[13] Shape-note sings do not require prior knowledge or singing ability. They are not a rehearsal or performance. They do include a traditional potluck dinner held at noon where much socializing occurs, as there is no talking allowed during the sings. All are welcome to participate in the daylong event, including adults and children of all ages. Shape-note sings are the essence of building community. The tradition continues across the United States (with strong roots in New York State and heavily concentrated in the rural south) and internationally in Canada and the United Kingdom.[14]

For the chorus's portrayal, the story of the lake was told through a spoken and sung narrative written by Coville. Using the traditional shape-note songs selected from *The Sacred Harp*, thirteen hymn tunes were selected for the various choirs to sing. The text used for the hymn tunes was created by Coville to tell the story of the life of the lake from its earliest known activity, eventual abuse, and recent remediation. All levels of the children's choir were involved, sometimes singing together, sometimes singing individually, and sometimes supplemented with adults who sang the tenor and bass parts of the traditional shape-note hymn tunes. The small ensembles of adults included an SATB quartet comprised of alumni members of the choir and a university student women's octet. Additional male singers included parents, grandparents, and uncles of the choristers, and university men who sang the tenor and bass parts with the young treble singers for many of the hymn tunes. The audience joined the choirs during the performance for the singing of "Amazing Grace," for which the original text was left unchanged.

The puppet theater portrayed the story using seventeen-foot-tall puppets. Scenery including a boat, birds, raindrops, clouds, and sun were on poles that moved about as required. Bands of blue silk fabric, stretched across the stage horizontally, were held by puppeteers who gently moved the fabric up and down to simulate the moving water of the lake. The entire concert hall space was used, with tall puppets on poles manipulated by three puppeteers (one each for the head and arms). Some of the puppets entered from the back of the high-ceilinged hall, moving down the center aisle onto the stage. Others came from side entrances or through doors at the back of the stage. Other puppets were used in front of the stage on the floor and in the side aisles.

Choirs moved about during the storytelling and sang from various locations, including the floor in front of the audience, the narthex at the back of the chapel space, the four corners of the concert space, and the three balconies. The author narrated the performance between songs to supplement the telling of the story. Because of the complexity of the production, which had choirs and puppets moving about the space throughout, extra rehearsal time was required to adequately prepare.

When artists meet to discuss possible collaborations such as this, the creative process begins. Each of the artists offers ideas about what might be possible. As ideas or concepts emerge, more ideas are generated. Discussions continue and eventually focus on the ideas that most intrigue the participants or seem most timely or realistically doable. After further discussions, one idea emerges.

For the project described above, each artistic medium, including the choir, puppeteer, and author, had specific requirements. For the puppeteer, this included the length of time required to construct the puppets and the scenery. All three offered input that was necessary for the selection of the shape-note hymn tunes to be used. For the author, the deadline for texts was determined by the date the choir needed the scores to begin rehearsing. For the treble choir, the vocal needs of shape-note music presented the challenge of not having tenors and basses in the choir. Additional singers would need to be recruited to supply the missing adult male voices. Time would also be needed to do the historical research upon which the authentic story was based.

Collaborations of this type take detailed planning well in advance of the event, and a timeline that takes into consideration the unique needs of each artist. The project took two years to complete, but it brought untold rewards to the creators, performers, and audience.

COMMISSIONING A NEW WORK

Commissioning a composer can be a rewarding project for both choir and conductor. Singing music that no one has ever sung before, having an opportunity to work closely with a composer, and taking a manuscript from the beginning of the creative process through to its premiere is an exciting and sometimes challenging task for all who participate. Components of such a project include the following:

- Beginning with the end in mind for the type of work and requirements for such a project
- The selection of the composer
- The timeline for the project
- The scope of the project
  - size of the choir
  - age of the singers
  - level of difficulty
  - length
  - text
  - context for the premiere
  - type of voicing (unison, SA, SSA, SSAA)
  - a cappella or accompanied, and type of instrumentation
- Budget expenses
  - commission fee
  - print costs (scores, parts)
  - performance costs
- Income to support the project
  - contributions
  - grants
  - ticket revenue
  - donations
  - corporate sponsorship
  - other funding sources
- Logistical considerations for the performance
  - space layout or stage area including approach to stage
  - risers, chairs, stands

- access to stage
- soloists, instrumentalists

The timeframe should be determined at the beginning of the commissioning process. As with many organizational matters, one should begin with the end in mind. What will the final product be? What will it look like with all the details in place? The tentative date (and possibly the time and location) of the performance will come first. The invitation to the composer to write for the choir follows. (This needn't always be the sequence, however. You might want to work with a particular composer who is not available for several years, and the project must be delayed to accommodate his or her availability.) Once the composer is confirmed, the deadline for the manuscript to be delivered should be established. It is wise to allow for some grace period in meeting the deadlines. It is also wise to allow additional time for copying and artistic preparation of the new manuscript in advance of the date the choir will be introduced to the new work.

Another consideration for a newly commissioned work deals with the selection of text. If the chosen text is by a living author, or if the text is a translation, adequate time should be allowed to obtain permission for its use. A further consideration concerns the printing of the text for the newly commissioned work if it is to be printed in the program at the time of the premiere. Permission must be obtained from the copyright holder to reprint the text in the program. A choir runs the risk of a copyright violation if it prints the text in the program without obtaining permission from the copyright holder.

The initial contact with the composer will most likely be made by the artistic director, who initiates a conversation with the chosen composer about the possibility of writing something for the choir. The composer may be a young, local artist who is eager to have his or her work performed, or the composer may be a distinguished artist with a well-established career in the United States or beyond. It is important to provide the composer with as much background information about the choir and the performance as possible:

- skill level of the singers
- ages of the young performers
- range and tessitura appropriate for the singers
- size of the choir
- anticipated type of concert location
- tentative date of the premiere
- text requirements or limitations, if any
- musical context for the proposed work

The more comprehensive the information given to the composer is, the more likely the resulting work will be written at an appropriate level of challenge for the singers and also meet the requirements of an appropriate work for the context of the premiere.

At the time of the initial contact, the composer will have questions:

- Is the text for the proposed work already selected?
- Will the composer research the text or will this be collaborative between composer and conductor?
- Who will pay for the rights to use a text if there is a cost involved, or should only public domain or self-written texts be considered?
- Will a librettist be hired, and who will fund this person?
- Does the director have a theme in mind?
- Is this to be premiered for a special occasion or specific concert theme?
- What is the length requirement of the proposed work?
- Will the instrumentation, if used, be piano only, or are other instruments an option?
- Will there be specific instrumentation requested by the choir, or is the composer free to determine instrumentation?
- How many singers will perform the new work?
- How advanced is the choir, and what are the ages of the singers?
- What does the choir expect to pay for such a work?

Sometimes the fee for the composer is a flat per-minute rate. Other times, the fee will be negotiated between the director and the composer. To assist with the cost of commissioning a new work, a grant may be written to support the hiring of a specific composer in part; or a donor may fund the commissioning of a work in memory or in honor of someone.

Regardless of the verbal negotiations, a written contract should be prepared that articulates the specifics of the agreement between the composer and director (or chorus administrator responsible for the contract). The basic details of the contract may include the following:

- composer's fee
- deadline for the completed manuscript to be delivered
- length of work to be written
- voicing and instrumentation (if determined by the time the contract is written)
- who will hire and pay the librettist, if needed
- who will pay for the licensing fee for use of a text, if needed
- who will pay for travel, lodging, and per diem (if offered) for the composer to attend the premiere performance
- any additional requirements as discussed in the negotiation between the director and composer

Premiering a new work may cost the choir very little, if anything at all, or the choir may pay a large predetermined sum of money based on the per-minute rate for performance time of the final work. The fee will most often depend on the expertise and experience of the composer. Young composers are often glad to have a choir perform their works and sometimes begin their careers by writing for specific groups that will perform their music. As they hone their craft and become more experienced, their fees increase. In-demand composers with well-established careers will most often have a flat per-minute rate of performance time for commissions. Sometimes a composer may be persuaded to take on a project because of the reputation of the choir or the uniqueness of a particular project and may be willing to negotiate the fee.

Encouraging young composers to write for the treble idiom may be important for choirs who often commission established composers or who have never commissioned a work. Holding a composition contest for young composers that may be regional, statewide, or national is a way to give encouragement to young composers. Mentoring and encouraging young and advancing composers should be part of what musicians do on an ongoing basis whenever possible. If a composition contest is held, the award for winning the contest may be the premiere of the work or perhaps a cash prize. Having the opportunity to work with composers at the beginning of their careers may inspire choristers to consider writing their own music.

Some established composers may have never written for a children's choir, or may not be aware of the artistic capabilities of young singers. With encouragement and increased awareness of the artistic capability of a fine children's choir, many significant composers have undertaken serious projects for young artists. Sometimes all it takes is having the courage to ask a composer whom you wish to commission. You never know if he or she has been waiting for you to initiate the conversation.

When possible, having the composer attend a rehearsal early in the process of preparing the new work enriches the choir's experience, and gives detailed information to the conductor and choir about the expectations of the composer. If it is not possible to have the composer in residence in advance of the premiere, a video or audio recording of the work may be exchanged between conductor and composer, if he or she is willing, to provide feedback to the choir about interpretation. The use of Skype or FaceTime is another way to build rapport between composer and choir. The dialog concerning text emphasis, tone color, articulations, dynamic adjustments, tempi, and the composer's concept for the work enhances the director's preparation of the work with the choir. The more comprehensive the communication between composer and conductor, the more likely the premiere will come closer to what the composer envisioned when writing the music.

If possible, having the composer in residence for the final rehearsal(s) of the work can provide a more in-depth understanding and polished premiere of the work. For the audience, having the composer offer remarks about the work before its premiere often enhances the initial listening experience of a new work.

HOSTING A GUEST COMPOSER

Inviting a composer to be present for the premiere of his or her new work can also provide an opportunity to share his or her work with other conductors, music educators, composers, and university students in the area. Invitations may be extended to observe an open rehearsal with the choir and composer as they prepare for the premiere. A question-and-answer session with the composer may follow for observers to discuss the new work, how the composer approaches the writing process, and other topics related to the composition. Invitations to these sessions may be extended to regional music educators, local composers, college and university composition and theory faculty members and students, college and university music education students, church choir directors, parents, and other area musicians who might be interested in attending.

Simple courtesies should be extended to a visiting composer to make the guest feel welcome during a potentially busy weekend schedule of events. If possible, meeting the guest composer at the airport and taking her or him to the rehearsal or hotel extends a warm welcome. Having a gift basket with food snacks in the hotel room is a welcome courtesy, particularly for someone who has had little time for food while traveling or one wishes to have an evening snack after a late rehearsal. It is wise to inquire about any food allergies or preferences in advance. A variety of healthful food items such as fruit, nuts, cheese, crackers, and the occasional chocolate are possible choices. Other host gifts may include fresh flowers with a welcome note, or a chorus coffee mug, water bottle, CD, or T-shirt.

The composer should be provided with a copy of the complete itinerary, including flight arrival and departure information, hotel name with address and phone number, rehearsal schedule, concert information, and any scheduled media interviews or guest appearances. The itinerary should include emergency contact numbers for the choir staff, and cell phone numbers for any key chorus staff members or volunteers who will be transporting the guest conductor during her or his stay. The itinerary may be e-mailed to the composer in advance, and an extra copy may be provided upon arrival for easy access and referral throughout the stay. The onsite itinerary may also reflect any last-minute changes in the schedule.

Properly hosting a guest composer is in keeping with the high musical standards and standards of excellence that pervade all aspects of a choral organization. Attention to the details of hosting guest artists is as important as attending to the details of the music score.

A reception for a visiting guest composer may follow a concert premiere and be part of the composer's residency commitment. Invited guests, or an informal small gathering of the conductor(s) and a few guests, may allow for social time and unwinding after a concert and premiere. Each organization determines what is most appropriate, and the composer should be asked in advance if she or he is willing to participate in such an event.

HOSTING A GUEST CHOIR

A children's choir may extend invitations to other choirs to join them for performances or festivals. One such example is that of inviting a guest choir to perform at a regular season concert of a community-based children's choir. The invited choir may be local, from within the state, from outside the state, or may travel from outside the country. The event may be planned a year in advance or, on occasion, little notice may be given for the opportunity to host a guest choir traveling through the region.

Your choir may receive an urgent request to host an international choir with a minimal amount of time to plan in advance of the choir's arrival. Planning time is sometimes very limited, and an overnight stay at choir members' homes may be all that is required for a choir passing through town unexpectedly. If time permits to arrange for a joint concert with the host choir and guest choir, it may be possible to have the choirs perform a song together at the end of the concert. A sound check and rehearsal should be scheduled for the visiting choir in the concert hall if time allows. Should a combined selection be possible, a rehearsal with both choirs should be scheduled before the concert.

It may also be possible to arrange for a dinner for the international choir prior to the rehearsal and concert. The host choir may or may not be part of this meal. When hosting an international choir, it is often possible to find a local community of people who were originally from that country, and they may be invited to provide traditional ethnic food for the visiting choir. For choirs whose food differs greatly from American food, this gesture of hospitality is appreciated.

Some touring choirs may prefer to stay overnight in a hotel. Others may prefer to be hosted in the homes of the choir members. Each choir will have its own preferences. The local hosting choir may help by making hotel recommendations to the visiting choir or touring company that is making the travel arrangements.

If the choir is to be hosted by choir member families, several criteria must be considered. For the safety of the choristers, it is standard policy among many choirs that no fewer than two choristers may stay overnight at a choir member's home. And, when possible, three or more choristers may stay in one home. Some choirs prefer hotels or other group facilities, such as a church camp or scout camp facility. Others do not allow overnight stays in private homes at all. It is for each organization to decide what the choir policy will be, and the choices may depend on the type of event, the specific location, and the policies and budget of the choirs.

When hosting visiting choristers in local homes, it is important to provide the host families with helpful information about the guest choir members. Matters such as pet allergies, medications, food allergies or dietary requirements, and religious requirements should be considered. When arranging overnight home visits, it is important to match the ages, interests, and special requirements of the visiting choir members as closely as possible to those of the host families. Providing the guest choir leaders in advance with a complete list of the phone numbers and addresses of the host families, and contact numbers for the host choir leadership, will facilitate communication should the need arise.

For international choirs, language can be a barrier if the guest choir does not speak English. In those instances, it is often remarkable to watch children communicate in creative ways by sharing family photographs, drawing pictures, singing to each other, sharing songs, and relying on a few known words in the other person's language. Words in a new language are always learned along the way, usually accompanied by lots of smiles, waving of hands, pointing, and giggles.

When language may be a challenge, having a local translator available throughout the duration of the choir's residency and having phone numbers available to all involved for needed consultations or translations are quite helpful.

For some choirs, the accommodations for the artistic staff, administrative staff, and chaperones may differ from where the choir members stay. Some may request to stay with a host family, while others may request that staff and chaperones be housed in a hotel. Each choir will decide what is best for the adults traveling with the choristers.

Another consideration for hosting a guest choir is that of the schedule. For choristers who have working parents, drop-offs and pick-ups of their children and the guest choir members who will be staying in their homes should be carefully timed to be convenient and sensitive to the parents' work schedules. A weekday early evening arrival for a guest choir works well. For the guest choir departure, an early morning drop-off before work or Sunday morning activities is also appreciated by the host families. Another kindness offered by some choirs is for the host families to provide bag lunches or healthful snacks for the departing choir members for their bus trip or upcoming flight. Choristers should also be prepared to exchange choir buttons, pins, or other small gifts with the guest choir members.

By hosting other choirs, much is learned about building bridges between countries and community-building within one's own city, state, or region. The choristers quickly learn that simple hand games, children's songs, and serious choral repertoire may be common among choirs. They learn through direct experience that music is a universal language, and that many songs are shared the world over. Music is the bridge to friendship, respect, and understanding of the similarities, differences, and richness of each culture. Learning about other families, other lives, and other homes broadens the choristers' understanding of the world around them.

COLLABORATION AS A RECRUITMENT OPPORTUNITY

There is sometimes an unforeseen benefit to hosting a guest choir from a local community, church, or school: recruiting new singers. By hosting a guest choir for an early fall school or church concert, each choir shares the responsibility for repertoire, creating less of a burden for a large quantity of music to be learned by each choir individually. Awareness about the host choir is increased. Guest choristers who like to sing may pursue future participation in the host choir. Holding a "Bring a Friend to Choir Day" may be an opportunity to collaborate with new singers, some of whom might be inspired to audition for or join the volunteer community or church children's choir.

OTHER TYPES OF COLLABORATING WITH MUSIC EDUCATORS

School music educators are some of the unsung heroes in the choral profession. Where music education programs exist in schools across the country, choral music educators often see every child in the school for general music classes and sometimes hold chorus rehearsals before or after school if it is not possible to do so during the school day. These dedicated professionals have the opportunity to nurture a child's love of singing and music that for some will last a lifetime. For students who find school work difficult, music class may be a place where they more easily achieve success. For others, music class may be a place where they excel. Lessons learned in music class support reading skills, mathematical skills, language skills, analytical skills, and creativity. A child who participates in choral music education may also learn to develop focused attention, a strong work ethic, leadership qualities, self-esteem, self-confidence, and poise.

Acknowledging school music educators for the work they do each day in the music classroom and educating the public about the continued importance of this subject in the school curriculum is an ongoing process. Creating an event that honors the music educators' work and provides an opportunity for them to share a day with colleagues from other schools provides a rich environment for instruction, inspiration, and dialog with colleagues. It is one way of saying thank you and honoring their work.

One such workshop day may be structured to include classroom choral teaching strategies, rehearsal techniques, repertoire suggestions, and choral performances by invited children's choirs. In a time of cutbacks in professional development funding for teachers, having a day that does not cost anything or only a minimal fee can be a boost to local music educators. One such example, Sharing the Choral Experience (SCE), was created by SCC for this purpose. Held on a weekday or Saturday, SCE was offered once every other year during the month of March. The daylong seminar for elementary and middle school music teachers provided a rich experience.

Unlike classroom teachers, where several teach the same grade level, the situation for choral music educators is often quite different. In many schools, the elementary or middle school music teacher may be the only person charged with this responsibility. Some choral music educators may travel to more than one school to teach every week. Depending on the school district, the general music teachers may or may not have monthly meetings with similar colleagues in their district. Some districts have formal district meetings for choral music educators once a month; others have all music disciplines (band, orchestra, and chorus) meet together; and others have no formal structure for the district music educators and no monthly meetings. Other districts have their music educators meet once or twice a year, or not at all.

Holding a workshop day for shared dialog and a variety of informative and educational sessions may be meaningful and appreciated. The music educators who register to attend the SCE event are sent two treble choir octavos and assigned a voice part to learn to sing in advance of the workshop day. The workshop begins with the teachers' chorus rehearsing the two selections. Breathing exercises, warm-ups, and demonstrated rehearsal strategies for the selected repertoire provide techniques appropriate for use in their own classrooms or choral rehearsals. The remainder of the morning is divided into sessions that include creative teaching strategies for the general music classroom, a repertoire reading session, and a performance by a university music ensemble (e.g., a Brazilian drumming ensemble). A lunch break provides time for the educators to connect informally with colleagues and share ideas. The afternoon session begins with a brief rehearsal of the teachers' chorus, continuing the work from the morning's rehearsal. A concert follows, which includes performances by two invited school choirs, the youngest level of the host community-based children's choir, and the teachers' chorus.

The community-based choir hosts this event in collaboration with the university school of music. Music education majors volunteer to assist throughout the day as greeters and attend events as their schedules permit. The comprehensive day concludes with an optional question- and-answer session. (See appendix 10.3 for varied schedules of two SCE events.)

REACHING BEYOND THE IMMEDIATE AREA

Sometimes a children's choir has an opportunity to reach out to a choir in another city during a time of crisis. Life's unexpected events may provide opportunities for a children's choir to demonstrate kindness towards another choir in small but significant and unexpected ways.

For each choir, ways of doing this will vary. What matters is what the choir does when something catastrophic occurs in the local community or far away. Some examples follow. Pennies were collected by choir members to go toward a scholarship fund for choristers whose choir was devastated by a hurricane. Messages of support were sent from the choristers to the director and members of the children's choir where a hurricane had occurred and the director had spent days driving around the city trying to locate his singers and their families. Messages of support from the choristers were gathered and sent to a children's choir in New York City at the time of 9/11. Sets of choral octavos were sent to a choir that had lost its music library in a flood. Choristers sang for or attended funerals of lost peers or parents. Clothing and funds were gathered and sent to a recent guest artist whose house and belongings were destroyed in a fire. A benefit concert was hosted by the children's choir to benefit a local charitable organization that feeds and shelters the homeless. The benefit concert included an emcee who was a local television personality and involved a variety of professional ensembles and solo performers. A colorful banner made by the choristers was hung in the hospital room of a much-loved composer. Accompanying the banner was a recording of the composer's yet-to-be-premiered work and another special song requested by the choristers. The gift of a video recording of a missed concert was sent to a chorister dad and a director's husband serving in the U.S. military in Operation Desert Storm. And a gift box and CD were sent to an alumni chorister serving in Afghanistan. For each choir, the list will be different. Choristers who do something to reach out to others will learn about extending kindness that goes beyond the music and is part of being human. And the choristers, directors, choirs, or individuals who are the recipients will be surprised by kindnesses extended during challenging times.

CHOIRS WITHIN CHOIRS

A frequent topic of discussion among music educators, church choir directors, and community children's choir directors is that of the recruitment of boys. It is not uncommon for there to be fewer boys than girls in the children's choir, particularly as the singers become older and reach more advanced levels. This is partly due to voice changes, but also due to declining numbers of male singers in some choirs. After-school activities, sports, and other types of activities increasingly compete for the student's time.

One strategy to increase awareness of how many boys are involved in the choir is to combine all the boys from the various levels of a multilevel choir into one choir of boys for a special performance. All the boys from grade level choirs in a school, or boys from various levels including elementary, middle school, and high school choirs in the church context, may be combined for a special performance. Having an all-boys choir performance may increase awareness and encourage other boys to join their friends. Inviting an all-male ensemble, such as a high school a cappella ensemble, collegiate all-male a cappella group, or men's glee club, to perform may also encourage boys to join the choir. With the current popularity of television shows such as *Glee* and *The Sing-Off*, there is an increased awareness of this style of singing, which may encourage others to seek out choral singing opportunities.

Another unique grouping of singers may involve combining all brothers and sisters who sing in the choir. Siblings may be combined for a particular song or set of pieces on a program. Sometimes there are twins or triplets who participate, or an alumni chorister brother or sister may wish to participate. There may be multiple siblings in the choir, singing in various levels or different grades. These occurrences may be celebrated in a unique sibling's choir. For the audience, it is entertaining to determine who the brother and sister combinations are. Additional family participation in a concert may be possible by programming a mother and daughter duet or a father and son duet. This is also very special for both parents and choristers who are talented singers.

Some choirs have a traditional song that is sung at the end of a December or spring concert each year in which alumni chorus members are invited to participate. This may be as formal as an alumni choir that is a featured part of an annual December concert, or it may be an informal invitation to join the choirs on stage at the end of a spring concert.

OTHER OPPORTUNITIES FOR COMMUNITY ENGAGEMENT

There are many types of events in which the children's choir may have an opportunity to engage other organizations in the community. These events, which differ from formal self-produced concerts, will give the choir an opportunity to extend its awareness in the community by interacting with different types of organizations. For these events, the choir may sing one or more songs or, on occasion, a complete concert.

The choir may sing the national anthem for a baseball, football, basketball, or hockey game at the college or professional level. Other opportunities may include singing for a community tree-lighting ceremony during holiday time or at the local zoo for a special event. For zoo events, directors have even been known to conduct in animal costumes such as penguins, cows, and owls, among others.

Further opportunities include singing for senior citizen residences, hospital patients, convention events, the opening of a hospital wing, a business dinner, a mall or hotel opening, a radio or television commercial, a service club (such as Kiwanis, Rotary, or Lions), a nonprofit foundation banquet, a museum, a chamber of commerce event, an opera club luncheon, a birthday party or anniversary for someone special to the chorus, a television or radio program (broadcast live or prerecorded), or funerals or weddings. Knowing what repertoire is appropriate to sing in each of these contexts and having it ready on short notice may be part of the choir preparation each year.

Chapter 11 will discuss collaborative performances with professional musicians, such as operas, symphony orchestras, and various types of small instrumental ensembles.

CONCLUSION

Building community through singing is a way to share our lives and our humanity. Choral singing is the essence of community. People gather to share the choral art, whether digitally or face to face. Singing is about sharing the human experience and collectively working toward a goal. It may be the goal of memorizing a piece, preparing for a concert or service, preparing a new work to premiere, or simply for the joy of singing together. It may be the goal of learning the solfeggio syllables, or which intervals are perfect, major, or minor. It may be learning dynamics or form. It may be learning a song in a new language or style. Whatever the goal is, singing is done in collaboration with others. When a choir shares a song, there may be emotional responses on the part of the listeners, as well as the singers. And when the choir experiences the miracle of that special moment when they know they were all together doing something quite extraordinary, they and we are transformed. The commitment of choral singers who are serious about their art is extraordinary. Singing celebrates life and the creation of beauty. The community of people is changed by the experience of hearing a children's/youth choir.

> *Music is alive. It is part of the living process of nature.*
> *When we join voices to sing, we transcend our everyday state of being*
> *and become communities filled with awe and compassion,*
> *celebrating the fire of life and the light of our being.*
> —NICK PAGE

11

PERFORMING WITH PROFESSIONALS

WHEN A CHILDREN'S choir has the opportunity to collaborate with professional musicians, the experience may be profound. Witnessing the faces of the choristers as they exit the stage following a performance with orchestra of Aaron Copland's *Old American Songs*, Béla Bartók's *Six Children's Choruses*, or the winter set of Ralph Vaughan Williams's *Folk Songs of the Four Seasons* reveals the choristers' excitement and joy. The purity and innocence of their voices singing the angel chorus in Benjamin Britten's *War Requiem* can be a moving experience for the audience.

Elementary or middle school children may have an opportunity to perform Anthony Powers's *Zlata's Diary* with a high school orchestra or the children's choral parts from the snow scene in *The Nutcracker* ballet. A school choir may perform Benjamin Britten's *Children's Crusade* with piano, organ, and percussion instruments. A church choir may present Andrew Carter's *Bless the Lord* involving adults, a children's choir, and an orchestra. A children's choir may be invited to sing Nick Page's multi-movement work *The Nursery Rhyme Cantata* with a professional orchestra. When a children's choir interacts with adult professional musicians, opportunities for experiencing music in new ways are created.

A chorister may solo with an adult choir for Leonard Bernstein's *Chichester Psalms* or assume the role of Amahl in Gian Carlo Menotti's *Amahl and the Night Visitors*. A child soloist may audition to sing with a professional symphony orchestra for Rob Kapilow's *Gertrude McFuzz* or *Green Eggs and Ham*. A chorister may audition to sing a national anthem for a college basketball game in a large stadium. The choir may be asked to record music with various instrumentation to be used for a children's book or television commercial. The opportunities for children's choirs to collaborate with professional musicians are many.

Collaborations with an adult chorus and orchestra may include Gustav Mahler's *Symphony No. 3* or *Symphony No. 8*, Modest Mussorgsky's *Boris Godunov*, Britten's *War Requiem*, John Adams's *On the Transmigration of Souls*, or Carl Orff's *Carmina Burana*.[1]

ording from a past performance with the orchestra conductor, if avail- gain insights into his or her possible musical interpretation and may ration of the choir.

choir conductor should have thorough knowledge of the complete before the rehearsing process begins with the choristers. It is benefi- ull orchestral score available for study prior to rehearsing. Choristers epared for all instrumental and vocal cues (especially for large sym- th adult chorus).

ery possible detail for success will lead to smoothly running rehears- nces. There will always be unanticipated events, but with good prepa- ing, they will usually be insignificant and manageable.

ration of the repertoire by the children's choir director is not signifi- from preparing a choral performance without orchestra. Preparation rough knowledge of the music, its historical context, and perfor- The choristers should be prepared to be completely off-book by the ey should understand the meaning of the text, make an emotional e text, and thoroughly know all entrance cues given by the orchestra). Phrasing, diction, breath support, pitch, dynamic contrast, vocal imation, and tonal energy are all part of the musical preparation of urse, the preparation does not end there. Matters beyond the prep- usic are equally important when getting ready for a concert with an

SICAL MATTERS

nusic for a performance is just the beginning. There are many addi- choristers will need. Choristers should be prepared for the serious estra rehearsal.

mportant for the choristers. The singers must be prepared for work- conductor and willing to follow the conductor's gestures and musical which may be new to them. Tempi might vary slightly from the way previously rehearsed. Balance issues may arise in the concert hall, and chestra and chorus may need to be adjusted. The choristers will be t quickly to any requested changes and retain that information for all s and performances.

ould be prepared for the solemnity of the rehearsal. During any orches- d concerts, they should be silent except when singing. The choristers xemplary behavior throughout the time shared with the orchestra. If s while waiting to perform, they should be taught how to sit quietly s on their laps, legs uncrossed, and feet flat on the floor. Fidgeting, r, or talking should not be allowed on the stage at any time. Yawns, et coughs should be done with a hand (or arm) up to the mouth, and n to the side to be minimally visible and audible.

To arrive at the performance point, there are many details that must come together to allow both musical and organizational excellence to shine. The seamless performance does not happen without attention to detail. This chapter focuses on the collaboration of children's choirs with other musicians. Topics to be discussed include how to prepare choristers for collaborations with symphony orchestras, operas, ballet companies, adult choirs, ethnic music ensembles, and chamber ensembles; and with small ensembles, such as string quartets, woodwind quintets, or brass ensembles. An in-depth discussion of preparing a children's choir for performance with an orchestra is presented.

PERFORMANCES WITH A SYMPHONY ORCHESTRA

Who initiates the conversation about a possible performance with a children's choir and orchestra? For a public school, it may be the conductor-teacher who contacts the director of the district's high school orchestra. If the school orchestra is not available, the conductor-teacher may contact a local adult chamber orchestra. This may be an orchestra composed of music educators from the region who may be semiprofessionals or volunteers. The local professional symphony orchestra may support a youth symphony orchestra that would be available for a collaborative performance. A nearby university may have a community music school that includes a high school orchestra. For some church programs, there may be a chamber orchestra that performs regularly with the adult choir for large works that would be willing to participate in a collaborative performance with the children's choir.

If a professional symphony orchestra exists in the region where a community-based children's choir is located, the conversation with the symphony orchestra manager or conductor may be initiated by the children's choir director. In the 1980s, at the beginning of the children's choir movement in America, in cities where there had been no history of children's choirs and orchestras performing together, children's choir conductors often contacted orchestra conductors to discuss possible future collaborations. Strong relationships grew. Initial discussions often focused on what repertoire would be appropriate, and how it might be integrated into the orchestra's concert season. Standard classical repertoire, such as boys' choir parts for major symphonic works, were often familiar to the orchestra managers and conductors. Often, new choirs were formed to fulfill those purposes. These choirs, in some cases, became the seed that grew into a sustainable community-based children's choir.

Other suggested works may not have been as familiar to the conductors or orchestra administrators. They may not have been aware of the availability of a newly formed children's choir in their area. As the number of children's choirs grew rapidly across America during the 1980s and 1990s, the number of children's choirs that performed with orchestras increased. At the same time, more composers became aware of these collaborations and increasingly began to write for this idiom. The body of repertoire for children's choirs and orchestras continually expanded.

Once it is determined that the choir and orchestra will consider collaboration, the discussions turn to the specific repertoire and other details:

- Type of work to be performed
- Title and length of the proposed work (including exact duration of each movement if a multi-movement work)
- Instrumentation required
- Number of singers required
- Availability of perusal scores and recordings
- Who will purchase or rent the choral scores (the choir or orchestra)?
- If scores are rented, does the rental agreement accommodate the orchestra's required rehearsal schedule?
- Number of performances (dates, times, locations)
- Performance fee

For an orchestral collaboration, the repertoire may be selected by the conductor in consultation with the orchestra's administrative staff. A list of possible repertoire may be requested from the children's choir director for consideration. Or the decision may be made mutually by the children's choir conductor and the orchestra leaders. Familiarity with the requirements of the repertoire (e.g., voicing, level of difficulty, number of treble parts, duration, size of choir needed) and knowledge of the artistic capabilities of both the orchestra and children's choir are important factors to be considered in planning a successful collaboration. The skills and abilities of the choir should match the level of the repertoire to be performed, or be within reach of what may be expected from the young singers.

For long-range planning, leaders of both groups should talk freely about artistic vision and possible collaborations. A symphony orchestra may choose to present a particular work that requires a boys' choir or children's choir for a brief part of an extended work, such as a symphony. Or, in some cases, a children's choir conductor might suggest that the choir is interested in performing a longer work scored specifically for children's choir and orchestra, such as a set of American, British, or Hungarian folk songs. The more knowledgeable a children's choir conductor is about the repertoire, the more likely an orchestra is to be interested in considering a possible collaboration.

Once there is interest in collaboration, there will be other matters to confirm. Selection of the repertoire is the most important and will determine the topics for future discussions. The level of challenge of the repertoire and the appropriate number of singers needed to balance the orchestration of the selected work are some of the important matters to be discussed early in the process. For example, if a children's choir has only forty singers, performing a work with heavy orchestration, such as Vaughan Williams's *Folk Songs of the Four Seasons*, is not realistic. If the selected work is Britten's *War Requiem*, a children's choir of forty-five singers is most appropriate, while a choir of one hundred is not.

To arrive at the performance point, there are many details that must come together to allow both musical and organizational excellence to shine. The seamless performance does not happen without attention to detail. This chapter focuses on the collaboration of children's choirs with other musicians. Topics to be discussed include how to prepare choristers for collaborations with symphony orchestras, operas, ballet companies, adult choirs, ethnic music ensembles, and chamber ensembles; and with small ensembles, such as string quartets, woodwind quintets, or brass ensembles. An in-depth discussion of preparing a children's choir for performance with an orchestra is presented.

PERFORMANCES WITH A SYMPHONY ORCHESTRA

Who initiates the conversation about a possible performance with a children's choir and orchestra? For a public school, it may be the conductor-teacher who contacts the director of the district's high school orchestra. If the school orchestra is not available, the conductor-teacher may contact a local adult chamber orchestra. This may be an orchestra composed of music educators from the region who may be semiprofessionals or volunteers. The local professional symphony orchestra may support a youth symphony orchestra that would be available for a collaborative performance. A nearby university may have a community music school that includes a high school orchestra. For some church programs, there may be a chamber orchestra that performs regularly with the adult choir for large works that would be willing to participate in a collaborative performance with the children's choir.

If a professional symphony orchestra exists in the region where a community-based children's choir is located, the conversation with the symphony orchestra manager or conductor may be initiated by the children's choir director. In the 1980s, at the beginning of the children's choir movement in America, in cities where there had been no history of children's choirs and orchestras performing together, children's choir conductors often contacted orchestra conductors to discuss possible future collaborations. Strong relationships grew. Initial discussions often focused on what repertoire would be appropriate, and how it might be integrated into the orchestra's concert season. Standard classical repertoire, such as boys' choir parts for major symphonic works, were often familiar to the orchestra managers and conductors. Often, new choirs were formed to fulfill those purposes. These choirs, in some cases, became the seed that grew into a sustainable community-based children's choir.

Other suggested works may not have been as familiar to the conductors or orchestra administrators. They may not have been aware of the availability of a newly formed children's choir in their area. As the number of children's choirs grew rapidly across America during the 1980s and 1990s, the number of children's choirs that performed with orchestras increased. At the same time, more composers became aware of these collaborations and increasingly began to write for this idiom. The body of repertoire for children's choirs and orchestras continually expanded.

Once it is determined that the choir and orchestra will consider collaboration, the discussions turn to the specific repertoire and other details:

- Type of work to be performed
- Title and length of the proposed work (including exact duration of each movement if a multi-movement work)
- Instrumentation required
- Number of singers required
- Availability of perusal scores and recordings
- Who will purchase or rent the choral scores (the choir or orchestra)?
- If scores are rented, does the rental agreement accommodate the orchestra's required rehearsal schedule?
- Number of performances (dates, times, locations)
- Performance fee

For an orchestral collaboration, the repertoire may be selected by the conductor in consultation with the orchestra's administrative staff. A list of possible repertoire may be requested from the children's choir director for consideration. Or the decision may be made mutually by the children's choir conductor and the orchestra leaders. Familiarity with the requirements of the repertoire (e.g., voicing, level of difficulty, number of treble parts, duration, size of choir needed) and knowledge of the artistic capabilities of both the orchestra and children's choir are important factors to be considered in planning a successful collaboration. The skills and abilities of the choir should match the level of the repertoire to be performed, or be within reach of what may be expected from the young singers.

For long-range planning, leaders of both groups should talk freely about artistic vision and possible collaborations. A symphony orchestra may choose to present a particular work that requires a boys' choir or children's choir for a brief part of an extended work, such as a symphony. Or, in some cases, a children's choir conductor might suggest that the choir is interested in performing a longer work scored specifically for children's choir and orchestra, such as a set of American, British, or Hungarian folk songs. The more knowledgeable a children's choir conductor is about the repertoire, the more likely an orchestra is to be interested in considering a possible collaboration.

Once there is interest in collaboration, there will be other matters to confirm. Selection of the repertoire is the most important and will determine the topics for future discussions. The level of challenge of the repertoire and the appropriate number of singers needed to balance the orchestration of the selected work are some of the important matters to be discussed early in the process. For example, if a children's choir has only forty singers, performing a work with heavy orchestration, such as Vaughan Williams's *Folk Songs of the Four Seasons*, is not realistic. If the selected work is Britten's *War Requiem*, a children's choir of forty-five singers is most appropriate, while a choir of one hundred is not.

Dates, locations, and the number of rehearsals and performances required must also be discussed. The children's chorus must be available for all scheduled performances of the orchestra, which may be one or several. The choir must also be available for any required orchestra rehearsals. In addition, there will be costs involved that should be discussed. The choral parts may need to be purchased or rented, and who will pay for this should be determined. An honorarium may or may not be offered to the choir depending on the budget of the orchestra. Typically, an honorarium is based upon the number of performances and how much involvement the children's choir has in each performance. For example, a holiday pops concert may involve the children's choir singing throughout most of the concert. For a classical concert, the children's choir may sing one multi-movement work, such as Randall Thompson's *The Place of the Blest*. For a Mahler symphony scored for a large adult choir, orchestra, and soloists, the children's choir will sing only a small section.

The details and understandings between the choir and orchestra should be stated in a signed agreement between the two parties. The written agreement, signed by both the orchestra administrator and the appropriate children's choir person (artistic director or executive director), should confirm the repertoire, the required rehearsal and concert dates, cancellation policies, who will provide music scores for the choir, and any monetary issues or other matters deemed necessary.

The opportunity for young singers to perform with an orchestra may be life-changing. Some choristers may have never attended a classical symphony orchestra concert and may be unfamiliar with a live performance of this type. The first time a young singer attends a classical orchestra concert may be the moment he or she shares the stage with a large orchestra. Other choristers may play instruments and may have attended orchestra concerts with their parents or school groups.

The preparation of the choir for collaboration with an orchestra entails great attention to the details of the music and more. The level of preparation of the choir, in all areas beyond the singing, is critical to a successful experience for the choristers. Excellence doesn't just happen. It is taught and nurtured. The skills learned will empower the choristers to be excellent.

MUSIC PREPARATION

Shortly after the repertoire has been determined and the performance invitation has been confirmed, a meeting with both conductors should be scheduled to thoroughly review the repertoire to be performed. The discussion should include tempi, vocal color, and other performance considerations. The more thorough the children's choir conductor's knowledge is about what the orchestra conductor expects, the better she or he can prepare the choir. The more prepared the choir is to be responsive to the orchestra conductor's interpretation, the more flexibility the conductor will have for shaping the music. When possible, it is wise to schedule a meeting with the orchestra conductor, particularly when interfacing with a new conductor or for a difficult work.

Requesting a recording from a past performance with the orchestra conductor, if available, is helpful to gain insights into his or her possible musical interpretation and may assist with preparation of the choir.

The children's choir conductor should have thorough knowledge of the complete orchestral score before the rehearsing process begins with the choristers. It is beneficial to have the full orchestral score available for study prior to rehearsing. Choristers must be well prepared for all instrumental and vocal cues (especially for large symphonic works with adult chorus).

Structuring every possible detail for success will lead to smoothly running rehearsals and performances. There will always be unanticipated events, but with good preparation and planning, they will usually be insignificant and manageable.

Musical preparation of the repertoire by the children's choir director is not significantly different from preparing a choral performance without orchestra. Preparation begins with thorough knowledge of the music, its historical context, and performance practice. The choristers should be prepared to be completely off-book by the performance. They should understand the meaning of the text, make an emotional connection to the text, and thoroughly know all entrance cues given by the orchestra (or adult chorus). Phrasing, diction, breath support, pitch, dynamic contrast, vocal energy, facial animation, and tonal energy are all part of the musical preparation of the choir. Of course, the preparation does not end there. Matters beyond the preparation of the music are equally important when getting ready for a concert with an orchestra.

BEYOND THE MUSICAL MATTERS

Mastering the music for a performance is just the beginning. There are many additional skills the choristers will need. Choristers should be prepared for the serious work of the orchestra rehearsal.

Flexibility is important for the choristers. The singers must be prepared for working with a new conductor and willing to follow the conductor's gestures and musical interpretation, which may be new to them. Tempi might vary slightly from the way they have been previously rehearsed. Balance issues may arise in the concert hall, and dynamics for orchestra and chorus may need to be adjusted. The choristers will be required to adapt quickly to any requested changes and retain that information for all future rehearsals and performances.

Choristers should be prepared for the solemnity of the rehearsal. During any orchestra rehearsals and concerts, they should be silent except when singing. The choristers should exhibit exemplary behavior throughout the time shared with the orchestra. If sitting on chairs while waiting to perform, they should be taught how to sit quietly with their hands on their laps, legs uncrossed, and feet flat on the floor. Fidgeting, fussing with hair, or talking should not be allowed on the stage at any time. Yawns, sneezes, and quiet coughs should be done with a hand (or arm) up to the mouth, and head tilted down to the side to be minimally visible and audible.

The distance between the orchestra conductor and the choir may be vast for the young singers, who are accustomed to standing relatively close to their own conductor. Frequent reminders to keep their eyes on the conductor may be given throughout the advance preparation process so that watching the orchestra conductor becomes automatic. Depending on the distance, there may also be a sound delay between the time the choristers sing and when the sound reaches the podium (much less the audience). The conductor may perceive that the choir is consistently singing behind the beat. The choir, if placed behind the orchestra, should be taught in advance to anticipate the beat.

To assist the singers' preparation for work with the orchestra, the conductor-teacher may stand a long distance away from the choir to simulate the sense of distance between conductor and singers when the orchestra is present. Advance training in "on time" singing will also be necessary. If the singers wait to hear the sound of the orchestra before singing, they will usually sing consistently late. It takes time for the orchestra's sound to travel through the air to reach the singers' ears. Skill development in getting their sound to the conductor *at the time of* the beat, rather than singing *with* the beat, will increase the likelihood that the singers will be precisely on time.

Choristers should be cautioned that some conductors may give little or no positive feedback about how they are doing during a rehearsal with orchestra. Some conductors speak very little, whereas others are more verbose. The singers should not interpret a serious conductor as one who is displeased with their performance. The better prepared the choir is, the less time the conductor will spend working with them during the rehearsal with orchestra. It is not good if the conductor has to stop frequently and work with the choir. The choir will know if it is doing well if the conductor keeps on rehearsing with few stops. The sign of a well-prepared children's choir during an orchestral rehearsal is when the only stops made are those to rehearse the orchestra. During this time, the singers should remain completely focused and ready to sing when the conductor resumes.

The use of scores is a distraction for young singers, who will be tempted to look often at them. If the choristers are looking down at their scores, or the scores are too high and cover their mouths, the balance between the orchestra and choir will be affected. Looking at scores instead of watching the conductor at all times causes the choir to be less precise. Memorization is not optional. The largest challenge will be when the conductor refers to a rehearsal number or letter to restart a section of the work. For the instrumentalists who have scores, this is standard procedure. For the singers who do not have scores, the conductor will have to give a specific text reference. Conductors who forget this will quickly be reminded when the choir is looking confused and doesn't sing. Sometimes, however, the choir will surprise itself and know exactly where to start singing based on the introductory material, a sign of a very well-prepared choir.

THE REHEARSAL PRIOR TO THE ORCHESTRA REHEARSAL

Ideally, the first rehearsal with the orchestra conductor should be scheduled before the first full orchestra rehearsal. Depending on the orchestra conductor's availability, this piano rehearsal may occur at the time and location of the choir's regular rehearsal.

Alternately, the piano rehearsal may immediately precede the orchestra rehearsal at its location.

The advantage of holding the piano rehearsal is that it provides the choristers with sequential learning about what to expect. They move from working with their own conductor to working with the orchestra conductor on the same repertoire. The choristers become familiar with the gestures and interpretations of the symphony conductor, and rapport is established before moving to the stage or large rehearsal hall with the full orchestra.

A well-prepared children's choir may be somewhat timid initially when working with a new conductor. This may also occur in the first few minutes of singing with a professional orchestra. Building rapport with the orchestra conductor prior to the downbeat of the full rehearsal promotes confidence in the choristers and gives them courage in an unfamiliar setting. If the choir is well prepared, they are empowered to sing with courage.

For the piano rehearsal with the orchestra conductor, the choristers should have their music scores in hand, if needed for referral. In most cases, they will not take the scores into the full rehearsal with the orchestra (depending on the unique requirements of the repertoire). This eliminates the scores as possible distractions and prevents noise if one is accidentally dropped during the rehearsal or concert.

Using scores for a performance may be recommended if a through-composed work includes spoken narration, interludes of varying lengths, numerous soloists, and multiple entrances at varying tempi. One such work is Samuel Jones's *The Shoe Bird: A Music Fable*, based on Eudora Welty's book *The Shoe Bird*. In this instance, it may be necessary for the singers to use scores to facilitate accuracy. For this engaging work for young audiences, familiarity with the spoken and orchestral cues is critical to the accurate negotiation of the numerous entrances by the choir. The scores are used only to remind the choristers of the sequence of musical passages and important verbal cues. The choristers should be encouraged to look away from their scores well in advance of the conductor's cue for each passage. Their precise entrances are necessary for maintaining a continuous flow of the musical narrative.

Occasionally, during a pre-orchestra rehearsal, the children's choir conductor may be asked by the orchestra conductor to lead the choir through the repertoire. For the orchestra conductor, the children's choir may be an unknown, similar to working with a soloist for the first time. The conductor may wish to gain a sense of how the children's choir has been prepared. The children's choir conductor may be asked to conduct a small portion, the beginning of key movements, or the entire work. The orchestra conductor may stop the choir intermittently to make changes. Sometimes the conductor may greet the choir and immediately begin working, without having heard the choir in advance. The choristers must understand that the orchestra conductor has the final authority for how the work is to be performed, and this is part of the rehearsal process. The choristers must adapt quickly and memorize the suggested changes. The choristers are considered professionals when working with an orchestra and are held to the same high artistic standards as the adult musicians.

THE REHEARSAL WITH THE ORCHESTRA

If the orchestra rehearsal is in the evening, it may be possible to request that the sections involving the young singers be rehearsed early, particularly if they fall on a school night. This request should be made in advance, though it may be denied if the conductor chooses to rehearse the concert repertoire in order from beginning to end. The decision about the order of the repertoire for the rehearsal may be made as much as ten months in advance of the rehearsal. Accommodating the choir's early dismissal request may involve rehearsing movements out of order. The orchestra conductor will determine if this is acceptable or not. The choir administration should be prepared for either decision and will be obligated to fulfill the commitment graciously, regardless of the conductor's final decision.

It is important to know if the orchestra is a union orchestra prior to the first combined rehearsal. If so, promptness is the rule, and watches should be synchronized with the official orchestra time source. Minutes and seconds matter in the context of a union orchestra rehearsal and concert. It could cost the orchestra thousands of dollars in additional wages if rehearsals or concerts exceed their designated time.

The children's choir must be in place in advance of the start time so there will be no delay with the downbeat of the rehearsal. The musicians cannot be kept waiting. The choristers must focus on everything that is happening around them and be prepared for rehearsing. They should know that when the music-making begins, there may be starts and stops during the rehearsal. Some pauses in the rehearsal process may require the choristers' patience during longer passages that involve only the orchestra. At other times, the conductor may work briefly with only the choir. This may be less likely to occur if the conductor has previously rehearsed with the choir. The singers' responsibility is to maintain concentration and energy, and to focus on making music throughout the rehearsal.

Choristers should be taught how to stand for long durations. The following points should be demonstrated:

- relaxed body
- proper posture
- knees slightly bent
- weight on both feet
- wiggle toes inside shoes periodically to keep the circulation going
- relaxed hands at their sides

Incidental movement by a chorister may seem normal or trivial, but to an audience, it is very obvious and may be distracting. It is wise to post chaperones offstage to watch the stage monitor if available, or to stand inconspicuously in the wings to monitor the choristers for any health issues.

Choristers should be reminded in advance of the rehearsal or concert that, once on the stage, they will not be able to leave. Bathroom and water breaks should be planned accordingly. Before long rehearsals, eating a nutritious meal is important. An additional healthful snack or lightly sugared cookie and juice or water may be needed for an energy boost during a rehearsal break. Chorister parents sometimes bring homemade cookies or cupcakes for the choir to have at the end of a long rehearsal, a gesture appreciated by the singers.

If chairs are available, the orchestra conductor may be gently reminded before the rehearsal to let the choristers sit during long passages of orchestral or adult chorus rehearsal. Cues for standing and sitting should be determined by the orchestra conductor in advance of the rehearsal, marked in both conductors' scores, and practiced by the choristers in advance for accuracy. The well-prepared choir will know when to stand in the event a cue is not given. The choir should not rely on the conductor to remember to give these cues. Standing and sitting cues are most often needed for a larger work, such as a symphony. The timing of the cue should allow enough time for choristers to stand, adjust their posture, and be ready to make a precise vocal entrance. If the children are the only guest artists with the orchestra for an entire work, they will stand for the full duration of the performance.

The rehearsal with the full orchestra will be run by the orchestra conductor, except on occasions when the children's choir conductor has been invited by the orchestra to conduct, or other performances where the children's choir conductor is the principal conductor. Once the rehearsal with the children's choir and orchestra begins, the conductor may not be interrupted.

Assuming that the orchestra conductor is leading the rehearsal, written rehearsal notes should be taken by the children's choir conductor regarding any comments made to the choir. These notes will be used for future review with the choristers. Any musical comments made by the conductor should be reviewed and completely rehearsed with the choir following the orchestra rehearsal, ensuring that changes will be made as requested. If time permits, rehearsal notes may be reviewed with the singers immediately after the orchestra rehearsal before dismissal; otherwise, they should be reviewed before the concert during the warm-up period.

Typically, there is one dress rehearsal with the orchestra before a performance. The children's choir conductor should be present throughout this rehearsal for any discussions with the orchestra conductor. The choral conductor may be asked by the orchestra conductor, or the orchestra's administrative staff, to comment on issues of balance between the choir and orchestra from various locations in the concert hall. Should issues of balance occur, if not mentioned, then the chorus conductor should tactfully intervene. This should be done by subtly approaching the orchestra conductor and speaking quietly to him or her only. At the conclusion of a rehearsal, the orchestra members may tap their stands or their feet as the choristers exit the rehearsal hall as a gesture of respect and appreciation for the young musicians' artistry and work ethic.

ENTERING AND EXITING THE STAGE

The level of musical excellence of a choir may be demonstrated by how well it enters the stage area. A choir that walks slowly and is lackadaisical in its gait may not be motivated to sing with energy and outstanding musicality. A choir that "walks tall, walks proud, and walks with a purpose" may be more likely to sing with outstanding artistry, a reflection of the comprehensive attention to musical and nonmusical details.

Preparing the choristers to walk onto the stage should be a carefully organized procedure. Which row enters first, in what order, and from what side (stage right or stage left) should planned in advance. The choristers should be in performance mode before leaving the warm-up space with the understanding that they are performers at all times once this process begins, not just when they are in front of the orchestra and audience. The orchestra may be rehearsing or performing while the choir is lining up and moving to the wings of the stage. The choir's movement should not interrupt the music-making in any way. Walking with "quiet feet" may also be rehearsed in advance of the concert.

The singers should be energized, but not overly so. They should be confident and poised. For a rehearsal or performance, the choir should be well warmed up and focused. Prior to moving to the performance area, the choristers should be sitting or standing in concert formation. This ensures that no last-minute confusion will occur while choristers get into the proper formation for proceeding to the stage.

Giving a choir a list of ten things to remember before going on the stage is not recommended. A list of three key words, given during the warm-up period, is adequate and can be easily remembered. Suggested words to use are joy, animation, resonance, beauty, focus, energy, smile, and courage. The words used should be contextual to the specific performance.

When the choir is called to the stage, it begins the musical journey with the orchestra. The following onstage protocol should be determined and practiced in advance:

- Where should the choristers look once on stage?
- Should the choristers remain standing if chairs are available?
- If chairs are available, should choristers sit immediately or be given a cue to sit simultaneously?
- Who will give the cue for sitting?

THE CONCERT

Prior to the orchestra rehearsal and concert events, choristers should be reminded to eat healthful foods that will sustain their energy for several hours of concentrated physical activity—singing. They should also be instructed not to consume candy, chocolate, or highly sugared foods before singing. They should not drink milk two hours before a performance, but should be well hydrated (preferably with water) at least two hours prior to singing.

On the day or night of the concert, the choristers may be excited, nervous, and full of energy. The warm-up preparation should be carefully planned to allow the choristers to maintain their focus prior to entering the stage. Knowing how much or how little to rehearse is important. Their best performance should not be in the rehearsal room, but rather before the audience.

If the choir has to wait until after intermission to sing, the warm-up may be done in two phases. A half hour or longer warm-up at the beginning of the call time prior to the start of the concert, and a ten-to-fifteen-minute refresher before going onstage, will refocus their attention back to musical matters.

If the call time is early, and the choir's performance does not occur until after intermission, it is important to know whether the orchestra conductor wishes to work with the choristers or speak to them prior to the start of the concert. If rehearsing is desired, the choir should be warmed up and prepared to work with the conductor at the appointed time. If the choristers do not sing until after intermission, they should do quiet activities and talk very softly in the warm-up room. If any monitors are available, they may listen to or view the concert until it is time for the final warm-up or rehearsing of any specific passages. The choristers must move from a focused vocal warm-up to the stage without losing concentration.

Following the performance, the children's choir conductor may be invited to the stage for a bow. This request may or may not be discussed in advance of concert night. Dress for the children's choir conductor should be appropriate for the context of the concert. If called to the stage, the children's choir director may shake the hand of the concert master as a gesture of appreciation to the orchestra. The choristers also appreciate their own conductor making eye contact with them and acknowledging them from the stage. The stage bows will be orchestrated by the conductor, including when to enter and exit the stage. The choir itself may or may not bow. This decision should be determined in advance so the choristers can be prepared accordingly. The choir should also be advised whether to clap, or not, at the conclusion of their performance.

UNANTICIPATED EVENTS

A four-foot-tall girl standing in the front row directly behind the bass drum may be suddenly surprised when the percussionist plays, and she feels the full force of the drum. Choristers standing in the front row behind the French horns may need a clear plastic screen placed between them and the horn section to protect their ears and allow them to hear the other singers. The request for a clear screen may be tactfully requested by the choir conductor or may be an orchestra decision. Balance may be an issue depending on the number of singers, the acoustics of the performance hall, the size of the orchestra, and the density of the orchestration. In certain contexts, the use of microphones may be necessary to improve balance and amplify the sound of the young voices. If sound amplification is necessary, it should be done artfully to maintain the acoustic sound of the choir. The eyes of the audience should not be drawn to the amplifiers at any time.

Positioning the choir may be a challenge depending on the configuration of the concert hall. For a cathedral performance, the risers for the choir may need to be placed on each side of a stationary altar with the orchestra placed on an elevated stage in front of the altar and choir. This scenario may be different with a three-part choir. Will the middle part be split on either side? Will the choir sing in a scrambled voicing formation? Will two parts sing from one side and one part from the other? Additional platforms may need to be constructed.

For a large stage, the choir may be placed on risers behind the full orchestra. For this setup, elevating the choir as high as possible above the orchestra will help with issues of balance and projection of sound. For Britten's *War Requiem*, the forces include full orchestra, chamber orchestra, soloists, adult choir, and children's choir. The children's choir may be placed in the location of box seating above and off to the side of the stage, or in a back balcony. For a work such as William Bolcomb's *Songs of Innocence and Experience*, the children's choir may sing while slowly walking, sing from the floor in front of the stage, or sing in other locations. Each concert hall and work will have its unique challenges and requirements.

What happens when a snowstorm occurs on a concert day, with blizzard warnings and travel advisories? If a choir lives in a geographic area that frequently has serious weather, sometimes contingency plans are necessary. If there is only one performance scheduled, and it is canceled due to a winter storm, it may be possible to reschedule. However, if the concert is on a very active symphony orchestra's season of concerts, rescheduling may not be an option. The orchestra may have a history of rarely, if ever, canceling a concert.

One such concert comes to mind. A children's choir was invited to participate in a pair of classical concerts with the local symphony orchestra. The Friday night performance occurred as scheduled. The Saturday night performance was another story. A sudden, unanticipated snow storm arrived on Saturday morning, crippling the city. Travel advisories were announced and "no unnecessary travel" was mandated. What would happen to the symphony orchestra concert that evening was causing great concern for the orchestra, the children's chorus staff, and the parents. Orchestra union rules dictated the time of day that the decision should be made to either go ahead with or cancel the performance. The orchestra manager and the children's choir conductor were on the phone several times during the day and continuously monitoring the weather information. A decision needed to be made by early afternoon. Finally, just before the appointed hour, it appeared the storm might subside. The decision was made to go forward with the concert, knowing that some participants (including orchestra players, singers, and audience) might be unable to attend.

A pre-concert lecture was to be given at 7:15 P.M., prior to the 8:00 P.M. concert. The conductors of the children's choir and the orchestra assumed their onstage positions, not knowing if any audience members would arrive. Approximately a dozen hearty souls appeared, taking off scarves, hats, heavy coats, and gloves as they made their way to seats near the stage. As the half-hour lecture progressed, more patrons gradually arrived. The children's choir conductor was concerned about not having enough singers for the concert. The orchestra manager worried about the musicians who traveled from outlying areas. Which key instrumentalists would be missing?

The snow banks outside the concert hall were six feet tall, the roads and sidewalks were snow-packed, the wind was blowing snow everywhere, and the city lights glistened against the white background. One by one, the instrumentalists, singers, and audience arrived. Although not quite a complete chorus or orchestra, and a slightly smaller audience than expected, all in attendance arrived safely and more or less on time. There was an energy in the hall that night that more than made up for the few missing personnel. Everyone was excited to be there, and a magical performance ensued.

PREPARING A CHORISTER SOLOIST FOR PERFORMANCE WITH AN ORCHESTRA OR ADULT ENSEMBLE

There are many opportunities for talented young singers to audition for solos beyond those within the children's choir. Some may be with full symphony orchestras, and some may be with smaller ensembles. Some orchestral works are scored for a child soloist, such as Rob Kapilow's *Gertrude McFuzz* (scored for soprano and girl soprano) and *Green Eggs and Ham* (scored for soprano and boy soprano). These are often programmed by a symphony orchestra for a family series concert and school concerts.

Solos for young singers that are performed with adult choruses include Leonard Bernstein's *Chichester Psalms* and Gian Carlo Menotti's *Amahl and the Night Visitors*, both scored for a boy soprano soloist. George Crumb's *Ancient Voices of Children*, a challenging contemporary work with adult soprano soloist and boy soprano, stretches the young singer musically.

Auditions for child soloists may be done within a limited window of time prior to a concert, or the call for auditions may be made well in advance of the audition date and subsequent performance. The audition may require a prepared song selected by the young singer or the person who is preparing the soloist. In some instances, the orchestra conductor or manager may provide an excerpt of the actual solo to be sung with the orchestra so that it may be learned in advance of the audition. Other times, a children's choir conductor may be asked to provide the soloist directly to the symphony orchestra, opera company, or other ensemble requesting the soloist.

When preparing a young soloist, it is always wise to prepare two:,one soloist and an understudy who can step in on short notice. A young singer may become ill prior to the performance, or an older boy may have a sudden voice change preventing him from singing. If the understudy has learned the solo and attended all the rehearsals, the substitution may be made easily. Understudying is a learning opportunity that can prepare the child for a future audition and possible solo performance.

To prepare the soloist for the audition, research should be done about the work. Knowing the full work, orchestration or instrumentation, historical background, and context of the work is helpful. Recordings may or may not be readily available or necessarily helpful. Many conductor-teachers prefer not to use recordings until after all the research and preparation is completed. Some prefer never to use recordings for reference, while others view YouTube performances for reference.

If a children's choir conductor or conductor-teacher is preparing a soloist or small group of soloists for auditioning, it may be beneficial to meet with the pre-selected students as a small group. Working this way to introduce the music may be most efficient, particularly if there is little time afforded to prepare. Matters such as the background of the work, phrasing, breath marks, tempi, diction, dynamics, memorization, and interpretation can be taught. Individual coaching can be done after the basics are learned. Attending the audition with the candidates may be appropriate to assist them with warm-up and to provide a calm, nurturing, and encouraging environment before auditioning. If they attend the audition as a group, this is also an opportunity to teach the singers how to support each other while competing for the solo.

Selecting choristers who have previously sung solos with the chorus is a wise place to begin when considering who should be recommended for an orchestral solo. A proven track record of how the singer will perform in front of a large audience will be an indication of how he or she will do when singing with an entire orchestra in a large concert hall. The solo is not only about a beautiful singing voice; it is also about the child's poise, confidence, courage, and inner spirit.

OTHER TYPES OF COLLABORATIONS

Opportunities to sing with professional musicians may be initiated by different types of ensembles. A national or international touring ballet company who presents Tchaikovsky's *The Nutcracker Suite* may invite school or community choirs to participate in local performances. A nationally known popular singing and recording artist who is touring with an orchestra may invite a local children's choir to join him or her while presenting a show in the local town or city.

An invitation to collaborate may come from a children's author who wishes to include a CD with a children's book. This might require hiring a chamber ensemble. The children's choir staff would put together a proposed budget for such a project upon request of the author. Budget items may include rehearsal and recording space rental, accompanist costs, a performance fee for the choir, cost of contracting and hiring the professional musicians, fee for the recording engineer (including recording, editing, and mastering the final audio), and any costs for renting or purchasing scores. There may be additional costs. Once a budget is prepared by the choir, negotiations with the author take place. Once finalized, instrumentalists are contracted, and the choir prepares. The scope and size of the project will determine the size of the budget, and a written contract between the chorus and the author should state all understandings and legalities.

Collaboration: Chamber Ensembles

When the children's choir director begins the process of selecting repertoire for the choir, selected works for performance may provide opportunities to collaborate with small ensembles. The instrumentation for selected repertoire may range from a few instruments, such as a jazz trio, string quartet, woodwind or brass quintet, to a chamber ensemble that incorporates more instruments. Sometimes during the process of commissioning a new work, there may be an opportunity to discuss possible instrumentation with the composer of the work being commissioned. The composer may have definite ideas about what instruments are to be used for the new work.

When working with small ensembles, there are several matters to be considered. What is the size of the choir? Will the instruments be stronger than the choir and overpower its sound, such as singing with a brass ensemble? Will the players be able to balance the choir by controlling the dynamics, or will larger choral forces be required? Will the children's choir conductor or a guest conductor direct? Where will the instrumentalists come from (high school musicians, professional musicians, or volunteer musicians)?

Works with unique combinations of instruments, such as William Mathias's *Salvatore Mundi*, Britten's "Psalm 150," or Derek Holman's *Sir Christëmas*, provide rich experiences for young singers. Rupert Lang's "Carol of the Child," scored for organ, piano, and handbells, includes a mother and child soloist, trio, and small ensemble in addition to full treble choir.[2] Multi-movement works are often scored for a small number of instruments, such as Gerald Cohen's Hebrew work *V'higad'ta L'vincha* (And You Shall Tell Your Child ...), scored for children's choir, clarinet and cello, or David Brunner's *Earthsongs*, scored for oboe and finger cymbals (later orchestrated). These represent a few of the many possibilities that may be considered when expanding the use of instruments beyond piano with a children's chorus.

Collaboration: Choral Consortiums

A new type of organization is developing in cities across the United States—the choral consortium. These groups comprise representative members of choral organizations in a particular city or geographic region who come together to pool resources, share lessons learned while growing their own organizations, share repertoire, collaborate for performances, publish choral concert event schedules, coordinate performance dates when possible to avoid conflicts, and share ideas about meeting the challenges of the current economic environment and more.[3] Cities such as Boston, San Francisco, New York, and Rochester, New York, have begun organizations of this type. At the time of this writing, a statewide choral consortium has been formed in New Jersey. Each organization will find its own mission and structure within its region and ideally increase awareness of choral singing opportunities for singers and audiences of all ages.

Collaboration: Opera

The experience of being in an opera may be life-changing for a young singer. If a children's choir conductor is asked to prepare a group of young singers for a professional opera company's production of Giacomo Puccini's *Tosca* and *La Bohème*, Mendelssohn's *A Midsummer Night's Dream,* Engelbert Humperdinck's *Hansel and Gretel*, or Georges Bizet's *Carmen*, to mention a few, the opportunity may be more than worth the investment of time and energy. For young singers, being part of an opera is a rich experience, both throughout the preparation process and as participants onstage.

Matters such as music direction, stage design, lighting, staging, costumes, makeup, musicians, schedules, and artistic personnel are managed by the opera company. The children's choir may be volunteer singers auditioned from school choirs, or selected from auditions announced in the local media or on the Internet. The singers may be selected for participation from an existing children's choir for which the choir may or may not be paid an honorarium for its involvement in the production. Regardless of how the singers are convened for participation, the commitment of a significant investment of time will be necessary.

Piano rehearsals for the opera may begin several weeks in advance of the production. Consideration for the children's schedules should be carefully monitored by the children's choir director throughout the process. Once the music is mastered, staging rehearsals begin. These rehearsals may take extensive hours of work, often with long breaks for the children, depending on how the scenes are sequenced. Time may be set aside during breaks for costume fittings. Extended rehearsals may be needed the weekend before the production begins, and every night leading up to the performances. The performances will require an early call time for applying makeup, donning costumes, and for adequate vocal warm-ups. Each step of the journey, from learning the music to performing the opera, will unfold one at a time. For the dress rehearsal and performances, all the components will come together including soloists, adult chorus members, costuming, scenery, lighting, orchestra, and the magic of the stage.

Another approach is having the children's choir produce its own opera for young voices. An opera for young singers only is Britten's *Golden Vanity*. Britten's *The Children's Crusade*, Stephen Hatfield's *Ann and Séamus: A Chamber Opera*, and Imant Raminsh's *The Nightingale* are examples of operas scored for young singers and a limited number of adult singers.

Self-producing an opera is a major undertaking for an artistic director, and the task may seem daunting for a first-time producer and the staff of a children's choir. Costuming, staging, lighting, scenery, and more must be organized and prepared to come together for a fully staged performance similar to that of a production by a professional opera company. People who are experienced in producing an opera and are willing to assist as advisers, volunteers, or hired personnel are valuable resources. For the children's choir director who has little or no experience in staging of any kind, the guidance and expertise of others may make the difference between an outstanding experience for the singers and one that is less satisfying.

People who understand costumes, scenery, arranging for appropriate lighting, what the costs will be, what may be donated, what must be purchased or borrowed, and other matters directly related to the production will be of great value to the artistic director when undertaking an opera for the first time. As always, the project begins with a budget and a timeline to determine if it is even feasible to consider undertaking.

The costs of presenting a fully staged opera will vary depending on the length of the opera, number of singers required, complexity of the costumes, scenery, and lighting, and the location where it will be performed. Taking on a smaller opera for a first production will afford the artistic director an opportunity to develop the expertise needed for directing a more complex opera in the future. Producing an opera is worth the investment of time and effort.

For some children's choirs, such as the Canadian Children's Opera Chorus founded in 1968, the primary mission is to present operas.[4] Choirs of this type may produce children's operas, commission new operas for young singers, and participate in adult opera productions when invited. Instruction for the singers may include drama training in addition to vocal training and music literacy. The joy on the faces of the choristers reveals how much they enjoy this type of artistry.

Once it is determined that the children's choir will present an opera, the number of performances should be considered. With some simplification of scenery and props, it may be possible to make the production portable. The opera may be presented at a school, community center, or other location, such as a community outreach project.

One such example of this occurred in 1996 when SCC presented Britten's opera *The Golden Vanity*. With partial support from the National Endowment for the Arts, the opera was performed for both an inner-city public school and the choir's concert series. Additional artists and a staging director were hired for the first-time opera production. A chorus staff member who had significant opera costuming experience oversaw the hiring of a seamstress to create the costumes. A volunteer parent who chaired a college theater department assisted with scenery, and a music director and professional musicians were hired to lead the concert series performance. For the school performance, the artistic director of the choir and the regular accompanist provided the artistic leadership.

Prior to the performance at the school, an instructional packet was created and sent to the music teacher with suggestions for preparing the students for the opera viewing experience. The comprehensive packet included such components as a synopsis of the story, opera vocabulary words, puzzles, a list of characters, word games, and a line drawing for coloring by the younger students.

The second opera the children's chorus undertook was *Rip Van Winkle: The Opera*, with music by Gregg Smith and libretto by Kim Rich.[5] This was a much larger production involving sixteen adult singers from the local opera company, a local professional singer, several additional soloists from the Gregg Smith Singers, and a professional staging director from New York City. Costuming was overseen by a chorus staff member, and Smith conducted the two performances.

A chorister mother who was a professional artist designed a poster and the program cover. Scenery was borrowed from the local opera company, and the fully staged production was performed for 2,700 school children during the school day, and an audience of 1,100 for the evening performance in the same location. Once again, instructional packets were sent in advance of the performance to all the music teachers in the schools who were to attend the performance. The packet included a synopsis of the opera, opera vocabulary terms and definitions, puzzles, and a guide for concert etiquette. Many were already familiar with the popular children's story "Rip Van Winkle," written by Washington Irving in 1819 and set in the Catskill Mountains of New York State.

Collaboration: Ballet Companies

In chapter 10, the commissioning of a work by Libby Larsen, *The Ballerina and the Clown: A Hans Christian Andersen Tale*, was discussed. The various performances of this work entailed collaborating with ballet companies who portrayed the story in dance as the chorus sang. For the preview performance, a local ballet dance studio was invited to collaborate. The dancers were advanced high school dancers, and the choreography was created by the dance school founder. For the premiere performance at the Music Educators National Conference (MENC, now known as NAfME) in Minneapolis in 2004, dancers from the University of Minnesota dance program from the department of theater arts and dance were invited to participate.

Particularly unusual considerations not typically on the list of criteria for choral concerts were the kind of floor in the concert space and whether there was enough physical space for the dancing to occur. For classical ballet dancers, the surface of the floor is critical. If the floor surface is not appropriate (too slippery, too sticky, too hard, too soft, uneven, etc.), the performers may be unable to dance or may be injured. The floor must be safe for the dancers and made of an appropriate surface. The open space must be adequate to allow the required number of dancers to move about easily. The volume level of the music is also important. For ballet dancers (who dance en pointe), there is an audible sound when the toe shoe hits the floor. The dancers must be able to hear the subtleties of the music at all times. Another consideration is that of tempi. For ballet dancers, the dance steps must be carefully choreographed to the music. The music must remain consistent in tempo to allow for the proper movement to occur. Pre-recorded music for the choreographer and dancers to use for rehearsing must be consistent with how the chorus will sing in performance. Additional rehearsal time will be necessary to rehearse with the chorus and dance company for this type of unique performance. On concert day, adequate space should be provided for the dancers to change into their costumes and warm up for the performance.

Collaboration: International Ensembles

For young singers living in a pluralistic society, the opportunities to collaborate with musicians of many cultures have increased dramatically. Providing shared musical experiences enriches young musicians' understanding of other cultures' music and traditions. Collaborations with ethnic ensembles may include singing with an *erhu* (ancient instrument) player from China, a Brazilian drumming ensemble, or experiencing African singing, dancing, and drumming. Collaborations may be done with Greek or Celtic dancers. School programs often combine learning about the food, clothing, geography, history, architecture, and art of a particular culture while preparing to perform the culture's music. Concert events often include a dessert reception for the audience in the school cafeteria following the concert. The featured country's food may be available for sampling.

Selecting and rehearsing repertoire for a collaborative performance may involve bringing the invited ensemble leader to the choral rehearsal to teach the appropriate dance steps, if movement is involved, or to teach how to play native instruments or the traditional songs passed down orally from generation to generation.

With other types of diverse choral repertoire found in printed format, a person from the country of origin of the selected repertoire (in Welsh, Serbian, or Russian, for example) may be invited to coach the language. This may be with the conductor initially and with the choir later. Bridging boundaries through song brings the world together in a timeless and profound way, collaborating on the most human level.

CONCLUSION

Opportunities for young singers to collaborate with adult musicians in various contexts expand their view of the world. For a child who experiences the joy of singing with an orchestra, a chamber ensemble, an opera company, a ballet company, or who sings and plays a *djembe* (drum), or who sings with a professional instrumentalist who plays the same instrument the young artist is studying, new ways of thinking about the world and its possibilities are created. Choristers share their artistry, but their horizons are also expanded beyond what they know.

After all, maps have boundaries, music has none.
—STEPHEN COLBERT

12

TOURING

Why would anyone want to spend six months doing the following in preparation for a three-week tour to a foreign country with fifty-five people?

- raise a very large sum of money in five months
- prepare forty chorister backpacks, daypacks, T-shirts, polo shirts, shorts, slacks, jackets, and formal concert attire items (for a three-week tour)
- prepare a detailed chorister suitcase packing list
- study, rehearse, prepare, and memorize twenty-eight pieces of music
- spend twenty-three hours on airplanes
- handle suitcases sixteen times
- travel for eighteen days in a country where few people speak your language
- stay in five different hotels
- present numerous workshops and concerts in four cities (sometimes with combined choirs of over two hundred singers and an orchestra)
- experience the culture of a foreign country with fifty-five people (including choristers, chaperones, artistic staff, and chorus staff)

The answer is simple: to bring children together to sing, dance, laugh, share, learn more about themselves, and experience life with others whose cultural traditions are different. The experience may be life-changing for both the children and the adults who accompany the young singers on their musical and cultural journey. Friendships are formed, and meaningful times are shared. Experiencing the richness of a country's culture—including its scenery, art, music, history, food, recreational activities, schools, and people—allows the travelers to learn more about themselves and the world around them.

Traveling with a choir is an enormous undertaking. The more thorough the advance planning is, the smoother the tour experience will likely be for all involved. There will inevitably be unanticipated events: A bus may break down, a suitcase containing a chorister's concert dress may be lost, or after singing for several large audiences, a three-day concert tour may end in a small town where only a handful of people attend the concert in a dingy, old school auditorium. A serendipitous meeting with a composer of a song the choir sang while on tour might occur at an airport while choristers are walking to a connecting flight (the composer spotted the chorus T-shirts that listed the tour repertoire on the back), or a concert may be given for an audience of five thousand people in a stadium. Even the most thoroughly planned tour may have unexpected good and bad surprises.

This chapter focuses on the organizational details of touring. For the conductor-teacher who is traveling for the first time, it may serve as a guide to what should be considered when planning a tour. For those who have already traveled with their choir, this chapter may inspire them to consider other types of tours or festival participation. Regardless of where anyone is on this collaborative choral journey, the experience of touring with a choir will have its extraordinary moments and challenges. Touring is always an adventure.

EARLY TOURING

Children's choirs in America have toured for many years. Pioneering choirs, such as the Columbus Boychoir (founded in 1937, now known as the American Boychoir), the Chicago Children's Choir (founded in 1950), the Glen Ellyn Children's Chorus (founded in 1964, now known as Anima), the Boys Choir of Harlem (founded in 1968), and the San Francisco Girls Chorus (founded in 1978), have toured throughout their existence. As the number of American community-based children's choirs rapidly grew in the 1980s and 1990s, more frequent touring occurred by the newly formed choirs. Conductor-teachers were eager to study repertoire and attend master classes, workshops, and professional conferences where techniques and resources were shared. With limited availability of children's choir recordings at the time, the motivation was strong to travel to hear other children's choirs.

Beginning in the early 1990s, festivals developed for young singers in increasing numbers in locations ranging from Hawaii to Carnegie Hall. Each festival was unique in length and format. Some included individual performances and combined choir performances. Some festivals included an adjudication component or performances with an orchestra.

In the early 1990s, one of the early professional companies to host a children's choir festival established a format that included the commissioning of a new work. The composer was invited to be in residence for the duration of the festival in order to interact with the festival's artistic director, accompanist, and the singers. This collaboration provided the young singers with detailed insights into the newly commissioned work.

Several auditioned school, church, and community children's choirs, selected from across the country and totaling over three hundred voices, gathered for this four-day festival of rehearsals, performances, and concerts. Each choir performed under its own director in various locations. The festival culminated with a combined choir performance that included the premiered work directed by the festival's artistic director.[1] This was one model for a children's choir festival; many others of varying types would follow.

JUSTIFYING TRAVEL

Once it is determined that the choir would like to tour, being able to justify why the choir should travel is important to the community that surrounds it. This community includes parents, administrators, staff, board, and funders. It is important to ask several questions: Why is the choir touring? Is it just to say it tours because other choirs tour? Are there sound educational reasons for providing this type of experience for the young singers? With whom will the singers collaborate? How will the singers be treated? Will it be worth the investment of time and expense to prepare for traveling with a large group? What will be gained by the experience? Is the schedule realistic for young singers? How much additional repertoire will need to be learned in addition to what the choir will sing for its own concerts during the year? Before any plans begin, questions should be raised and answered to justify the feasibility of a concert tour for the choir.

The choir's goal may be to participate in a competition against other choirs, or critiqued and adjudicated based on musical standards. Or the choir's goal may be to sing with other choirs at a state, national, or international festival. Or the goal may be to study repertoire and sing with a well-known conductor of children's choirs in a workshop or master class. The invitation to travel may come from a children's choir that will host the invited choir for a combined concert. The choir may audition to perform for a professional music conference or to enter an international competition. Or the choir may be invited to be part of a concert series in a nearby city. Each tour will be unique.

The frequency of traveling should also be considered. Will touring become a regular part of the schedule of events for each year? Who will bear the financial burden for the cost of touring? How will funds be raised? Will the choir provide ways for individual singers to earn money for their tour fees? Will there be group fundraising activities to benefit the entire choir? Will there be scholarship assistance for those who may not be able to afford the cost of the tour? Will there be an honorarium offered for a performance? Will tickets be sold for performances while on tour?

Some choirs plan a three-year rotation: a state tour in year one, a domestic tour in year two, and an international tour in year three. For others, tours are based on what opportunities or invitations are presented to them each year. Some choirs travel every other year, whereas others choose to never travel.

For large choirs with multiple levels, the intermediate-level choir may travel for short events, such as a weekend state festival. This opportunity allows the younger singers to develop touring experience in preparation for longer choir tours once they advance to the next level. For older singers, tours may last more than a few days and possibly include international festivals, performances, or competitions.

Some choirs base decisions about touring on specific performance goals. A choir may apply and audition for a performance at a professional music conference or apply to compete in an international festival. The decision to travel should be based on strong reasons for the organization, the community, and most important, the choristers.

BEGINNING TO TOUR

Most choirs begin with a small day trip to a nearby city and travel by bus to present a workshop or give a concert. A subsequent tour might include traveling to a city within its state for an overnight concert event or to a city located several hours away. This may occur on a long weekend and may be a performance or festival that includes more than one choir. For this type of festival, choirs often travel out of state to a festival led by a colleague or recognized leader in the choral profession. The festival may include individual choir performances and a combined choir performance.

Extended tours may include traveling to many cities within the United States or internationally. Regardless of the type and length of a choir tour, there are certain organizational matters to be considered, as described below.

DOMESTIC TOURS AND FESTIVALS

A first travel experience may be to visit another choir for a collaborative performance, to present a concert for a music series, or to be the guests of another choir. If the choir is being hosted by a choir in another city, the weekend event may include rehearsals, shared meals and social time, and a combined performance by the two choirs for a concert. It may also include a combined-choir concert finale. For this type of tour, typical expenses may include hotel, travel, meals, and an entertainment or sightseeing activity while in the destination city. Or, in some cases, some of these expenses may be assumed by the host choir.

Another type of travel is for a choir to participate in one of the numerous children's choir festivals held across the country. Most often, children's choir festivals occur during the months of June, July, and early August when young singers are not in school. The festivals may involve several choirs. For traveling to a domestic children's choir festival (including Hawaii and Alaska), the participant package fee may include rehearsals and a combined concert with a guest conductor, hotel, and meals (some may be optional or not included). Festival participation may also include performances in nearby locations, sightseeing, or other recreational activity; there may also be a social event, such as a reception, dinner, or boat cruise for the combined choirs. Participation fees may be based on a choir fee or a fee per participant, and additional costs for optional meals or activities may be required.

For some festivals, the host organization (or tour company) may not arrange the long-distance travel to the festival location. In this case, the participating choir may use a travel agency to arrange for a group flight or secure a motor coach to the festival location. If the festival package does not include local transportation, such as to and from the airport, the hosts may recommend local bus companies for use during the festival.

PLANNING YOUR TOUR

An alternate to attending a prearranged festival is for the choir to plan its own tour. Doing this will give the choir the ability to shape the itinerary to accommodate its own requirements. The choir will determine the complete itinerary, where the choir will be housed, where concerts will be given, and the sightseeing or recreational activities. The choir will be responsible for all expenses. It is challenging to secure performance venues, make all concert arrangements, and prepare publicity when you are not located in the destination city. Although it is possible to do, it is time-consuming and requires thorough knowledge of the geographic location.

Another option is for the choir to hire a professional tour company to work collaboratively with the choir. A tour company may have extensive knowledge, based on years of experience, and may be a strong resource for a choir that has not done extensive touring. If the choir determines it will hire a tour company, there are several topics to consider before selecting one.

SELECTING A TOUR COMPANY

There are many companies that plan tours for children's choirs. Some specialize in arrangements for domestic and international tours. Others present only festivals domestically or internationally. Some tour companies plan a variety of tours and festivals.

Selecting a tour company should begin with thorough research. When interviewing more than one company, use the same set of questions. This will provide useful information about each company's philosophy and procedures. The data gathered will assist in making an informed decision during the selection process. Sample questions to ask might include the following:

- How many choirs traveled with your company last year?
- How many of these choirs were children's choirs? Could you name some of the choirs?
- How long have you been in the tour business?

- Can you recommend three children's choir directors to contact who have toured with you (or attended your festivals) over the past two years?
- Will we have a tour guide? Will our tour guide be with us at all times?
- Will our tour guide be fluent in the language of the destination country?
- What expenses are included in the individual tour package?
- Are there any complimentary packages based on the total number of singers and chaperones traveling?
- If the choir allows parents to travel with the choir, is there a travel package for parents? If so, what does it include?
- Can you describe the type of hotels where the choir will stay?
- Can you guarantee that the chaperones will be located on the same floor as the choristers for all hotel stays?
- Will the choir be housed together, or will it be split on many floors throughout a hotel?
- Can you give an idea of what a typical day's schedule would be like?
- What type of buses do you hire? Local school buses or motor coaches?
- What airlines do you typically use for group travel?
- How long will it take to put a proposal together?
- Once the tour package is prepared, will the company send a representative to attend the informational meeting with parents about the choir's first international tour?

It is appropriate to ask a company to provide names of choirs and directors who have recently participated in their festivals or for whom they have arranged a recent tour. Colleagues who have traveled with a particular tour company may give helpful insights into their travel experiences. All data that can be gathered in advance of hiring a company will assist in making an informed decision about which company will be the best fit for the choir. There will be additional questions, and the questions will be unique to each choir and each type of tour.

INTERNATIONAL TOURS

Many choirs hire a professional travel company that specializes in arranging international choir tours and one that has experience in planning tours for young singers, in particular. There is a strong advantage to doing this. A company may be familiar with the unique needs of children's choirs and may have strong contacts with people in specific geographic regions. These contacts may adeptly facilitate securing concert venues, promoting the concerts, finding unique performance opportunities, arranging for sightseeing tours, and all other accommodations.

There are many ways to arrange an international tour. One option is to specify a destination city or country and have a tour company complete all the planning. Another option is for a choir to participate in a children's choir festival that is planned by a tour company. An additional option occurs when a choir is accepted for participation in an international festival or competition and there is no existing relationship with a tour company. In this case, a selected tour company may be hired to make all travel arrangements.

International children's choir festivals are often sponsored by tour companies in various locations throughout the world. If the company has a strong history of sponsoring successful festivals, it will be accustomed to working with children's choirs of various sizes and types. If it is possible to have a conversation with a choir director who has participated in one of these festivals, much can be learned about that choir's experience.

GOVERNMENT TRAVEL REQUIREMENTS FOR INTERNATIONAL TRAVEL

The choir must be thoroughly informed about all government requirements for traveling. This will include citizenship documentation, visas, and immunizations. Specific documentation of citizenship (such as birth certificates, passports, and photo identifications) may be required and may vary depending on the age of the traveler, the international destination, and the mode of travel. For certain countries, a visa and/or specific immunizations may be required.

Passport photos will be required when applying for a passport. The application for a passport and any required visas should be completed well in advance of the travel date. Travel requirements, or advisories, may change while the choir tour is being planned and should be checked regularly for current information. The government website http://www.travel.state.gov/travel/ provides current information about international travel. Information about passports and visas may be found at http://travel.state.gov/passport/.[2]

Travel cancellation insurance and health insurance coverage (while out of the United States) should be researched and procured by the choir. Each organization should make its own decisions about these matters. Some choirs may request that a registered nurse or physician travel with them at all times.

The number of pieces of luggage each individual is allowed to take on tour is another consideration. The specific suitcase size (including height, length, width, and weight) must be carefully followed so that overweight baggage fees are not incurred. There will also be specifics regarding the number and size of the carry-on pieces that will be allowed on the airplane. The tour company (or airline if the choir is making its own flight arrangements) should provide information about specific requirements.

THE TOUR BUDGET

Prior to announcing a tour to the choristers and their families, an itinerary and budget should be prepared. (See appendix 12.1 for a sample tour budget.) Written information should include the travel dates, destination, accommodations, cost, tentative schedule, performances, modes of transportation, the procedure for parents to apply to be a chaperone, and the rationale for why it is important for the chorus to travel to the specified location. Usually, the choir participants will bear the expense for international travel. On rare occasions, the costs (excluding airfare) might be covered by the host country. For choirs who are represented by a professional arts management company, the structure will be completely different, and the choir's performance fees may cover the cost of touring.

The choir's complete tour budget will be prepared incorporating the company's proposed tour costs and any additional expenses not included in its proposal. For example, some meals may be included, and others may not. The costs of a tour will be based on the total number of singers and adults traveling and include (but may not be limited to) the following:

- Choir or individual singer participation fee (if applicable for a festival or competition)
- The number of singers who will travel (proposals may be based on a minimum number of participants)
- The number of adult chaperones who will travel
- The number of artistic and administrative staff (or volunteers) who will travel (e.g., administrative staff and tour coordinator, conductor, accompanist, and any additional musicians or personnel)
- Airfare and associated fees such as fuel taxes
- Ground transportation (motor coach, bus, train, subway)
- Hotel (based on the number of choristers/chaperones per room as requested by the choir)
- Meals (included or not)
- Entertainment (preplanned group-guided sightseeing, special dinner event, concert or theater tickets, museum admission, etc.)

Additional choir budget items that may not be included in the tour company proposal may include the following:

- Wardrobe items (e.g., tour T-shirts, polo shirts for choristers, or additional casual or concert attire)
- Laundry or dry-cleaning costs (for extended tours)
- Miscellaneous expenses
- Insurances (travel, international health, trip cancellation, and others as needed)

The choir may also include a 10 percent administrative fee to cover staff time, tour preparation costs, and other expenses directly related to tour expenses (printing, stationery, programs, telephone calls, postage, etc.). It is wise to build miscellaneous expenses into the budget that will provide a small fund for unexpected expenses (e.g., extra meals due to a delayed flight). If any funds remain at the conclusion of the tour, refunds may be made to the participants or retained for the next tour.

The tour planning may be overseen by the artistic director, chorus administrative staff, or volunteer(s), depending on the size of the organization. Preparing a list of tasks for each person involved in planning will help eliminate duplication of efforts. Communication among the planners should be encouraged throughout the planning process and should be clearly defined and coordinated with the choir tour manager who will be responsible for making all final decisions.

It is important to determine if the choir families can financially support a touring endeavor before committing to a tour. There may be some choristers who need financial assistance, and scholarship funds may be necessary to accommodate this need. (See appendix 12.2 for a board and staff fundraising overview.)

FUNDING THE TOUR

There are many ways to fund a tour. Some are more labor-intensive than others. Some may be done individually by the choristers and parents, and others may be done by the choristers and parents working side by side. Typical fundraising ideas may include the following:

- Fundraisers to benefit the entire choir (car wash, pizza sale, spaghetti dinner)
- Individual chorister fundraisers to help with individual tour fees (cookie dough sale, pie sale, candy sale, plant sale, gift wrap sale, candle sale, etc.)
- A commitment from the board of directors to sponsor a fundraising activity (dessert reception, dinner, etc.)
- A school booster club raising funds to support the choir's tour (fruit sale)
- Choristers asking family members for money instead of gifts for birthdays or other special occasions
- Chorus grants may be secured from private or national foundations
- Auctions
- A gift basket raffle
- A plant sale
- A benefit concert (possibly the dress rehearsal preceding the tour)

The possibilities are endless when using creativity and imagination. For some tours, a fundraiser may follow a theme that matches the tour destination, such as having a tea party to help sponsor a trip to China or a spaghetti dinner to help sponsor a trip to Italy. Another way to gather ideas is to talk to other colleagues who have toured.

ANNOUNCING THE TOUR

If the choristers hear any discussion about a tour being planned, excitement will brew among them. The most frequently asked chorister question will be, "Where are we going?" Then the parents will ask, "What are the dates, and how much will it cost?" It is important to instill confidence in the parents about tour matters. An information packet, provided to parents at the time the tour is announced, will be helpful. The packet should reflect the highest level of preparation, with attention to details, and it should confirm that the children's safety is foremost.

The formal announcement may be made to the parents by letter, by e-mail, or in a meeting called for the purpose of announcing the tour. (See appendix 12.3 for a sample staff agenda for the chorister and parent tour announcement meeting.)

Once the tour is announced, the choir should be prepared to give the chorister families comprehensive information including the dates, location, type of event, performances, concert locations, cost (including a description of what the tour fee will cover), payment schedule, and any additional clothing that will be necessary to purchase. There should be no changes made to the tour fee once it is presented to the parents; if a change is made, it should be only to reduce the cost, never increase.

A payment schedule may accompany the packet. Depending on how far in advance the tour dates are announced, the payment schedule might include a nonrefundable deposit (due soon after the tour announcement is made) and deadlines for two or three additional payments spread over several weeks or months. The nonrefundable deposit formally commits a chorister to participating in the tour. Deadlines for subsequent tour payments should be planned to accommodate the external deadlines for nonrefundable payments for airfares, hotels, and festival participation fees. (See appendix 12.4 for a tour commitment agreement, appendix 12.5 for a tour payment strategy, and appendix 12.6 for a tour countdown calendar.)

The payment schedule should be given to chorister families as far in advance as possible. A safety factor should be built into the stated choir deadlines. This allows for the occasional late payment and will still accommodate the choir's on-time payment to the vendor. If possible, the choir should avoid making any payment to a vendor if no funds have been received from a chorister family.

If a choir is taking its first international tour, it may request that the tour company send a representative to meet with the parents at the first tour meeting. The professional may easily answer questions from parents based on past experiences with other touring choirs.

THE RATIO OF CHAPERONES TO CHORISTERS

Each choir will determine what the appropriate ratio of chaperones to choristers will be based on the needs of the tour. For some tours, the choir will follow a scheduled itinerary and move as a group from the time it leaves the hotel in the morning until it returns at night. For this type of tour, fewer chaperones may be required, and the ratio may be one chaperone for every eight or ten choristers, depending on their age. For an international tour that includes free time, choristers may spend time in small groups with a chaperone for each group. The ratio for these tour conditions may be one chaperone for every four or five choristers. Overall, the ratio of chaperones to choristers will vary, depending on the nature of each tour and what seems most comfortable for the choir. (See appendix 12.7 for "About Chaperoning" excerpted from a tour handbook, and appendix 12.8 for a chaperone application.)

FAMILY GROUPS

For some tours, the choristers will have a recreational activity built into the itinerary. This might include visiting a museum, zoo, or amusement park, or attending a theater performance. For such an activity, it may be wise to break into smaller units called "family groups" that will have one chaperone per group. Decisions about the size of each family group will depend on the type, length, and structure of the tour.

Family groups should be assigned well in advance of a tour with decisions about who will be in each one based on the chorister's request form and the preferences of the staff and conductor. It is not always possible to accommodate all the choristers' requests, but having at least two friends together will be appreciated. Some choirs mix the age levels of the family group members, while others keep students of similar ages together. Sometimes, the boys and girls are in mixed groups during the day, but are separated into all-boy or all-girl groups for the night. Sometimes choristers have no preference and are willing to be placed with any group. By the time the tour ends, the choristers often develop many new friends. Prior to the tour, each chaperone is encouraged to host a social gathering where choristers can become better acquainted and build camaraderie. (See appendix 12.9 for a tour book excerpt titled "About Family Groups.")

In addition to being part of a family group for the duration of a tour, each chorister should be assigned a buddy within its family group. Buddies should always stay together. A chorister should never be left alone, even for a quick restroom stop or to buy a souvenir. Choristers should be encouraged to travel in pairs, or in a group of three, or with their family group, at all times.

CHAPERONE SELECTION AND TRAINING SESSIONS

The selection of chaperones is an important process. Some choirs do not travel with parent chaperones, but with adults or staff members who are not related to the choristers. Some choirs have application forms for parents to complete if they wish to be selected as chaperones for a choir tour. Often, those who apply have previously volunteered as chaperones for concert events, auditions, or other chorus activities. Some who apply may not be well known to those responsible for planning the tour; however, the use of an application form allows anyone to be considered. Chaperones who are accepted should understand the requirements of chaperoning and be willing to assume all chaperone responsibilities. They should not view a tour as a vacation.

In addition to an application process, some choirs require a background check for each chaperone who will travel with the choir. And some choirs require a medical professional, either a nurse or physician, to be one of the chaperones.

After the chaperones have been selected, it is wise to have a chaperone training session for them. If not well prepared for their responsibilities, chaperones can cause a conductor and staff much unnecessary stress and extra work. Chaperones should understand the tremendous responsibility they assume for the safety and well-being of the choristers. The chaperone meeting will provide an opportunity to address questions and review the itinerary and procedures with the tour manager. This meeting may occur during or following a regularly scheduled choir rehearsal, as a convenience to the parents, or at a separate date and time.

Chaperones should be available at all times throughout the tour. When the choir is rehearsing, it may be possible to rotate a small number of chaperones on and off duty, thereby giving a break to a few chaperones at a time. For some tours in extreme climates, it may be wise to have an extra person available for an emergency, such as a serious illness.

Clear delineation of the chain of command is also important for chaperones to understand before departure. Chaperones for most choirs will not be allowed to make independent decisions to change meeting places, take their group somewhere not cleared by the head chaperone, or act independently without communicating with those in charge. Chaperones should understand who is responsible for various matters while on tour and who the appropriate person is to speak to for making any decisions. This can be part of the pre-departure training. Careful and thorough preparation is appreciated by the chaperones and is a comfort to the parents at home.

THE TOUR HANDBOOK AND TIMELINE

There are many facets of tour preparation, including travel arrangements, wardrobe, schedules, repertoire, and personnel. For the choir that travels regularly, it may be helpful to develop a detailed tour handbook that includes important details about touring; it can be revised and updated as each tour occurs. (Appendix 12.10 provides a detailed list of possible topics for a tour handbook for both domestic and international choir tours.)

A tour timeline may be helpful for all tour matters. A countdown calendar, prepared at the beginning of the tour planning process, may include the following:

- financial deadlines
- fundraising events
- wardrobe ordering deadlines
- passport deadlines
- deadlines for materials to be submitted to host choir/festival
- deadlines for program printing
- dates to submit press releases for a benefit concert

The amount of detail may seem overwhelming, but doing one task at a time, from a carefully constructed timeline, will keep everyone less stressed and on schedule with preparations.

MEDICAL CONSIDERATIONS

The health and well-being of each chorister is an important consideration for any tour, either domestic or international. Both adults and choristers should complete a medical information form (to be kept confidential unless needed in an emergency). It is important for all adults, both staff and chaperones, who will be responsible for the choristers throughout a tour to be well-informed about any allergies or medical conditions of any of the travelers.

Concerns such as food allergies or reactions to insect bites or stings should be conveyed to the staff and chaperones prior to traveling. Any medications to be taken should be discussed with parents before traveling, and decisions should be made about how, when, and who will administer them. Current contact information for parents or guardians should be readily available throughout the tour.

Health insurance information should be carried with the staff and chaperones at all times in case of an emergency. International health insurance may be needed for international travel. (See appendix 12.11 for a sample tour medical and personal information form.)

ORGANIZING REPERTOIRE FOR A TOUR

Depending on the type of tour, a variety of repertoire may be required. This may include the choir's own repertoire for independent concerts or a competition, or additional repertoire for a massed choir performance with other choirs at a festival. Lessons learned from touring are offered as suggestions for improving the flexibility of the choir performances while on tour. Selecting the appropriate diversity of tour repertoire may prepare the choir for almost any performance opportunity, formal or informal. The following repertoire may be considered for inclusion:

- Sacred repertoire
- Secular repertoire
- American music (both composed and folk songs)
- Canons or rounds
- Repertoire of various styles, periods, and tempi
- A cappella repertoire
  - An a cappella song that may be sung as a thank-you to someone (bus driver, tour guide, translator, restaurant staff, chef, host choir)
  - An a cappella song that may be sung before a meal

- Repertoire with piano or additional instruments such as drums, flute, etc.
- Repertoire with organ accompaniment (if a performance is scheduled in a church where an organ is available)
- Repertoire in a variety of languages
- A selection in the language of the country where the choir will tour

Often, a choir will want to sing spontaneously while touring. Choristers might sing on the bus for fun, learn a new song from another choir in a hotel lobby, or be emotionally moved and request to sing at an outdoor historic or memorial site. Preparing for any unexpected moments with repertoire is all part of organizing the tour and will enrich the shared experience of the singers.

Whether to memorize music or not is an important decision to be made by the conductor-teacher. If the choir does not memorize its music, folders or envelopes will be needed for the music while on tour. In some cases, music and pencils will be required by a festival guest conductor. Some choirs memorize their complete tour repertoire before departure. Taking music scores on tour will depend on the situation.

OTHER ORGANIZATIONAL DETAILS

Sometimes the preparation for an international tour has nothing to do with the music, itinerary, clothing, or budget. The preparation for this tour may include learning about the currency, food, and cultural traditions. Learning the words for "hello," "goodbye," "please," and "thank you" in the language of the country where the choir will travel is beneficial. Familiarity with the country's national anthem prepares the choristers to stand respectfully if the anthem is played.

Some choirs require choristers to wear lanyards with photo identification holders, which may also include emergency phone numbers and other important information. Some choirs have a code of behavior. Some choirs have chaperones, or staff members, hold the passports, airline tickets, and other important travel documents for the choristers. This avoids potential loss and allows for distribution of these items when needed.

Another component of choir traveling includes the tradition of choristers exchanging small gifts with choir members from other choirs. Lapel pins with the choir logo, city logo, or recognizable city landmark or American flag may be given as gifts. Shiny American pennies or stamps are sometime given. Another type of small gift may be something that the choristers' home city is known by or something handmade by the choristers. There are many possibilities for small gifts to be exchanged.

It is wise to have a person assigned to public relations for the tour prior to traveling. The local news media may be contacted about an upcoming tour, festival, or performance invitation. This may encourage press coverage in print, on the web, or with television stations that will create community interest. Press coverage may include interviews, filming a rehearsal, an interview with the director to promote an upcoming tour benefit concert, a feature article in the local newspaper, or a segment on a television news or daytime program.

An appropriate gift for the host choir director or festival guest conductor may be a framed photo of the choir with a personal dedication, a framed certificate of appreciation, a book about the choir's home state or region, or something made by a well-known artist or craftsman from the choir's home city. CDs from the choir are also appropriate.

Before the international tour, choristers should be coached on how to react to unexpected situations. For example, if punch with alcohol is served at a reception, choristers should feel comfortable asking chaperones how to graciously decline so the host organization does not feel offended.

A professional or volunteer photographer or videographer may be assigned to follow the choir while on tour. Photographs and a journal of daily events may be put on a blog for families and friends to follow at home. Video from the tour may be used for a special documentary film for a local public broadcast station or for a DVD to be given to choristers as a remembrance from the trip.

Cell phones may be required or banned while on tour. Each choir will determine its own policy about use of cell phones and texting while on tour.

A choir tradition may include a poem or bedtime story at the end of the day, a yoga session, or a quiet gathering of the choristers and the director for reflections about the day's events. Depending on the tour schedule and facilities, this may or may not be possible every day.

On the last night of the tour, the choir may have a special banquet for those who have traveled together. Everyone can share fun photographs, favorite times, and reflections about the adventures of the tour. There may be a retrospective slide show and a time to present humorous awards based on tour events. The banquet may also include a humorous skit about the tour created by the choristers or a song sung by the chaperones. Appropriate thanks may be extended to chaperones, staff, and musicians.

A choir tour reunion may be held several weeks after the tour. The tour reunion may be a covered dish supper or dessert reception for choristers and their families. Tables can display the choristers' tour photograph albums or scrapbooks. Each choir will develop its own traditions.

CONCLUSION

The transformative power of music for young singers may be profound. When choristers have an opportunity to share their joy of singing with others of a similar age, their worlds are expanded. If choristers tour across state boundaries or to other countries, the young singers understand that they are both very different from and very similar to other children who love to sing. And they learn that where they call home may be quite similar to or quite different from where young singers from another culture call home. Simple things, such as how a shower operates, what a refrigerator looks like, if ice is readily available, what foods are eaten, or which eating utensils are used, may be very different from what they experience at home. And yet, all the young singers have a common language: music. Friendships are formed regardless of language barriers. Photographs of home, family, and pets are shared, games are played, songs are sung for each other, and communication is facilitated. When sharing music, cultural boundaries do not exist. Providing enriching musical experiences for young singers away from home makes borders invisible.

Musical artistry is not a privilege for the few, but a necessity for all.
—ROBERT SHAW

13

IN THE WORDS OF OTHERS

THROUGHOUT LIFE'S JOURNEY we are influenced by others. From the mother whose love of music nurtures a talent, to the teacher who inspires, to the choir that has a transcendental moment while singing, to being challenged to the depths of our cores—these are the things that shape us as human beings. Often it is a nurturing spirit, a kind hand, a faithful friend, a word of encouragement, or a nudge from others that gives us the courage to take steps we never thought possible. The influence of others is profound.

Part of being human is learning about ourselves and the world around us, aspiring to dreams, making dreams a reality, and handling the many challenges that life presents. Without others, we are incomplete. Creating music, making music, and encountering the beauty of choral singing as a performer or listener are elemental to the supporting structures that allow choral singing to occur. Singing is basic to humanity and culture.

Distinguished colleagues were invited to offer their thoughts about children's choirs. Each was asked to write about one of two topics: why organizational excellence is as important as striving for musical excellence or the importance of children's choirs for the future of choral singing in America. The following essays were written by composers, conductors, symphony orchestra conductors, an organizational consultant, and leaders in the choral field who have influenced many through their life's work.

TOPIC 1: WHY ORGANIZATIONAL EXCELLENCE IS AS IMPORTANT AS STRIVING FOR MUSICAL EXCELLENCE IN SCHOOL, CHURCH, AND COMMUNITY CHOIRS.

Tom Hall

America is a country of doers, and choral singing is something we do with great passion and frequency. Nearly 20 percent of all households in America include someone who has performed publicly in a chorus in the last twelve months. From *American Idol* to *The*

Voice, we seem to have an insatiable interest in singing and those who sing. College campuses are rife with a cappella groups, and high school music teachers report that *Glee* has inspired a renaissance of interest in vocal music. Singing isn't just fun, it's hip.

The cornerstone of any successful performing arts organization is a commitment to artistic excellence. There is simply no reason to go to the trouble of rehearsing and funding a chorus that isn't going to sing well. This is particularly important for a children's chorus. A child who sings in a good chorus learns not only lessons in music-making, but also important lessons in life-living. She learns what it means to work cooperatively. She learns to focus on the task at hand. She learns when it's appropriate to be out front and when it's best to be in the background. She learns that skills are developed over time, and she learns the delight of improving. She learns that in a group, if everyone does her part, the result is greater than anything any individual could create.

Successful children's choruses, like successful adult choruses and orchestras, have a culture of excellence that imbues every endeavor of the organization. That culture is established and advanced by the director and the musical staff, and that same culture must permeate all that the board and administrative staff do as well. Creativity and imagination should be as important to boards and administrators as they are to artistic directors. Resources are limited. Time is tight. People are busy. The challenges of keeping an organization fiscally sound need to be addressed by a thoughtful, committed governance and management team. Boards need to govern according to best practices. Administrators must be responsible, cooperative, supportive stewards of the organization's resources. Parents and members of the community should see the same model of excellence in the way an organization is run that the children experience in rehearsals and performances. It is hard to imagine that an organization that is sloppy and amateurish in its approach to its fiscal and organizational structure can be committed to excellence in it artistic work. And there are plentiful examples, across North America and beyond, of children's choruses who embrace excellence as a fundamental tenet of all aspects of their work, and whose contribution to the cultural lives of their communities is invaluable.

Our children learn a lot when they are part of a hardworking group of like-minded kids who have fun when they perform beautifully. And those opportunities for learning and growth are made possible when the organizations they sing with are transparent, strategic, and systemically sound. Excellence begins on the stage, but it shouldn't stop there.

Ann Howard Jones

Some organizational factors for the conductor to consider that will help ensure the highest quality performance:

- *Repertoire*. Choose excellent music that employs the most appropriate range, dynamics, tone color, and text for the ensemble, music that helps the singers acquire sophisticated skills and taste, and music in which the conductor believes.

- *Responsibility*. Share the work. The conductor has exclusive responsibility for solving conducting/musical problems, but the success of the group depends on the attention to other details too, and some responsibilities can be effectively shared (setting up chairs, taking roll, making announcements, organizing trips, etc.).
- *Rules*. Establish expectations clearly and firmly, and make sure everyone knows them.
- *Rehearsal Planning*. Know the score. Musical structure, harmonic and rhythmic complexities, mental and vocal demands on the singers, and places of tension and release both in the music and in the rehearsal require study and affect the way the rehearsals unfold.
- *Effective Rehearsal Techniques*. Spend time on vocal training, sight-reading, language precision, and all the other technical issues of bringing the music to life. The pacing of the rehearsal, the understanding of the time it takes to master the music, and the ability of the conductor to employ humor when appropriate are of critical importance.

Donald Neuen

Organizational excellence is a necessary ingredient in building a choral program because artistic endeavors based on a foundation of chaos never materialize in a successful, artistic manner. As Robert Shaw once told me, "Our music will always be a reflection of our lives." Therefore, if the surrounding entities are disorganized, the music will surely reflect that. There is a scripture that reads: "God is not the author of confusion; let all things be done decently and in order."

Furthermore, artists—due to their basic right-brained instincts—are a bit inclined to be disorganized and need to pay special attention to efforts of organization and order. If help is needed, through assistants in the program—whether they be student volunteers or parent volunteers—by all means get them.

Advertising for and holding auditions must be effective and sensitively carried out in a consistent manner. Rehearsal rooms must be neat, clean, well-lit, and orderly. Singers must have their own individual music (not sharing), marking the directions of the conductor and then following them. Posture and personal behavior must be professional—for singers of any age. Rehearsals and concert details must be well planned, short and long range, in advance so everyone (including parents) knows what to expect and when to expect it.

Spend time—hours—planning and organizing. Only then will vocal artistry and expressive musicality thrive on a sure and solid foundation.

Nick Page

The Chicago Children's Choir is an example of a choir that has remained true to its twin goals of musical excellence and cultural diversity since its founding. I had the honor of being a conductor with the Chicago Children's Choir in the early 1980s. Their founder, the Reverend Christopher Moore, was still alive and full of the same fire and compassion that impelled him to found the children's choir in 1956. The choir was born of the Civil Rights era and for over fifty years, through many changes and much growth, they have remained committed to their twin goals of creating the highest standards in performance while representing the true diversity, both racially and economically, of the city of Chicago.

The chorus's staff now teaches over 3,000 students in fifty Chicago public schools, actually going into the schools and teaching children to read music and sing with great beauty and heart. From these schools, the more talented and highly charged students are drawn into eight different neighborhood after-school programs throughout the city. These programs are the true heart of the choir. They tour and routinely perform throughout the city. From these eight satellite choirs, the middle and high school age singers are drawn into a top concert choir that records professionally and performs for dignitaries like Nelson Mandela, President Clinton, and many others. At their fiftieth anniversary, I met alumni who went back to the early days of the choir. They were thrilled to see that the goals of the choir's founder and of the many conductors who had served since were still alive today.

David Patrick

Organizational excellence is an essential component of any successful venture and a key component of a successful choral program. The choral conductor's ability to accomplish musical excellence is inextricably linked to how successfully the mechanics of the organization are handled. Some conductors are fortunate enough to possess excellent organizational and musical skills. Others understand the need to secure that individual who exhibits the attention to detail, discipline, follow-through, and big-picture vision needed to keep the organization healthy and moving forward. All musicians, novice to pro, function on a more creative level when calendars are up to date, music is ordered and prepped, communication is clear, and ongoing and financial matters receive the necessary oversight and attention.

A first step should involve turning your vision into a mission and/or action statement. What is the goal? How do you get there? Brainstorm these basic questions, then refine and craft your answers into a workable statement. Practical questions should be answered next: Where will the choir rehearse? When will the choir rehearse? How many singers do we need/want/dream of? Financial questions that need to be answered will present themselves at each step of the process. A budget will need to be created that covers both income and expenses. What revenue sources are currently available? Corporations, arts organizations, and local businesses often contribute to community and civic organizations. Will there be a participation fee? Will there be a formal board of directors? Those choruses that have a clear mission and financial plan usually fare best.

Parents are one of your greatest resources. A formal parent organization should be formed in tandem with the choir. Establish responsibilities, form committees, empower, encourage, and lead.

Patrick Dupré Quigley

There is an underlying truth when it comes to performers: The difference between a superstar and a starving artist is marketing. Whether it be a singer or a painter, this maxim holds true—the most talented author, who is unable to find a way to publish his or her work, is forever forced to place an adjective in front of his or her profession: *aspiring* author, *unpublished* writer, *amateur* poet. Without dissemination of work, without the broadcasting of new thought or sound, the artist remains a dilettante. The same is true for any arts organization, and doubly true for a chorus.

As choral musicians, we do not have a page on which to write or a canvas on which to paint; rather, our canvas is the ear of the listener. The listener is essential to our art. Therefore, finding the listener is the primary charge of the organization behind the chorus. The excellent organization is able to locate potential listeners and communicate to them what they will experience, thereby assuring an outlet for the creative process of the choral artist.

Organizational excellence is not a bonus to a top-level ensemble: It is a necessity. Without the backing of an efficiently operating organization that brings in an audience, the ensemble is forever limited in its scope.

Sherry Schiller

Founders of children's choruses are naturally driven by their artistic vision. In the beginning, they may be able to create magic without charters, board meetings, strategic plans, budgets, or clarity about roles and responsibilities.

Over time, however, organizations cannot live on vision alone. In order to continue to flourish, organizational order must be intentionally created to nurture artistic vision. The purpose of strategic planning should be to define artistic vision and then align the most effective programs, structures, and processes to achieve it. (Please refer to Figure 13.1).

Leaders of children's choruses must be sure that every decision they make builds organizational order that advances their artistic vision. When the programs, structures, and systems they create support their artistic vision (see figure 13.1), they open the floodgates to unimaginable innovation, audience delight, and sustainability.

Gregg Smith

You cannot have musical excellence without having organizational excellence because organizational excellence enables you to do the music to the best of your ability.

In 1967, the Gregg Smith Singers (GSS) and Texas Boys Choir (TBC) recorded four albums of Gabrieli in the place for which the music was written, the Basilica of San Marco in Venice, Italy. Months of preparation involved choosing, copying, and preparing the music. George Bragg prepared the children and I prepared the adults. Once together, the challenge was to unify the sound—the boys working with the GSS men,

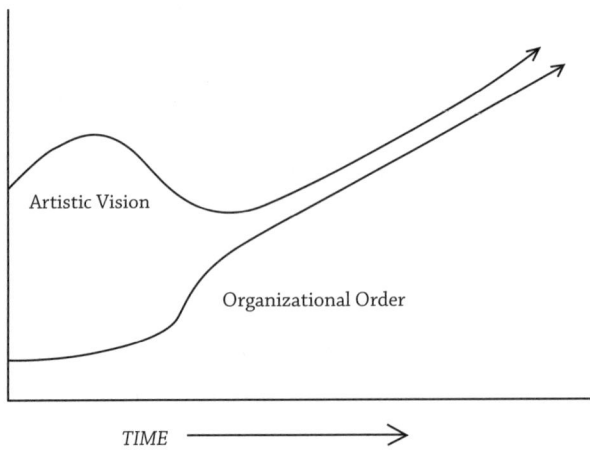

FIGURE 13.1 **Artistic Vision—Organization Order Chart**

the GSS women supporting the boy soprano sound. We worked first in a rehearsal room and later in the complex acoustic of San Marco, where the glorious cathedral sound wrapped around us, carrying us and showing us the correct tempi and final space separation—choirs and brass in balconies, conductor on the floor below, and organ elevated on a special platform. Because of tourists in the cathedral during daytime hours, the ten-day recording sessions began after 9:00 P.M. and often continued until 3:00 A.M.

To be rewarded with a Grammy for this incredible musical journey, and to have these recordings still considered groundbreaking after almost half a century, was and is one of the most satisfying aspects of the whole project. Think of the forces that were involved: GSS, TBC, the Edward Tarr Brass Ensemble, John McClure and all his associates at Columbia Records, E. Power Biggs, and the cathedral itself. That was organizational excellence making the music happen!

TOPIC 2: WHY CHILDREN'S CHOIRS IN SCHOOLS, CHURCHES, AND COMMUNITIES ARE IMPORTANT FOR SUSTAINING THE FUTURE OF CHORAL SINGING IN AMERICA.

Ann Meier Baker

The vast majority of those who sing in adult choruses today started singing as young children, so it is obvious that, without opportunities for young people to sing in schools, in places of worship, and in independent choruses, the future of tomorrow's choruses is in question.

But the most compelling case for choral music is how choruses enrich their whole communities. In a time when society is more and more fragmented and people are feeling increasingly isolated, choral singing provides a powerful means of shared expression that brings people together. By pointing out the value of singing with regard to broader issues of concern in our world, we make choirs relevant—even to those decision-makers who may not have experienced the beauty and power of choral music firsthand.

Tens of millions of children and adults sing in hundreds of thousands of choruses of all kinds in North America. Arm yourself with data (available from Chorus America and others) about the value of singing for communities and help keep choral music the most popular form of participation in the performing arts.

Shawn Crouch

A lifelong relationship with music begins from the moment an infant hears the soothing voice of his mother. The melodic risings and fallings of her voice are his first communications with the outside world. As children grow older, they learn language through songs. They play and experiment with sounds of words that lead to phonic awareness. Over time, children will lose their relationship to singing if it is not continued in some part of their lives, and they will break their natural voice/ear connection. As these young students grow into mature adults, they may feel that they do not have the ability to sing. They forget the joy of making music with their voices.

But the young child who is raised in a world full of singing as part of games, religious services, assemblies, and ensembles knows that singing is as natural as speaking. He or she will not shy away from using his or her voice as an instrument, and most important, he or she will continue to have a lifelong relationship with music as a performer and listener. To keep the choral tradition alive in America, we must create choirs for all age levels of children and encourage their participation in them.

Daniel Hege

The ability to respond instinctively to music appears to be present in children very early in life, similar to the way they already have the mental capacities for language. It is incumbent on us, as adults, especially those who are involved in the arts as a vocation or avocation, to help cultivate this musical instinct. Being part of a children's chorus in a school, church, or broader community enables young people to have the opportunity to encounter at least two major life lessons, musical and nonmusical, that can be carried into maturity:

1. If young people acquire musical skills early on, they will be better enabled to enjoy the great art of music throughout their lives, in any capacity.
2. Young people will encounter the rich diversity of talents, cultures, religions, etc., that are often part of a children's choir experience—and this is a microcosm of society at large. Learning to be a good citizen in this environment is natural because ensemble singing, in most cases, helps to ensure a level of "equality," where everyone is held to a high standard of musical justice, regardless of personal differences.

Children's choirs are often the catalyst to light the fire within young people, which helps to ensure the future of choral singing in America.

Libby Larsen

Our culture is, in the best and most challenging way, perpetually fluid, constantly mixing and remixing ideas, beliefs, and traditions in pursuit of what it means to be American. As a nation of many cultures, we make a daily leap of faith that the Many are in concert as One, and vice versa.

We are a culture built on the leap of faith that we can organize ourselves to practice fluidity and change while we progress and produce objects that are lasting and valuable to us.

To my way of thinking, when a chorus gathers to sing and takes its collective breath anticipating the downbeat of the conductor, it is a living metaphor for the leap of faith we experience as a culture. There is no scientific reason a chorus should arrive precisely together on any downbeat or come in together after a rest or cutoff together. None at all—yet it happens. When many choristers sing as one, it is brilliant and beautiful in its practice of unity in the presence of possible chaos. What could be more symbolic and more real than the cooperation of choristers displaying this leap of faith over and over again on each beat of each measure of each piece of music?

I would put it this way: Choral singing is important to the future of America. Children's choirs are important to choral singing.

Jim Papoulis

The importance of making a positive influence in a young person's life is too often underestimated. Exposure to art, humanity, and kindness are essential parts of helping anyone become a responsible, caring, and evolved individual. Because of an overwhelming trend in today's society to move away from the stimulation of art as a means of development, this becomes increasingly difficult.

The opportunity to participate in a choir is a wonderfully fulfilling and effective way to introduce anyone to the joys of art, collaboration, and creativity.

The concept of understanding that activities in life are not just an end result, but an ongoing process, is slowly becoming extinct in our society. Instant gratification is becoming the norm for today's youth, and it is essential to maintain a means to explore an activity that promotes the element of a process that takes time.

A choir does just that: learning music, experiencing harmony, being part of something larger than oneself, working with others, and experiencing learning in small steps. This art will be lost as programs are cut, and emphasis is placed on purely academic stimuli. There is no way to quantify the depth of development that singing can contribute to a young person. Choir directors and educators have a very important task to keep this wonderful forum alive for our youth for years to come.

Alice Parker

I think we are the only society in the world where families do not sing together every day, where people don't join in song at work and at play, at births and weddings and funerals. Songs are the language of the heart. They express our innermost feelings and share them with others. It's not just the future of choral singing in America that is at stake: It is our society, which is founded on the sense of community that is so wonderfully strengthened when we sing. *All* children should sing!

Doreen Rao

The future of choral singing in America is now.

The vision we shared thirty years ago has taken root in the exceptional work of hundreds of conductors and choral teachers leading young choirs today. Many of our new generation of choral leaders sang in community children's choir programs like the Glen Ellyn Children's Chorus (Anima), the Toronto Children's Chorus, and the Chicago Children's Choir, to name only a few. Today, the next generation of choral leadership is taking the inspiration of their youthful singing experiences to the next level of artistic achievement, educational innovation, and social change across North America.

While speaking recently at a conference at Yale University, I met a young violinist, a Yale alumna and former singer with the Glen Ellyn Children's Chorus. She announced to the conference that her life took its direction through the inspirational experience she'd had as a young chorister in Glen Ellyn. Michelle's story is common throughout North America as community, school, and church choirs dedicated to children and youth engage and inspire musicianship and social sensitivity through a diverse and distinctive choral repertoire.

Some of the most exceptional and innovative performance and educational initiatives today derive from choral programs dedicated to the musical experience of children and youth. These organizations have made an impact not only on the children for whom they exist, but on the communities they serve. Children's choirs define the future of our profession and the humanity of our culture. The future of choral singing in America is now.

Sandra Snow

The children's choir movement in North America has steadfastly challenged stereotypes associated with music-making by children. Community-based children's choirs largely comprise elementary and middle level singers, and the superior vocalism and development of musicianship of signature programs continue to set the standard for the music-making capabilities of these young artists. Factor in the most active commissioning and engagement efforts with living composers in the profession, and community-based children's choirs have in many ways led growth in the choral art.

We cannot deny, however, the luxury of a community-based, tuition-driven program, with largely supportive and engaged parents, and the tremendous advantage of a pool of singers eager and motivated to participate. Our public school colleagues are subject to increasingly difficult working conditions that include systemic budget cuts resulting in fewer hours of contact, as well as a lessening importance in an educational environment concerned with high-stakes testing and accountability.

The future of community-based children's choirs in North America must include an intimate assessment of local needs and a commitment to partnership and meaningful engagement. There are challenges to be faced, particularly the charge of elitism that stems from programs that serve those who can best afford the experience. Finding points of access that allow a greater proportion of the local population to participate is a starting point.

Access, however, is the tip of the iceberg. Community-based programs must strive to find cultural relevance in a way that honors the special and unique aspects of the community in which the program resides. Partnership requires a deep commitment to listening and action, and often requires participants on both sides to step outside the comfort and safety of the familiar.

I learned this lesson intimately when the Glen Ellyn Children's Chorus instituted an outreach program to communities we were not actively serving. It became immediately obvious that I did not have the tools to make the needed connection. I remember feeling inadequate and self-serving as I tried to use the same approaches that I did in our regular rehearsal setting. I had not taken the time to talk with area teachers. I had not sought out the desires of parents and families. I did not understand families that didn't bring their children to rehearsal regularly. In short, I failed a group of children in great need of mentorship and a transforming experience.

Community-based children's choirs *can* support both public school programs and the local, situated needs of the community by growing their understanding of how to connect and partner effectively. There are strong models, both inside and outside of music, that can lead the way. Community-based children's choirs are more relevant and needed than ever, and it resides within the imagination of the organization to foster healthy and ongoing relationships with the communities in their stead.

CONTRIBUTOR BIOGRAPHIES

Ann Meier Baker is president and CEO of Chorus America. Prior to joining the Chorus America staff in 2000, she held leadership positions at the National School Boards Association Foundation, the League of American Orchestras, and the National Association for Music Education.

Shawn Crouch is an award-winning composer, conductor, and educator. He is the founding director of Seraphic Fire's Miami Choral Academy, a tuition-free after-school music program for students and their families from underserved communities of Miami-Dade County.

Tom Hall is the music director of the Baltimore Choral Arts Society and a host on WYPR Radio, the NPR affiliate in Baltimore, Maryland. He also serves on the faculty of Goucher College.

Daniel Hege is the music director of the Wichita Symphony Orchestra and was the music director of the Syracuse Symphony Orchestra from 1999 to 2011. Mr. Hege guest-conducts frequently throughout the United States and abroad, and he has served on the faculties of Syracuse University and Roosevelt University.

Ann Howard Jones is professor of conducting at Boston University, where she conducts the Chamber Chorus and the Symphonic Chorus and teaches graduate conducting. She is recognized nationally and internationally for her work in healthy singing, conducting pedagogy, score preparation, and rehearsal techniques.

Libby Larsen is one of America's most performed living composers, with a catalogue of over four hundred works spanning virtually every genre from intimate vocal and chamber music to massive orchestral works and over twelve operas. Grammy Award-winning and widely recorded, with more than fifty CDs of her work, she is highly sought after for commissions and premieres by major artists, ensembles, and orchestras around the world, and is establishing a permanent place for her works in the concert repertory.

Donald Neuen, former assistant conductor for Robert Shaw and professor of conducting with the Eastman School of Music, has been the director of choral activities for UCLA since 1993 and the minister of music for the internationally televised Crystal Cathedral from 2000 to 2010. A featured guest conductor in Europe, Asia, Mexico, Canada, and nearly every state in the United States, his main emphases have been the performance of major works for chorus and orchestra and the development of collegiate graduate conducting (M.M. and D.M.A.) programs.

Nick Page is a Boston-based composer, conductor, and author best known for his song leading. He is the author of three books and has more than eighty published choral works.

Jim Papoulis composes music from many genres and is known for work that combines contemporary, classical, and world sounds and rhythms, writing for choirs, orchestras, films, dance, and artists of many genres. He has made significant contributions to choral music by revitalizing the choral repertoire with songs that fuse classical, world, and contemporary styles, and firmly believes that music can heal, educate, celebrate, and empower the humanity in all of us.

Alice Parker has for six decades earned her living as a composer, conductor, and teacher of vocal and choral music. She has written in forms from folk song to opera, conducted groups from symphonic choruses to church congregations, and taught at all levels of age and ability. She believes that all the world should sing.

David Patrick was president and owner of Keynote Arts Associates from 2000 until 2012, where he led a talented staff in the creation and production of exceptional choral events and festivals. As a much-sought-after conductor, music director, vocal coach, and accompanist, Patrick has filled these roles for the Walt Disney Company since 1981. He is a member of the adjunct faculty in the department of theatre and dance at

Rollins College in Winter Park, Florida, where he served as chapel organist from 1999 to 2002.

Patrick Dupré Quigley is the twice Grammy-nominated founder and artistic director of Seraphic Fire and the Firebird Chamber Orchestra. He is the recipient of Chorus America's Louis Botto Award for Innovative Action and Entrepreneurial Zeal, as well as the National Endowment for the Arts/Chorus America Robert Shaw Conducting Fellowship.

Doreen Rao has changed the landscape of choral music education in America. Her seminal work as a conductor and master teacher fostered the children's choir movement and inspired a generation of conductors and teachers to lead young choirs in schools and communities around the world. Toronto music critic Robert Everett-Green wrote: "For her, every note has an urgent meaning, not just within the composition, but within the wider world."

Sherry Schiller, founder and president of the nonprofit organization Schiller Center for Connective Change, has been helping people and organizations around the world work with greater purpose and harmony for more than twenty years. A world-renowned expert on organizational culture, Schiller has developed an approach to strategic planning that has helped many nonprofits clarify their unique identities and deliver effective programs that demonstrate their value. She has been a consultant for many choral organizations, as well as Chorus America.

Gregg Smith, founder of the Gregg Smith Singers in 1955, has written more than four hundred compositions ranging from choral music to operas and is a founding member of Chorus America. Referred to by the *New York Times* as "one of the great choral conductors of our time," Smith and his professional vocal ensemble have recorded more than one hundred albums, won three Grammy Awards, and toured throughout the world.

Sandra Snow is professor of choral conducting and music education at Michigan State University. She interacts with undergraduate and graduate students in conducting pedagogy, teacher training, and as conductor of the MSU Women's Chamber Ensemble.

> *The circle is complete
> when the creator, performer, and listener
> are made one through song.*
> —ALICE PARKER

14

SUGGESTED TREBLE REPERTOIRE

REPERTOIRE IS THE heart and soul of the music-making of a choir. Once the organizational structure is in place for the choir, the singing begins. What the artist-teacher chooses for the young singers to sing, study, practice, analyze, and perform in classroom, festival, school, church, or community choirs may reflect a variety of languages, styles, cultures, and musical challenges. This chapter's repertoire list is a small sampling of the possibilities for treble choirs. (See chapter 7 for a discussion of the music library and the structural analysis of a score.)

The approximately seven hundred titles are listed alphabetically by voicing, composer/arranger, title, and publisher. They reflect many cultures, styles, and periods of choral music. Whether sharing the simplest song with the youngest singers or challenging older singers, it all starts with a song. And for our singers, we must always share music of excellent quality.

UNISON

Composer	Title	Publisher
Adler, Samuel, arr.	The Chanukah Story	Oxford University Press
Anderson, W. H.	In the Barnyard's Southerly Corner	Gordon V. Thompson Music
Anderson, W. H.	The Piper and the Chiming Peas	Gordon V. Thompson Music
Armstrong, Kathy	Songs from Gahu	Boosey & Hawkes
Bach, Johann Sebastian	Come, Together Let Us Sing	E. C. Schirmer Music Co. Inc.
Bach, Johann Sebastian	Et exultavit	Oxford University Press
Bach, Johann Sebastian	Rejoice, O My Spirit	G. Schirmer, Inc.
Bach, Johann Sebastian	Two Cradle Hymns	Alliance Music Publications, Inc.

Composer	Title	Publisher
Bach, Johann Sebastian (Doreen Rao, ed.)	Bist du bei mir	Boosey & Hawkes
Bach, Johann Sebastian (S. Calvert, arr.)	Bist du bei mir	Gordon V. Thompson Music
Bacon, Denise	How Can I Keep from Singing?	Alliance Music Publications, Inc.
Bacon, Denise	Wondrous Night	Kodály Center of America
Bacon, Ellen (Ernst Bacon, arr.)	Let Me Be Your Friend	Oxford University Press
Bacon, Ernst	Sourwood Mountain	Delborn Music Publ. Co.
Bacon, Ernst, setting	Ye Shepherds, Leave Your Flocks	Oxford University Press
Baynon, Arthur	Mrs. Jenny Wren	Boosey & Hawkes
Berg, Ken, arr.	This Little Light of Mine	Colla Voce Music, Inc.
Bernstein, Leonard	Simple Song (from *Mass*)	Boosey & Hawkes
Bernstein, Leonard	There Is a Garden (from *Trouble in Tahiti*)	Boosey & Hawkes
Binkerd, Gordon	An Evening Falls (from *Sung Under the Silver Umbrella*)	Boosey & Hawkes
Boole, Roy	The Owl and the Pussycat	Gordon V. Thompson Music
Boshkoff, Ruth	I Will Bring You Brooches	Boosey & Hawkes
Brahms, Johannes (Jean Ashworth Bartle, ed.)	Wiegenlied (Lullaby)	Hinshaw Music, Inc.
Brahms, Johannes (Mary Goetze, ed.)	Marienwürmchen (Lady Bug)	Boosey & Hawkes
Britten, Benjamin	Friday Afternoons, Op. 7 (collection of 12 songs)	Boosey & Hawkes
Britten, Benjamin	Oliver Cromwell	Boosey & Hawkes
Britten, Benjamin	The Sally Gardens	Boosey & Hawkes
Britten, Benjamin	The Birds	Boosey & Hawkes
Broughton, Marilyn	No Mouth	Gordon V. Thompson Music
Broughton, Marilyn	Nursery Rhyme Nonsense	Gordon V. Thompson Music
Brunner, David L.	On Christmas Morn	Boosey & Hawkes
Brunner, David L.	Winter Changes	Boosey & Hawkes
Burleigh, H. T.	Steal Away	Belwin-Mills Publishing Corp.

Composer	Title	Publisher
Caldwell, Paul, and Sean Ivory, arr.	Ani ma'amin	Earthsongs
Carter, Andrew	Bless the Lord	Oxford University Press
Cary, Henry (Doreen Rao, ed.)	Spring Morning	Boosey & Hawkes
Cockshott, Gerald, arr.	Three French Carols	Robertson Publications
Coghlan, Michael	December's Rose	Gordon V. Thompson Music
Cohen, Gerald	Adonai roi lo echsar (Psalm 23)	Transcontinental Music Publications
Copland, Aaron, arr.	At the River (from *Old American Songs*, Set II)	Boosey & Hawkes
Copland, Aaron, arr.	The Boatman's Dance	Boosey & Hawkes
Copland, Aaron, arr.	Ching-a-Ring Chaw (Minstrel Song)	Boosey & Hawkes
Crawley, Clifford	The Penguin Dance	Leslie Music Supply, Inc.
Daley, Eleanor	And God Shall Wipe Away All Tears	Hinshaw Music, Inc.
Daley, Eleanor	Sweet Was the Song the Virgin Sang	Hinshaw Music, Inc.
Daley, Eleanor	The Birds	Gordon V. Thompson Music
Davies, Peter Maxwell	Kirkwall Shopping Songs	Boosey & Hawkes
DeLong, Richard	Lullaby, Oh Lullaby	ECS Publishing
Dinkin, Jonathan	Mi chamocha	Boosey & Hawkes
DiOrio, Dominick	My Shadow	Roger Dean/The Lorenz Corporation
Dolloff, Lori-Anne	A Great Big Sea	Boosey & Hawkes
Dolloff, Lori-Anne	She's Like the Swallow	Boosey & Hawkes
Dolloff, Lori-Anne	Manx Lullaby	Boosey & Hawkes
Ebel-Sabo, Victoria	Wind on the Hill	Boosey & Hawkes
Enns, Leonard	Sing Me a Song	Gordon V. Thompson Music
Fauré, Gabriel	Pie Jesu (from *Requiem*)	Boosey & Hawkes
Floyd, Carlisle	Rain	Boosey & Hawkes
Goetze, Mary	Dormi Dormi (Sweetly Slumber)	Boosey & Hawkes
Goetze, Mary	The Little Birch Tree	Boosey & Hawkes
Green, A. H., arr.	Little Bull	Oxford University Press
Grieg, Edvard (Henry Leck, arr.)	The Last Spring (Varen)	Plymouth Music Company, Inc.

Composer	Title	Publisher
Gritton, Eric	Welcome, Yule	E. C. Schirmer Music Co. Inc.
Grundman, Clare	Zoo Illogical	Boosey & Hawkes
Handel, G. F. (Doreen Rao, ed.)	Where'er You Walk	Boosey & Hawkes
Handel, G. F. (Doreen Rao, ed.)	How Beautiful Are the Feet of Them	Boosey & Hawkes
Handel, G. F. (Doreen Rao, ed.)	Oh Let the Merry Bells Ring	Boosey & Hawkes
Handel, G. F. (H. Clough-Leighter, ed.)	Where'er You Walk	E. C. Schirmer Music Co. Inc.
Handel, G. F. (Jean Bartle, ed.)	Art Thou Troubled?	Hinshaw Music, Inc.
Hatfield, Stephen	Blonde in a Black Skirt	Alliance Music Publications, Inc.
Henderson, Ruth Watson	À la ferme	Gordon V. Thompson Music
Henderson, Ruth Watson	A Tree Toad (and Lone Dog)	Gordon V. Thompson Music
Henderson, Ruth Watson	Bless the Lord, O My Soul	Hinshaw Music, Inc.
Henderson, Ruth Watson	Don't Ever Squeeze a Weasel (and The Boar and the Dromedar)	Gordon V. Thompson Music
Henderson, Ruth Watson	Eletelephony (and The Wise Frogs)	Gordon V. Thompson Music
Henderson, Ruth Watson	Four Is Wonderful (and My Dreams)	Gordon V. Thompson Music
Henderson, Ruth Watson	The Donkey and the Barn Owl	Gordon V. Thompson Music
Henderson, Ruth Watson	You'll Never Guess What I Saw	Gordon V. Thompson Music
Hess, Juliet	By the Sea	Boosey & Hawkes
Holst, Gustav	I Vow to Thee My Country	G. Schirmer/Curwen
Holst, Gustav	The Saviour of the World Is Born (from *Four English Carols*)	Treble Clef Music Press
Ives, Charles	A Christmas Carol	Merion Music, Inc.
Ives, Charles	The Circus Band (from *The Ives Collection*)	Peer Southern
Ives, Charles	Memories (from *The Ives Collection*)	Peer Southern

Composer	Title	Publisher
Ives, Charles	On the Counter (from *The Ives Collection*)	Peer Southern
Ives, Charles	Serenity (from *The Ives Collection*)	Peer Southern
Ives, Charles	Side Show (from *The Ives Collection*)	Peer Southern
Ives, Charles, compiled by Barbara Tagg	*The Ives Collection: Five Songs by Charles E. Ives*	Peer International Corp.
Jergenson, Dale	Quiet Silence	Laurendale Associates
Kabalevsky, Dmitri (Doreen Raom, arr.)	Good Night, a Russian Song	Boosey & Hawkes
Kallman, Daniel	The Mending Song	Mark Foster Music Co.
Kallman, Daniel	The Pasture (no. 1 of *Country Scenes*)	Mark Foster Music Co.
Kay, Ulysses	The Little Elf Man	Duchess Music Corp.
Lau, Robert C.	Run to the Manger	Hinshaw Music, Inc.
Miller, Mandy, arr.	Dream Angus	Boosey & Hawkes
Mourant, Walter	Gimme Some Jazz	Laurendale Associates
Mulholland, James Quitman	When I Lay Me Down to Sleep	Colla Voce Music, Inc.
Norton, Christopher	Music Makes Me Feel It More	Boosey & Hawkes
Núñez, Francisco J.	What the Grey-Winged Fairy Said	Boosey & Hawkes
Núñez, Francisco J., arr.	Three Dominican Folk Songs	Boosey & Hawkes
Ouchterlony, David	The Gentle Donkey	Leslie Music Supply, Inc.
Ouchterlony, David	On the Night When Jesus Was Born	Gordon V. Thompson Music
Page, Nick	Fairest Lady	Boosey & Hawkes
Page, Nick	*Sing with Us Songbook*	Hal Leonard
Parker, Alice	Christmas Stars	Choristers Guild
Parker, Alice	Hand Me Down Songs	GIA Publications, Inc.
Purvis, Richard	A Manger Carol	Harold Flammer, Inc.
Rachmaninoff, Sergei	Vocalise	Boosey & Hawkes
Raminsh, Imant	My Heart's Friend	Boosey & Hawkes
Ridout, Godfrey, arr.	Ah! Si mon moine voulait danser	Gordon V. Thompson Music
Rowley, Alec, arr.	Sleep My Baby (Suo Gan)	Boosey & Hawkes
Rutter, John	Jesus Child	Oxford University Press
Rutter, John	Nativity Carol	Oxford University Press

Composer	Title	Publisher
Rutter, John	Shepherd's Pipe Carol	Oxford University Press
Rutter, John	Star Carol	Oxford University Press
Scarlatti, Domenico (Henlenclair Lowe, arr.)	We Will Sing for Joy	Choristers Guild
Schram, Ruth Elaine	The Song that Nature Sings	BriLee Music Publishing Co.
Schubert, Franz	An die Musik	Boosey & Hawkes
Schubert, Franz	Der Musensohn	Gordon V. Thompson Music
Schubert, Franz	Fischerweise	Gordon V. Thompson Music
Schubert, Franz	Heidenröslein	Plymouth Music Company Inc.
Schubert, Franz	To Music (An die Musik)	Boosey & Hawkes
Schubert, Franz	To the Moon (An den Mond)	McGroarty Music Publishing
Shaw, Martin	The Song of the Music Makers	J. B. Cramer & Co., Ltd.
Smith, Gregg	Little Lamb (from *Songs of Innocence*)	G. Schirmer, Inc.
Sprenkle, Elam	A Farewell	Boosey & Hawkes
Stone, David	Space Travellers	Boosey & Hawkes
Tate, Phyllis, arr.	Three Moravian Carols	Oxford University Press
Telfer, Nancy	The Magi	Neil A. Kjos Music Co.
Telfer, Nancy	Mary Wondered What It Meant	Gordon V. Thompson Music
Thiman, Eric	A Carol of Peace	Boosey & Hawkes
Thiman, Eric	The Path to the Moon	Boosey & Hawkes
Tilley, Alexander	Our Very First Song	Boosey & Hawkes
Tilley, Alexander	Vagabond Song (from *Songs for the School Year*)	Leslie Music Supply, Inc.
Vaughan Williams, Ralph	God Bless the Master	Oxford University Press
Vaughan Williams, Ralph	Let Beauty Awake	Boosey & Hawkes
Vaughan Williams, Ralph	Linden Lea	Boosey & Hawkes
Vaughan Williams, Ralph	On Christmas Night	Galaxy Music Corp. (ECS)
Vaughan Williams, Ralph	Orpheus with His Lute	Oxford University Press
Vivaldi, Antonio (Janet Galván, ed.)	Domine Deus, Agnus Dei	Roger Dean Publishing Company
Vivaldi, Antonio (Janet Galván, ed.)	Et exultavit (from *Vivaldi for Treble Voices*)	Roger Dean Publishing Company

Suggested Treble Repertoire — 221

Composer	Title	Publisher
Walters, Edmund	A Child's Prayer at Christmas	Boosey & Hawkes
Warlock, Peter	What Cheer? Good Cheer!	Boosey & Hawkes
Watson, Ruth	Lullaby for the Christ Child	Gordon V. Thompson Music
Wetzler, Robert	Shepherds Come A-Running	Art Masters Studios
Wetzler, Robert	Still, Still, Still	Augsburg Publishing House
Whittemore, Joan, arr.	Pat-a-Pan	Boosey & Hawkes
Wiliams, Lyn	Ferry Me Across the Water	Boosey & Hawkes
Williams, Frances	Let There Be Music	Gordon V. Thompson Music
Williamson, Malcolm	Ode to Music	Boosey & Hawkes
Wolf, Hugo (Mary Goetze, ed.)	Mausfallen Sprüchlein (Moustrap Saying)	Boosey & Hawkes

CANON

Composer	Title	Publisher
Bacon, Ernst	Rest in the Mountains (from *Two Rounds*)	Oxford University Press
Bacon, Ernst	Sierra High Trip (from *Two Rounds*)	Cameo Music Publishing Co.
Bertaux, Betty	Thank You for the World So Sweet	Boosey & Hawkes
DeLassus, Rolande	Musica Dei donum optimi	Boosey & Hawkes
Forsblad, Leland	*Rounds for Beginning Choirs*	Pro Art Publications
Fulleylove, James, arr.	This Old Man	Oxford University Press
Jennings, Paul and Theresa	The Round Book	Jenson Publications
Mason, Lowell, and George J. Webb	A Dozen Rounds (from *Cantica laudis*)	Carl Fischer, Inc.
Mason, Lowell (Doreen Rao, ed.)	O Music	Boosey & Hawkes
Praetorius, Michael (Doreen Rao, ed.)	Jubilate Deo	Boosey & Hawkes
Praetorius, Michael (Wallace DePue, arr.)	Sing dem Herrn	Warner Bros. Publications

Composer	Title	Publisher
Rao, Doreen, arr.	Friendship Song (Czech canon)	Boosey & Hawkes
Rao, Doreen, arr.	Hashivenu	Boosey & Hawkes
Schuman, William	Caution	Merion Music, Inc.
Sharlin, William	Tzor te'udah	Laurendale Associates
Sleeth, Natalie	Go Now in Peace	Hinshaw Music, Inc.
Smith, Gregg	Fifteen Rounds by Gregg Smith	Laurendale Associates
Smith, Gregg	Now I Walk in Beauty (Canon/SATB)	G. Schirmer, Inc.
Sweelinck, J. P.	Vanitas, vanitatum	Boosey & Hawkes
Terri, Sali	*Rounds for Everyone from Everywhere*	Lawson-Gould Music Publishers, Inc.

TWO-PART TREBLE

Composer	Title	Publisher
Adams, Lydia	Mi'kmaq Honour Song	McGroarty Music Publishing
Ades, Hawley	Let There Be Peace on Earth	Shawnee Press, Inc.
Adler, Samuel	Who Can Retell?	Oxford University Press
Adolphe, Adam	Cantique de Noël, O Holy Night	Plymouth Music Company, Inc.
Agnestig, Carl-Bertil, arr.	Vem kan segla forutan vind? (Who Can Sail?)	Walton Music Corp.
Althouse, Jay	Bye Bye Blackbird	Alfred Publishing Co.
Atkinson, Conrad	Little Lamb	Galaxy Music Corp. (ECS)
Bach, Johann Sebastian	Christe eleison	Boosey & Hawkes
Bach, Johann Sebastian	Jesu, Joy of Man's Desiring	E. C. Schirmer Music Co. Inc.
Bach, Johann Sebastian	O Jesu, So Sweet	E. C. Schirmer Music Co. Inc.
Bach, Johann Sebastian	The Peasant Cantata	Paterson's Publishing, Ltd.
Bach, Johann Sebastian	Wir eilen mit schwachen, doch emsigen Schritten	E. C. Schirmer Music Co. Inc.
Bach, Johann Sebastian (Doreen Rao, ed.)	Domine Deus	Boosey & Hawkes

Composer	Title	Publisher
Bach, Johann Sebastian (Doreen Rao, ed.)	Duet (from Cantata no. 15)	Boosey & Hawkes
Bach, Johann Sebastian (Doreen Rao, ed.)	Duet (from Cantata no. 9)	Boosey & Hawkes
Bach, Johann Sebastian (Doreen Rao, ed.)	Duet (from Cantata no. 93)	Boosey & Hawkes
Bacon, Ernst	A Cradle Song	Lawson-Gould Music Publishers, Inc.
Bacon, Ernst	Bennington Riflemen	Boosey & Hawkes
Bacon, Ernst	Buttermilk Hill	Boosey & Hawkes
Bacon, Ernst	Mid Winter's Snow	Lawson-Gould Music Publishers, Inc.
Bacon, Ernst	Return of Spring	Lawson-Gould Music Publishers, Inc.
Bacon, Ernst	Years End (Fum, Fum, Fum)	Boosey & Hawkes
Bacon, Ernst, setting	Hold On	Oxford University Press
Bacon, Ernst, setting	Low Bridge	Oxford University Press
Bacon, Ernst, setting	The Infant Jesus	Oxford University Press
Bartók, Béla	Don't Leave Me	Boosey & Hawkes
Bartók, Béla	Six Children's Choruses	Boosey & Hawkes
Berger, Jean	Ah, Summer! (The Dragonfly)	Neil A. Kjos Music Co.
Berger, Jean	Oh, Spring! (The Caterpillar)	Neil A. Kjos Music Co.
Berger, Jean	The Bumblebee	Neil A. Kjos Music Co.
Bernon, Amy F.	I Am Music, Music Is Me	Roger Dean Publishing Company
Bernstein, Leonard	Gloria tibi (from *Mass*)	Boosey & Hawkes
Bertaux, Betty	Blossoms	Boosey & Hawkes
Bertaux, Betty	Esa noch yo baila (Come With Me, Let's Dance Tonight	Boosey & Hawkes
Bertaux, Betty	Pick a Bale of Cotton	Boosey & Hawkes
Bertaux, Betty	To Music	Boosey & Hawkes
Bertaux, Betty, arr.	I Had a Little Nut Tree	Boosey & Hawkes
Billings, William (Russell Robinson, arr.)	Alleluia on a Theme by William Billings	Warner Bros. Publications
Binkerd, Gordon	The Christ Child	Boosey & Hawkes
Bishop, Jeffrey	Tis Iver on a Visit	Brichtmark Music, Inc.

Composer	Title	Publisher
Bissell, Keith	When I Set Out for Lyonnesse	Gordon V. Thompson Music
Bouman, Paul	Three Rhymes—Set I	Earthsongs
Bouman, Paul	Three Rhymes—Set II	Earthsongs
Britten, Benjamin	A New Year Carol	Boosey & Hawkes
Britten, Benjamin	Rossini Suite (movement 2 and 5 for trebles)	Boosey & Hawkes
Britten, Benjamin	The Golden Vanity	Boosey & Hawkes
Brunner, David L.	Toucans Two	Boosey & Hawkes
Brunner, David L.	Earthsongs (three movements)	Boosey & Hawkes
Brunner, David L.	Hold Fast Your Dreams	Boosey & Hawkes
Brunner, David L.	Yo le canto todo el Dia	Boosey & Hawkes
Caldwell, Paul, and Sean Ivory	Grace Fell Like the Rain	www.caldwellandivory.com
Carter, John	Will You Walk a Little Faster	J. Fischer & Bros.
Chass, Blanche	Hanerot halalu (A Song for Hanukah)	Mark Foster Music Co.
Chen, Nira (Doreen Rao, arr.)	Dodi Li	Boosey & Hawkes
Chilcott, Bob	Can You Hear Me?	Oxford University Press
Chilcott, Bob	Farewell! Advent (and Hey Now)	Oxford University Press
Chilcott, Bob	Hey Now!	Oxford University Press
Chilcott, Bob	Like a Singing Bird	Oxford University Press
Chilcott, Bob	Mid-winter	Oxford University Press
Chilcott, Bob	Peace Mass	Oxford University Press
Chilcott, Bob	This Old Man	Hal Leonard
Chilcott, Bob	Two Singing Songs	Oxford University Press
Collins, Charles A.	Mary Had a Little Blues	Boosey & Hawkes
Copland, Aaron, arr.	At the River (Hymn Tune)	Boosey & Hawkes
Copland, Aaron, arr.	Simple Gifts (Shaker Song)	Boosey & Hawkes
Copland, Aaron, arr.	The Little Horses	Boosey & Hawkes
Curtright, Carolee R.	Listen, Shepherds, Listen	Choristers Guild
Daley, Eleanor	The Sugar Plum Tree	Alliance Music Publications, Inc.
Dalglish, Malcolm, arr.	Bye Oh Baby	Boosey & Hawkes
Davis, Katherine K.	Carol of the Drum	Belwin-Mills Publishing Corp.

Composer	Title	Publisher
Debussy, Claude	Noël des enfants qui n'ont plus de maison	Durand/Theodore Presser
Debussy, Claude	Salut printemps	Editions Choudens
DeCormier, Robert, arr.	The Erie Canal	Lawson-Gould Music Publishers, Inc.
Dennard, Brazeal W., arr.	Hush, Somebody's Callin' My Name	Shawnee Press, Inc.
Dilworth, Rollo A.	The Dream Keeper	Hal Leonard
Dufay, Guillaume	Trumpet Gloria	Mark Foster Music Co.
Dusing, David	The Riddle Song	Lawson-Gould Music Publishers, Inc.
Dvořák, Antonín (Robert Allen, arr.)	The Christmas Tree	Galleon Press Music Publisher
Dwyer, Ruth, and Judith Waller	Go Tell It on the Mountain	Colla Voce Music, Inc.
Dwyer, Ruth, arr.	El pequeño niño	Colla Voce Music, Inc.
Ebel-Sabo, Victoria	Miss Rumphius	Santa Barbara Music Publishing, Inc.
Ebel-Sabo, Victoria	The Trees Stand Shining	Boosey & Hawkes
Elliott, David J.	The Boston Trot (adapted American folk song)	Boosey & Hawkes
Elliott, David J., arr.	Jingle Bell Swing	Boosey & Hawkes
Elliott, David J., arr.	Lady Green Leaves	Boosey & Hawkes
Engdahl, Richard and Audrey (Lee Larsen, arr.)	Caterpillar	Kandinsky Music
Fauré, Gabriel	Holy, Holy, Holy (Sanctus)	HT Fitzsimmons Co. Music Publ.
Finkelstein, Meir (Rebecca Thompson, arr.)	L'dor vador	Hal Leonard
Finzi, Gerald	Ten Children's Songs	Boosey & Hawkes
Floyd, Carlisle	Long, Long Ago	Boosey & Hawkes
Franck, César (István Bogár, arr.)	Panis angelicus	Mark Foster Music Co.
Gerber, Thomas (Henry Leck, arr.)	Haida	Plymouth Music Company, Inc.
Glick, Saul Irving	Psalm Trilogy (Psalms 92, 47, and 23)	Earthsongs
Goemanne, Noel	Sing of America	Alliance Music Publications, Inc.
Goetze, Mary	Black Snake Wind	Boosey & Hawkes

Composer	Title	Publisher
Goetze, Mary	Glory to God	Boosey & Hawkes
Goetze, Mary, arr.	Ca' the Yowes	Boosey & Hawkes
Govedas, John E., arr.	I'se the B'y	Alfred Publishing Co.
Gray, Cynthia	Hush, My Babe	Heritage Music Press
Gretchaninoff, Alexandre	The Name Game	Musica Russica, Inc.
Grundman, Clare	Pat-a-Pan	Boosey & Hawkes
Grundman, Clare	Three Songs for Christmas	Boosey & Hawkes
Handel, G. F.	Oh Lovely Peace	Boosey & Hawkes
Handel, G. F.	Praise the King	Belwin-Mills Publishing Corp.
Harris, Robert A.	Little David, Play on Your Harp	Boosey & Hawkes
Harris, Robert A., arr.	This Little Light of Mine	Boosey & Hawkes
Hatch, Winnagene	Korean Carol Lullaby	Hal Leonard
Hatfield, Stephen	Camino, Caminante	Boosey & Hawkes
Hatfield, Stephen	Crimson, Ivory, Aquamarine	Boosey & Hawkes
Hatfield, Stephen	Foggy Birthday Shuffle	Hal Leonard
Hatfield, Stephen	Run Children Run	Boosey & Hawkes
Hatfield, Stephen	Two Minutes Before Sleep	Boosey & Hawkes
Heitzeg, Steve	O Colored Earth	Stone Circle Music
Hemberg, Eskel	The Alunda Song	Boosey & Hawkes
Henderson, Ruth Watson	Five Fat Fleas	Hinshaw Music, Inc.
Henderson, Ruth Watson	My Heart Soars	Hinshaw Music, Inc.
Henderson, Ruth Watson	Orange (from *Adventures in Color*)	Earthsongs
Henderson, Ruth Watson	Psalm 100	Hinshaw Music, Inc.
Henderson, Ruth Watson	Two Insect Songs—Fireflies and Whirligig Beetles	Earthsongs
Herrington, Judith (Sara Glick, arr.)	Hotaru, Koi (Fireflies)	Pavane Publishing
Herrington, Judith (Sara Glick, arr.)	Cherry Riddle Song	Pavane Publishing
Herrington, Judith (Sara Glick, arr.)	Dance Laddie	Pavane Publishing
Hirokawa, Joy Ondra, arr.	My Favorite Things	Hal Leonard
Hirsh, Nurit (V. Pasternak, arr.)	Bashana haba-a	Posthorn Press

Composer	Title	Publisher
Holst, Gustav	In the Bleak Midwinter	Plymouth Music Company, Inc.
Holst, Gustav	The Corn Song	E. C. Schirmer Music Co. Inc.
Howell, John Raymond, arr.	The Angel Gabriel	Boosey & Hawkes
Humperdinck, Engelbert	Prayer (from *Hansel and Gretel*)	G. Schirmer, Inc.
Jacobson, Joshua	Niggun	Transcontinental Music Publications
Jager, Robert	I Dream of Peace	Hal Leonard
Johnson, David N., arr.	The Lone Wild Bird	Augsburg Publishing House
Kabalevsky, Dmitri	One Fine Morning	MCA Music Publishing
Kemp, Helen	Prayer Litany	Choristers Guild
Kesselman, Lee R.	Shalom, Friends	Boosey & Hawkes
Kesselman, Lee R.	The Skye Boat Song	Boosey & Hawkes
Kesselman, Lee R., arr.	Ae Fond Kiss	Boosey & Hawkes
Kirk, Theron, arr.	Kling Glöckchen (Ring! Little Bells)	Pro Art Publications
Kodály, Zoltán	Christmas Dance of the Shepherds	Universal Edition
Kowalski, Crystal LaPoint	My Own Song	Hinshaw Music, Inc.
Kuzmenko, Larysa	Winds	Boosey & Hawkes
LaPoint, Crystal	Little Bird	Roger Dean Publishing Company
Lassus, Orlando de	Serve Bone	Mark Foster Music Co.
Lawson, Philip	Three English Madrigals	Boosey & Hawkes
Lewis, Aden G., arr.	African Noel	Plymouth Music Company, Inc.
Lightfoot, Mary Lynn	The Arrow and the Song	Heritage Music Press
Lübeck, Vincent	Christmas Cantata	Chantry Music Press
Luboff, Norman	A Capital Ship	Walton Music Corp.
MacGillivray, Allister, and Diane Loomer	Song for Peace	Cypress Publishing
MacGillivray, Allister (Lydia Adams, arr.)	Here's to Song	McGroarty Music Publishing
Mahler, Gustav	The Cuckoo, the Nightingale, and the Donkey	Oxford University Press
Mayo, Becki Slagle, arr.	Sing We Now of Christmas	Choristers Guild

Composer	Title	Publisher
Mendelssohn, Felix	Herbstlied (Autumn Song)	National Music Publishers
Messick, Pat	A Time for Singing	Alliance Music Publications, Inc.
Mezzogorri, Giovanni	Jubilate Deo (Sing to God)	Concordia Publishing House
Möller, Friedrich	The Happy Wanderer (Val-De-Ri Val-De Ra)	Sam Fox Publishing Co.
Mozart, W. A. (Maurice Gardner, arr.)	Two Mozart Canons (Ave Maria, The Weather Song)	Staff Music Pub. Co., Inc.
Mozart, W. A.	Laudate Dominum	Boosey & Hawkes
Mulholland, James Quitman	Diary of Dickinson	Colla Voce Music, Inc.
Naplan, Allan E.	Al shlosha d'varim	Boosey & Hawkes
Naplan, Allan E.	Hine ma tov	Boosey & Hawkes
Naplan, Allan E.	Let Me Know Beauty	Boosey & Hawkes
Naplan, Allan E.	Shiru	Boosey & Hawkes
Naplan, Allan E.	Sim shalom	Boosey & Hawkes
Nelson, Ron	Ask the Moon	Boosey & Hawkes
Neukomm, Sigismund (Doreen Rao, ed.)	Mass in C	Boosey & Hawkes
Niles, John Jacob	I Wonder as I Wander	G. Schirmer, Inc.
Norton, Christopher	In Praise of Music	Boosey & Hawkes
Norton, Christopher	Music in the Air	Boosey & Hawkes
Núñez, Francisco J.	Cantan	Boosey & Hawkes
Núñez, Francisco J.	De colores (All the Colors)	Boosey & Hawkes
Page, Nick	Baby Song of the Four Winds	Boosey & Hawkes
Page, Nick	She Shall Have Music	Boosey & Hawkes
Page, Nick	Sing and Shine On	Boosey & Hawkes
Page, Nick	Stars, Songs, Faces	Boosey & Hawkes
Page, Nick	The Holly and the Ivy	Boosey & Hawkes
Page, Nick, arr.	Bowling Green	Boosey & Hawkes
Page, Nick, arr.	Thula s'thandwa	Boosey & Hawkes
Papoulis, Jim	Kusimama	Boosey & Hawkes
Papoulis, Jim	Small Voices	Boosey & Hawkes
Parker, Alice	Irish Lullaby (from *Three Christmas Carols*)	Lawson-Gould Music Publishers, Inc.
Parker, Alice	The Children's Call for Peace	Treble Clef Music Press
Parker, Alice	Three Christmas Carols	Lawson-Gould Music Publishers, Inc.

Composer	Title	Publisher
Patriquin, Donald, arr.	J'entends le moulin (I Hear the Millwheel)	Earthsongs
Paulus, Stephen	All My Heart This Night Rejoices	Carl Fischer, Inc.
Paulus, Stephen	Hallelu!	European American Music Corp.
Paulus, Stephen	Silver the River	European American Music Corp.
Pergolesi, Giovanni B.	Stabat Mater	G. Schirmer, Inc.
Pergolesi, Giovanni B. (Doreen Rao, ed.)	Pergolesi Suite (from *Stabat Mater*)	Boosey & Hawkes
Pfautsch, Lloyd	The Laughing Song	Lawson-Gould/Alfred Music Publ.
Pinkham, Daniel	Company at the Creche	E. C. Schirmer Music Co. Inc.
Pinkham, Daniel	In Youth Is Pleasure	E. C. Schirmer Music Co. Inc.
Poorman, Berta and Sonja	Tue, Tue (Come Sing a Song)	BriLee Music Publishing Co.
Porterfield, Sherri	Something Told the Wild Geese	Heritage Music Press
Poston, Elizabeth, arr.	Dance to Your Daddie	Boosey & Hawkes
Powers, Anthony	Zlata's Diary	Oxford University Press
Praetorius, Michael	How Brightly Shines the Morning Star	Boosey & Hawkes
Protheroe, Daniel	Y Mae Afon (There Is a River)	Cwmni Gwynn
Purcell, Henry	Sound the Trumpet	Lawson-Gould Music Publishers, Inc.
Raminsh, Imant	Agnus Dei	Plymouth Music Company, Inc.
Raminsh, Imant	I'll Give My Love an Apple	Boosey & Hawkes
Raminsh, Imant	Song of the Stars	Boosey & Hawkes
Raminsh, Imant	White Feathers	Boosey & Hawkes
Ramsey, Andrea	Heaven Unfolding	Boosey & Hawkes
Read, Paul	Birdsong	Boosey & Hawkes
Rorem, Ned	Afternoon on a Hill (four movements)	Boosey & Hawkes
Rutter, John	All Things Bright and Beautiful	Hinshaw Music, Inc.
Rutter, John	Angels' Carol	Hinshaw Music, Inc.

Composer	Title	Publisher
Rutter, John	Carol of the Children	Hinshaw Music, Inc.
Rutter, John	Donkey Carol	Oxford University Press
Rutter, John	For the Beauty of the Earth	Hinshaw Music, Inc.
Rutter, John	I Will Sing with the Spirit	Hinshaw Music, Inc.
Rutter, John	The Lord Bless You and Keep You	Hinshaw Music, Inc.
Saint-Saëns, Camille	Praise Ye the Lord (Tollite hostias)	Boosey & Hawkes
Sargon, Simon	Feast of Lights	Transcontinental Music Publications
Sargon, Simon, arr.	Mah yafeh hayom	Transcontinental Music Publications
Sarmanto, Heikki (Auvo Sarmanto, arr.)	Hanget soi (Singing Snow)	Edition Fazer
Schillo, Emile	There Was a Little Maiden	Lawson-Gould Music Publishers, Inc.
Schubert, Franz	May Song	Boosey & Hawkes
Schultz, Donna	Bring a Torch, Jeanette, Isabella	Boosey & Hawkes
Schultz, Donna	Orkney Lullaby	Boosey & Hawkes
Schultz, Johann A. P. (James H. Sutcliffe, arr.)	O Come Little Children	Boosey & Hawkes
Schütz, Heinrich (Bradley L. Almquist, ed.)	Der Herr ist gross	Alliance Music Publications, Inc.
Shaw, Martin	With a Voice of Singing	G. Schirmer, Inc.
Shields, Valerie, arr.	Ding Dong Merrily on High	Mark Foster Music Co.
Shields, Valerie, arr.	Eliyahu hanavi	Boosey & Hawkes
Shields, Valerie, arr.	Mayim, mayim	Earthsongs
Showers Crenscenz, Valerie	Things I Learned from a Cow	Alliance Music Publications, Inc.
Shur, Bonia, arr.	Three Songs for Hanukah	Walton Music Corp.
Singh, Vijay	Blue Jay	Warner Bros. Publications
Singh, Vijay, arr.	Reuben, Reuben	National Music Publishers
Sirett, Mark	Sunny Bank	Hinshaw Music, Inc.
Sirett, Mark, arr.	Irish Lullaby	Boosey & Hawkes
Sirett, Mark, arr.	J'entends le moulin (I Hear the Millwheel)	Boosey & Hawkes

Composer	Title	Publisher
Sirett, Mark, arr.	Ma come bali bene bela bimba (La Villanella)	Boosey & Hawkes
Sleeth, Natalie	O Come, O Come Immanuel	Choristers Guild
Smith, Gregg	Bible Songs	G. Schirmer, Inc.
Smith, Gregg	Holiday Harmonies (suite)	Laurendale Associates
Smith, Gregg	Songs of Innocence	G. Schirmer, Inc.
Smith, Gregg	Suogân (Sleep My Baby)	G. Schirmer, Inc./Hal Leonard
Smith, Gregg	The Cuckoo	G. Schirmer, Inc.
Smith, Gregg	The Lord Is My Shepherd	G. Schirmer, Inc.
Stroope, Z. Randall	Inscription of Hope	Heritage Music Press
Stroope, Z. Randall	Resonet in laudibus	Mark Foster Music Co.
Stroope, Z. Randall	I Had a Paint Box	Colla Voce Music, Inc.
Terri, Sali	Alunde aluya	Lawson-Gould Music Publishers, Inc.
Thiman, Eric	When Cats Run Home	Boosey & Hawkes
Thompson, Randall	Two Childhood Songs	Thorpe Music Publishings
Thompson, Randall	Velvet Shoes	E. C. Schirmer Music Co. Inc.
Tilley, Alexander	In Flanders Fields (from *Songs for the School Year*)	Leslie Music Supply, Inc.
Tilley, Alexander	The Magic Store (from *Songs for the School Year*)	Leslie Music Supply, Inc.
Tormis, Veljo	Lauliku lapsepöli	Earthsongs
Tormis, Veljo, arr.	Three Ugric Folk Songs	Boosey & Hawkes
Vance, Margaret	Here We Come a Caroling	Lawson-Gould Music Publishers, Inc.
Varner, Joan C.	Dance with the Elephants	Alliance Music Publications, Inc.
Varner, Joan C.	When I Am Silent	Alliance Music Publications, Inc.
Vaughan Williams, Ralph	John Barleycorn	Oxford University Press
Vivaldi, Antonio	Gloria in excelsis Deo	Jenson Publications
Vivaldi, Antonio	Laudamus Te (from *Gloria*)	Walton Music Corp.
Vivaldi, Antonio (Janet Galván, ed.)	Esurientes (from *Vivaldi for Treble Voices*)	Roger Dean Publishing Company
Vivaldi, Antonio (Janet Galván, ed.)	Vivaldi for Treble Voices	Roger Dean Publishing Company

Composer	Title	Publisher
Walker, Gwyneth, arr.	How Can I Keep from Singing?	E. C. Schirmer Music Co. Inc.
Washburn, Jon	Mary and the Baby	Gordon V. Thompson Music
Webb, Joy, arr.	Hand Me Down My Silver Trumpet	Hinshaw Music, Inc.
Wilberg, Mack	One December, Bright and Clear	Oxford University Press
Wilder, Alec (Donald Lang, arr.)	Lullabies and Nightsongs	Boosey & Hawkes
Williamson, Malcolm	Little Mass of Saint Bernadette	Josef Weinberger, Ltd.
Wolfman, Barbara	Little One, Little Chickadee	Boosey & Hawkes
Zerbe, Dorothy, arr.	I Wonder as I Wander	Roger Dean Publishing Company

THREE-PART TREBLE

Composer	Title	Publisher
Adler, Samuel	Never Was a Child So Lovely	Hinshaw Music, Inc.
Adler, Samuel	The Flames of Freedom	Ludwig Music
Agnestig, Carl-Bertil	Quiet Solitude	Walton Music Corp.
Alexander, Elizabeth	If You Can Walk You Dan Dance	Seafarer Press
Armstrong, Kathy	Ghana Alleluia	Boosey & Hawkes
Bach, Johann Sebastian	Alleluia (from *Christmas Cantata*)	Galaxy Music Corp. (ECS)
Baker, Barbara, and David J. Elliott, arr.	Feel Good	Boosey & Hawkes
Bara, Charlotte, arr.	Away in a Manger	Santa Barbara Music Publishing, Inc.
Bart, Katie Moran	Blessing	Curtis Music Press
Bartók, Béla	Teasing Song	Boosey & Hawkes
Bernon, Amy F.	When the Earth Sings, Her Children Sing Along	Roger Dean Publishing Company
Bertaux, Betty	Rejoice My Friends	Boosey & Hawkes
Bertaux, Betty	Who Killed Cock Robin?	C. T. Wagner

Composer	Title	Publisher
Billingsley, Alan, arr.	A Nightingale Sang in Berkeley Square	Hal Leonard
Boone Allsbrook, Nancy, and Glenda Goodin, arr.	Shady Grove	Boosey & Hawkes
Britten, Benjamin	A Ceremony of Carols	Boosey & Hawkes
Britten, Benjamin	Missa brevis in D	Boosey & Co., Ltd.
Broeker, Jay, arr.	Cedar Swamp	Santa Barbara Music Publishing, Inc.
Brunner, David L.	O Music	Boosey & Hawkes
Brunner, David L.	Jubilate Deo	Boosey & Hawkes
Burge, John	Praise the Lord for Dancing	Boosey & Hawkes
Burt, Alfred	The Alfred Burt Carols	Shawnee Press, Inc.
Byrd, William (Jean Bartle, ed.)	Non nobis, Domine	Hinshaw Music, Inc.
Caldwell, Paul, and Sean Ivory, arr.	Get on Board!	Earthsongs
Caldwell, Paul, and Sean Ivory, arr.	Go Where I Send Thee!	Earthsongs
Caldwell, Paul, and Sean Ivory, arr.	Lay Earth's Burden Down	www.caldwellandivory.com
Carey, Paul, arr.	I Saw Three Ships	Oxford University Press
Cary, Paul	Where Go the Boats?	Roger Dean Publishing Company
Chilcott, Bob	Friends	Oxford University Press
Chilcott, Bob	Gifts (from Three Christmas Songs, no. 3)	Oxford University Press
Chilcott, Bob	The Skye Boat Song	Oxford University Press
Chilcott, Bob	The Time of Snow (from *Three Christmas Songs*, no. 1)	Oxford University Press
Chilcott, Bob	This Joy (from *Three Christmas Songs*, no. 2)	Oxford University Press
Cohen, Gerald	V'higad'ta L'vincha, from *V'higad'ta L'vincha* (And You Shall Tell Your Child,	Oxford University Press
Cohen, Gerald	Avadim hayinu (We were slaves to Pharaoh), from *V'higad'ta L'vincha*	Oxford University Press

Composer	Title	Publisher
Cohen, Gerald	Ha lachma anya (We were slaves to Pharaoh), from V'higad'ta L'vincha	Oxford University Press
Cohen, Gerald	Dayeinu (It would have been enough) from V'higad'ta L'vincha	Oxford University Press
Cohen, Gerald	B'chol dor vador (In every generation) from V'higad'ta L'vincha	Oxford University Press
Cohen, Gerald	L'fichach (Therefore we should thank) from V'higad'ta L'vincha	Oxford University Press
Copland, Aaron, arr.	At the River (Hymn Tune)	Boosey & Hawkes
Copland, Aaron, arr.	I Bought Me a Cat	Boosey & Hawkes
Copland, Aaron, arr.	The Little Horses	Boosey & Hawkes
Credit, André Roosevelt	When the Saints Go Marching In	Yaweno Publishing
Curtright, Carolee R.	The Way to Start a Day	Hinshaw Music, Inc.
Curtright, Carolee R., arr.	Kookaburra	Boosey & Hawkes
Daley, Eleanor	Angels Will Guide You Home	Alliance Music Publications, Inc.
Daley, Eleanor	Child with the Starry Crayon	Alliance Music Publications, Inc.
Daley, Eleanor	The Song of the Music Makers	Alliance Music Publications, Inc.
Daley, Eleanor	What Sweeter Music	Alliance Music Publications, Inc.
Dalglish, Malcolm	Woody Knows Nothin'	Boosey & Hawkes
Dalglish, Malcolm, setting	Reel à bouche	Plymouth Music Company, Inc.
Davidson, Charles	I Never Saw Another Butterfly	Ashbourne Music Publications
Doyle, Mark, arr. (trad. from Torres Strait Islands)	Sesere eeye	Mark O'Leary
Elliott, David J., and Doreen Rao, arr.	Swing Around Suite (adapted American folk songs)	Boosey & Hawkes
Elliott, David J., arr. (adapted American folk songs)	Old MacDoodle Had a Band	Boosey & Hawkes
Elliott, David J., arr. (traditional)	Christmas Lites	Boosey & Hawkes

Composer	Title	Publisher
Elliott, David J., arr.	A-Tisket, A-Tasket (Ella Fitzgerald and Al Feldman)	Boosey & Hawkes
Fauré, Gabriel	Messe basse	Theodore Presser Co.
Finley, Brian, arr.	Danny Boy	Boosey & Hawkes
Franck, César (Howard Cable, arr.)	Panis angelicus	Hinshaw Music, Inc.
George, Earl	O Clap Your Hands	Circle Blue Print Co.
Goetze, Mary	Fire	Boosey & Hawkes
Goetze, Mary	Sing Alleluia, Allelu	Boosey & Hawkes
Goetze, Mary	Sing We Noel	MMB Music, Inc.
Goetze, Mary, arr.	Crawdad Hole	Boosey & Hawkes
Goetze, Mary, arr.	Infant Holy	Boosey & Hawkes
Goetze, Mary, arr.	Old Joe Clark	Boosey & Hawkes
Goetze, Mary, arr.	Shenandoah	Boosey & Hawkes
Gregoryk, Joan, arr.	Kalinka	Boosey & Hawkes
Grundahl, Nancy, arr.	Hebrew Rounds for Peace	Alliance Music Publications, Inc.
Guillaune, Sydney	Koudjay	Walton Music Corp.
Hagen, Jocelyn	Joy	Boosey & Hawkes
Handel, G. F.	Awake the Trumpets Lofty Sound (from *Samson*)	Edward B. Marks Music Corp.
Handel, G. F.	Verdant Meadows	J. Fischer & Bros.
Haydn, Michael	Laudate pueri (Come Children, Praise Our Lord)	G. Schirmer, Inc.
Henderson, Bill (David J. Elliott, arr.)	When I Sing	Boosey & Hawkes
Henderson, Ruth Watson	Come, Ye Makers of Song	Gordon V. Thompson Music
Henderson, Ruth Watson	Creation's Praise	Gordon V. Thompson Music
Henderson, Ruth Watson	Music Comes	Roger Dean Publishing Company
Henderson, Ruth Watson	The Song of the Music Makers	Alliance Music Publications, Inc.
Henderson, Ruth Watson	Twelve Days of Christmas	Gordon V. Thompson Music
Henderson, Ruth Watson	The Wise Frogs	Gordon V. Thompson Music

Composer	Title	Publisher
Hiorkawa, Joy Ondra, arr.	Lullaby of Birdland	Hal Leonard
Hogan, Moses, arr.	Music Down in My Soul	Hal Leonard
Holman, Derek	Sir Christëmas	Novello
Holmes, Brian	Roger Bobo Plays the Tuba	Roger Dean Publishing Company
Holmes, Martha	Rumjana	Boosey & Hawkes
Holst, Gustav	A Babe Is Born (from *Four Old English Carols*)	Treble Clef Music Press
Holst, Gustav	Four Old English Carols	Treble Clef Music Press
Holst, Gustav (Z. Randall Stroope, arr.)	Homeland	Colla Voce Music, Inc.
Holst, Gustav	Now Let Us Sing (from *Four Old English Carols*)	Treble Clef Music Press
Hyökki, Matti	On suuri sun rantas autius	Fazer Musik
Johnson, Craig Hella	Will There Really Be a "Morning"?	Alliance Music Publications, Inc.
Jones, Nigel	Lullaby (Suo-gân)	Boosey & Hawkes
Jordanoff, Christine, arr.	Appalachian Suite 1	Boosey & Hawkes
Kodály, Zoltán	Ave Maria	Universal Edition
Kodály, Zoltán	Dancing-Song	Oxford University Press
Kodály, Zoltán	Ladybird	Boosey & Hawkes
Kodály, Zoltán	Mountain Nights I–IV	Boosey & Hawkes
Kodály, Zoltán	Psalm 150	Oxford University Press
Kountz, Richard	Sleigh (à la russe)	G. Schirmer, Inc.
Kowalski, Crystal LaPoint	Beautiful Rainy Day	Boosey & Hawkes
Kowalski, Crystal LaPoint	I'm Gonna Shine Today	Hinshaw Music, Inc.
Kowalski, Crystal LaPoint	The Fairy Folk	Boosey & Hawkes
Kowalski, Crystal LaPoint	When the Mists Have Rolled Away	Hinshaw Music, Inc.
Kuzmenko, Larysa	Night	Boosey & Hawkes
Kuzmenko, Larysa	Stars	Boosey & Hawkes
Lang, Rupert	Cantate Domino	Boosey & Hawkes
Lang, Rupert	Carol of the Child	Boosey & Hawkes
Lang, Rupert	Spirit of the Child	Boosey & Hawkes
Larsen, Libby	Ring the Bells	Oxford University Press
Larsen, Libby	The Ballerina and The Clown	Oxford University Press
Lassus, Orlando de	Echo Song (double chorus)	E. C. Schirmer Music Co. Inc.
Lassus, Orlando de	Two Short Motets	Brichtmark Music, Inc.

Composer	Title	Publisher
Leck, Henry, arr.	Freedom Is Coming	Walton Music Corp.
Leontovich, M.	Carol of the Bells	Carl Fischer, Inc.
Leslie, Kenneth	Cape Breton Lullaby	Gordon V. Thompson Music
Lotti, Antonio	Miserere mei	Boosey & Hawkes
Lowry, Robert (Robert Hugh, arr.)	How Can I Keep from Singing?	Boosey & Hawkes
Lutoslawski, Witold	Three Children's Songs	J. & W. Chester
Lutoslawski, Witold	About Mr. Tralalinsky	J. & W. Chester
MacGillivray, Allister	Song for the Mira	Gordon V. Thompson Music
MacGillivray, Allister (Stuart Calvert, arr.)	Away from the Roll of the Sea	Gordon V. Thompson Music/Warner Bros.
Mathias, William	Salvator mundi	Oxford Universtiy Press
McClure, Glenn	Kyrie (from *St. Francis in the Americas, a Caribbean Mass*)	Earthsongs
McCray, James	Gloria in excelsis Deo	Roger Dean Publishing Company
McRae, Shirley W.	Fair Warning	Plymouth Music Company, Inc.
McRae, Shirley W., arr.	Old Dan Tucker	Colla Voce Music, Inc.
Mendoza, Michael D.	Three Nursery Rhymes	Alliance Music Publications, Inc.
Mulholland, James Quitman	Life Has Loveliness to Sell	Colla Voce Music, Inc.
Mulholland, James Quitman	Set of Three Scottish Songs	Colla Voce Music, Inc.
Nahirniak, Taras	Hodie Christus	Roger Dean Publishing Company
Naissoo, Uno	Metsa Telegramm (The Woodpecker's Warning)	Shawnee Press, Inc.
Naplan, Allan E., arr.	An American Anthem	Boosey & Hawkes
Núñez, Francisco J.	Kadiq	Boosey & Hawkes
Núñez, Francisco J.	Los primeros pastores (The First Shepherds)	Boosey & Hawkes
Núñez, Francisco J.	Misa pequeña para niños	Boosey & Hawkes
Núñez, Francisco J.	Creo en Dios (from *Misa pequeña para niños*)	Boosey & Hawkes
Núñez, Francisco J., arr.	Amazing Grace	Boosey & Hawkes
Osmond, Marcella	Petty Harbour Bait Skiff	Boosey & Hawkes
Page, Nick	Explore, Dream, Discover	Hal Leonard

Composer	Title	Publisher
Page, Nick	Fantasy on Two English Carols	Boosey & Hawkes
Papoulis, Jim	A Light Inside	Boosey & Hawkes
Papoulis, Jim	Can You Hear	Boosey & Hawkes
Papoulis, Jim	Give Us Hope	Boosey & Hawkes
Papoulis, Jim	Oye	Boosey & Hawkes
Papoulis, Jim	Stand Together	Boosey & Hawkes
Papoulis, Jim	We Will	Boosey & Hawkes
Papoulis, Jim, and Jacques Sebisaho	Amani (Song of Peace)	Boosey & Hawkes
Parker, Alice, and Robert Shaw, arr.	Fum, Fum, Fum (trad. Spanish carol)	Hal Leonard
Patriquin, Donald	I Went to the Market (from *World Music Suite*)	Earthsongs
Patriquin, Donald, arr.	Deep River (from *World Music Suite*)	Earthsongs
Patriquin, Donald, arr.	Kali's Song	Earthsongs
Paulus, Stephen	Day Break	Paulus Publications
Paulus, Stephen	Hope Is the Thing	Paulus Publications
Paulus, Stephen	Sing Creation's Music On (from *Songs Eternity*)	Paulus Publications
Paulus, Stephen	The Land of Nod	Paulus Publications
Peterson, Oscar (Seppo Hovi, arr.)	Hymn to Freedom	Gordon V. Thompson Music/Warner Bros.
Poulenc, Francis	Petites voix	Editions Salabert
Praetorius, Michael	Psallite (Now We Sing!)	Bourne Co.
Raminsh, Imant	Daybreak Song	Boosey & Hawkes
Raminsh, Imant	Vestigia	Boosey & Hawkes
Ramsey, Andrea	From a River's Edge	Boosey & Hawkes
Rao, Doreen, ed.	Siyahamba (Zulu song)	Boosey & Hawkes
Reger, Max	The Virgin's Slumber Song (Mariä Wiegenlied)	G. Schirmer, Inc.
Robinson, Karen Linford	High Flight	Santa Barbara Music Publishing, Inc.
Rogers, Wayland	Cantate! Sing!	Boosey & Hawkes
Rorem, Ned	Angels Are Everywhere	E. C. Schirmer Music Co. Inc.
Rorem, Ned	What Is Pink?	Boosey & Hawkes
Rouéché, Michelle	Lux aeterna	Alliance Music Publications, Inc.

Composer	Title	Publisher
Rutter, John	Dancing Day (from *Tomorrow Shall Be My Dancing Day*)	Oxford University Press
Rutter, John	Nativity Carol	Oxford University Press
Rutter, John	Shepherd's Pipe Carol	Oxford University Press
Rutter, John	Tomorrow Shall Be My Dancing Day	Oxford University Press
Schafer, R. Murray	Two Songs (from *The Spirit Garden*)	Arcana Editions
Schein, Johann Hermann	Kikkehihi	Boosey & Hawkes
Shields, Valerie	All My Heart This Night Rejoices	Colla Voce Music, Inc.
Sirett, Mark	All Winter Long	Boosey & Hawkes
Sirett, Mark	Blake's Cradle Song	Gordon V. Thompson Music
Sirett, Mark	The Lamb	Gordon V. Thompson Music
Smith, Gregg	Fear Not, Good Shepherds (from *Bible Songs for Young Voices*)	G. Schirmer, Inc.
Stroope, Z. Randall	Lux aeterna	Alliance Music Publications, Inc.
Stroope, Z. Randall	Psalm 23	Alliance Music Publications, Inc.
Talley, Barry	He Is Born	Alliance Music Publications, Inc.
Telfer, Nancy	Butterfly	Earthsongs
Telfer, Nancy	Missa brevis	Lenel Music Publishing
Thompson, Randall	A Girl's Garden (from *Frostiana*)	E. C. Schirmer Music Co. Inc.
Tindley, Charles A.	The Storm Is Passing Over	Boosey & Hawkes
Tolmage, Gerald, arr.	Ding Dong Merrily on High	Staff Music Pub. Co., Inc.
Varner, Joan C.	Sing Softly a Lullaby	Alliance Music Publications, Inc.
Vaughan Williams, Ralph	Folk Songs of the Four Seasons (collection of fifteen songs)	Oxford University Press
Vecchi, Orazio	Fa una canzone (Sing, Sing a Song for Me)	Bourne Co.

Composer	Title	Publisher
Walker, Gwyneth	I Thank You God	E. C. Schirmer Music Co. Inc.
Washburn, Robert	Scherzo for Spring	Oxford University Press
Whitacre, Eric	Seal Lullaby	Hal Leonard
Zaninelli, Luigi	The Water Is Wide (adapted folk song)	Shawnee Press, Inc.

FOUR-PART TREBLE

Composer	Title	Publisher
Armstrong, Kathy, and Rory Magill	Bobobo Suite	Boosey & Hawkes
Berkey, Jackson	Cantata 2000	SDG Press
Berkey, Jackson	Ride the Wind	SDG Press
Berkey, Jackson	Sacramento—Sis Joe	SDG Press
Bertaux, Betty	S'vivon	Boosey & Hawkes
Bogas, Ed	I Hear America Singing	Laurendale Associates
Chilcott, Bob	Look to this Day!	Oxford University Press
Copland, Aaron, arr.	Ching-a-Ring Chaw (Minstrel Song)	Boosey & Hawkes
Deibler, Sean	I'm Goin' Home on a Cloud	Kodály Center of America
Dubinsky, Leon (Lydia Adams, arr.)	We Rise Again	Gordon V. Thompson Music
Elliott, David J., arr.	Kentucky Jazz Jam	Boosey & Hawkes
Franck, Melchior (Mary Goetze, arr.)	Da pacem Domine	Boosey & Hawkes
Galuppi, Baldassare	Dixit Dominus	Roger Dean Publishing Company
Goetze, Mary	There Is Ever a Song	Boosey & Hawkes
Hatfield, Stephen	African Celebration	Boosey & Hawkes
Hatfield, Stephen	Nukapianguaq	Boosey & Hawkes
Hatfield, Stephen	Ower the Hills	Boosey & Hawkes
Hatfield, Stephen, arr.	Dubula	Boosey & Hawkes
Hawkins, Walter	I'm Goin' Up a Yonder	Boosey & Hawkes
Henderson, Ruth Watson	Cantate Domino	Roger Dean Publishing Company
Henderson, Ruth Watson	Watts' Cradle Songs	Hinshaw Music, Inc.
Holst, Gustav	Jesu, Thou the Virgin-born (from *Four Old English Carols*)	Treble Clef Music Press

Composer	Title	Publisher
Kodály, Zoltán	See the Gypsies	Oxford University Press
Kodály, Zoltán	The Straw Guy	Oxford University Press
Kowalski, Crystal LaPoint	Come Ho! (from *Four English Songs*)	Lawson-Gould Music Publishers, Inc.
Kowalski, Crystal LaPoint	Hey Nonny No! (from *Four English Songs*)	Lawson-Gould Music Publishers, Inc.
Kowalski, Crystal LaPoint	Memory (from *Four English Songs*)	Lawson-Gould Music Publishers, Inc.
Kowalski, Crystal LaPoint	Missa humilis	Roger Dean/The Lorenz Corporation
Kowalski, Crystal LaPoint	Ode to Solitude (from *Four English Songs*)	Lawson-Gould Music Publishers, Inc.
Lange, Kinley	Esto les digo	Alliance Music Publications, Inc.
Larsen, Libby	Chang McTang McQuarter Cat (from *Mind You, Now*)	Libby Larsen Publishing
Larsen, Libby	Giving Thanks, a Native American Good Morning Message	Libby Larsen Publishing
Larsen, Libby	Mind You, Now (from *Mind You, Now*)	Libby Larsen Publishing
Larsen, Libby	Summer Song (from *Mind You, Now*)	Libby Larsen Publishing
Larsen, Libby	Warning (from *Mind You, Now*)	Libby Larsen Publishing
Leck, Henry, arr.	South African Suite	Plymouth Music Company, Inc.
Macha, Otmar	Hoj, Hura Hoj	Alliance Music Publications, Inc.
Neaum, Michael	Scottish Lullaby	Alliance Music Publications, Inc.
Núñez, Francisco J., arr.	Guayacanal	Boosey & Hawkes
Page, Nick	Niška banja	Boosey & Hawkes
Page, Nick	Solomon Grundy	Boosey & Hawkes
Page, Nick	Was Ever a Dream a Drum?	Boosey & Hawkes
Parker, Alice, arr.	Tis the Gift to Be Simple	Lawson-Gould Music Publishers, Inc.
Paulus, Stephen	Faith, Hope, and Laughter	Paulus Publications

Composer	Title	Publisher
Raminsh, Imant	Cantate Domino	Hinshaw Music, Inc.
Seiber, M.	Three Hungarian Folk Songs	G. Schirmer, Inc.
Sirett, Mark	Watane	Boosey & Hawkes
Szymko, Joan	I Dream a World	Santa Barbara Music Publishing, Inc.
Taylor-Howell, Susan, arr.	I'm Going Home on a Cloud	Boosey & Hawkes
Thompson, Randall	The Place of the Blest	E. C. Schirmer Music Co. Inc.
Vasiliaukaiten, Kristina	Kyrie and Gloria	Santa Barbara Music Publishing, Inc.
Ward, Samuel J. (Gregg Smith, arr.)	America the Beautiful	Laurendale Associates
Washburn, Jon	Tango to Evora	Walton Music Corp.
Wessman, Harri	Water Under Snow Is Weary	Walton Music Corp.
Willcocks, David	Psalm 150	Gordon V. Thompson Music
Zhuang, Liu, arr.	Da mai hao zi (from *Three Chinese Songs*)	Boosey & Hawkes
Zhuang, Liu, arr.	Lan hua hua (from *Three Chinese Songs*)	Boosey & Hawkes
Zhuang, Liu, arr.	Yang guan san die (from *Three Chinese Songs*)	Boosey & Hawkes

TREBLE/ADULT AND TREBLE—MULTIPLE VOICINGS

Composer	Title	Publisher
Britten, Benjamin	Saint Nicolas (treble/adult)	Boosey & Hawkes
Brunner, David L.	In the Beauty Way (treble/adult)	Boosey & Hawkes
Caparotta, Kevin	May the Road Rise to Meet You (treble/adult)	Boosey & Hawkes
Chilcott, Bob	Salisbury Vespers (treble/adult)	Oxford University Press
Hatfield, Stephen	As Above, So Below (treble/adult)	Boosey & Hawkes
Jergenson, Dale	This Train (treble/adult)	Laurendale Associates

Composer	Title	Publisher
Leek, Stephen	Riawanna (multiple voicings)	Hal Leonard
Leisring, Volkmar	O filii et filiae (treble/adult)	
Papoulis, Jim	Kolenna sawa (All of Us Together) (treble/adult)	Boosey & Hawkes
Schafer, R. Murray	Snowforms (multiple voicings)	Arcana Editions
Smith, Gregg	Welcome Home (from *Rip Van Winkle*, the opera) (treble/adult)	Music 70/Warner Chappell Bros.
Willcocks, David, and John Rutter, eds.	*Carols for Choirs,* Book 4 (multiple voicings)	Oxford University Press

SKILLS RESOURCE

Composer	Title	Publisher
Bacon, Denise	Fifty Easy Two-Part Exercises	European American Music Corp.
Baldwin, Eileen, Jean Bartle, and Linda Beaupré	*A Young Singer's Journey,* Vols. 1–5	Hinshaw Music, Inc.
Crowe, Edgar, ed.	Folk Song Sight Singing Series, Books 1, 2	Oxford University Press
Hemmenway, John, Mary Belle Leach, and Nan Wehrung	*The Keys to Sight Reading Success*	AMC Music
Houlahan, Micheál, and Philip Tacka	Sound Thinking	Boosey & Hawkes
Jennings, Kenneth	Sing Legato	Neil A. Kjos Music Co.
Juilliard School Project, The	*Juilliard Repertory Library Vocal Volume 1–6*	Canyon Press, Inc.
Kodály, Zoltán	333 Elementary Exercises	Boosey & Hawkes
Kodály, Zoltán	*Pentatonic Music: 100 Hungarian Folk Songs,* Vol. I	Boosey & Hawkes
Rao, Doreen	We Will Sing	Boosey & Hawkes
Szőnyi, Erzsébet	*Bicinia Americana 1* (22 traditional American children's songs)	Boosey & Hawkes
Telfer, Nancy	*Successful Sight Singing*	Neil A. Kjos Music Co.
Telfer, Nancy	*Successful Warmups,* Books 1 and 2	Neil A. Kjos Music Co.

Notes

CHAPTER 1

1. Doreen Rao, "Children and Choral Music in ACDA: The Past and the Present, The Challenge and the Future," *Choral Journal* 29, no. 8 (March 1989):6.

2. The National Board of ACDA invited Doreen Rao to organize a National Committee on Children's Choirs (as distinct from the National Committee on Boy Choirs) in 1979. Rao identified and appointed chairs in each of the seven divisions of ACDA. The first formal convention meeting of the newly formed National Committee on Children's Choirs was held at the ACDA national convention in New Orleans in March 1981. By 1981, division chairs were being appointed, many state chairs were already appointed, long-term goals were established, and the work of the committee began.

3. Membership numbers obtained from the ACDA indicate an increase in the number of ACDA members who work with children's choirs during this time. Membership figures from the ACDA National Committee on Children's Choirs' 1994–1995 annual report indicated that forty percent of the membership listed professional involvement with children's choirs on their membership forms, and forty-nine out of fifty state chairs (plus the District of Columbia) had been appointed.

4. Dr. Cornelia Yarbrough was director of the School of Music, and Arthur Freundlich was dean of the College of Visual and Performing Arts at Syracuse University at that time.

5. Annual summer workshop sessions for conductors began in August of 1984 with Jean Ashworth Bartle and the Toronto Children's Chorus.

6. Other music organizations supporting the work of children's choirs include and are not limited to Choristers Guild, Organization of American Kodály Educators, the Orff Schulwerk Society, and Music Educators National Conference.

7. The June 15, 1989, report of the ACDA National Committee on Children's Choirs, prepared by National Chair Barbara Tagg for the *ACDA Standing Committees for Choral Repertoire*

and Standards Annual Report 1988–1989, indicated that the national membership for ACDA had increased over the prior year with approximately twenty percent of the organization's membership listing an interest in children's choirs. Forty-four R&S children's choir state chairs had been appointed to serve by that time. National Committee Guidelines for state chairs were also prepared in March of 1989 under Tagg's leadership.

The 1990–1991 report of the ACDA National R&S Committee on Children's Choirs prepared by Tagg states, "Children's Choirs continue to be one of the fastest growing R&S areas with significant increases in ACDA membership." Statistics in the report indicated over 2,000 new members who work with children.

The 1994–1995 ACDA National R&S Committee on Children's Choirs annual report prepared by Tagg states, "With forty percent of the membership indicating involvement with children's choirs on their ACDA membership forms, this R&S area continues to grow in membership." By 1995, forty-nine out of fifty state children's choir chairs (plus the District of Columbia) had been appointed. Numbers were obtained for the report from the ACDA National Headquarters in Lawton, Oklahoma.

The 1995 ACDA national convention in Washington, D.C., held the first Children's Choir Research Session (and poster session), proposed by Tagg and the ACDA National Committee on Children's Choirs. The same year, the revised *Directory of Children's Choirs in America* was published, indicating a significantly more comprehensive listing of ACDA members who reported working with children in school, church, and community contexts. This was also the year that Chorus America held the first children's choir series of sessions at its national convention in Seattle (as indicated in the ACDA report).

8. The first concert of American children's choirs presented at Carnegie Hall in New York City was held in May 1990 and included (in order of performance) the Syracuse Children's Chorus (Barbara Tagg), Amadeus Children's Choir (Irene Schmor, Canada), Los Angeles Children's Choir (Rebecca Thompson), St. Louis Children's Choir (Ethelyn Sparfeld), Red River Boy Choir (Linda Ferreira), Northwest Girlchoir (Rebecca Rottsolk), Winnipeg Mennonite Children's Choir (Helen Litz, Canada), Vox Aurea (Kari Ala-Pöllänen, Finland), and the Indianapolis Children's Choir (Henry Leck). Each choir performed individually under its own director and, following intermission, the choirs combined under the direction of Doreen Rao to perform works by Pergolesi, Debussy, Fauré, Copland, and Oscar Peterson.

9. The two issues of the *Choral Journal* devoted to the topic of children's choirs include Rao, Doreen, ed., *Choral Journal* Special Issue on the Children's Choir, 28, no. 8 (March 1989), and Tagg, Barbara M., and Linda Ferreira, guest eds., "Focus: Children's Choirs/ ACDA," *Choral Journal* 33, no. 8 (March 1993). Copies are available from ACDA, 545 Couch Drive, Oklahoma City, OK 73102. An additional article by Barbara Tagg titled "The Early History of the National Committee on Children's Choir 1981–1995" may be found in the *Choral Journal* 52, no. 11 (June/ July 2012):45–47.

10. Laurel Jones, Heather Peeler, and Morrie Warshawski, eds., *National Endowment for the Arts Advancement 95/96* (The Bay Group International, 1995), 3.

11. Ibid.

12. http://www.nea.gov/resources/Lessons/warshawski.html

13. Syracuse University, "History of Crouse College," College of Visual and Performing Arts   http://vpa.syr.edu/newsroom/college-information/history-vpa/history-crouse-college (accessed July 27, 2010).

CHAPTER 2

1. *The Chorus Impact Study: How Children, Adults, and Communities Benefit from Choruses* (Washington, D.C.: Chorus America, 2009), 4.
2. Ibid., 5–6.
3. "Fiduciary" is defined as "law involving trust, especially with regard to the relationship between a trustee and a beneficiary." *Oxford English Dictionary Online*, http://www.oxfordreference.com.libezproxy2.syr.edu/views/SEARCH_RESULTS.html?y=0&q=fiduciary&category=t23&x=0&ssid=550825552&scope=book&time=0.0820011811862997 accessed February 22, 2012.
4. The website for Board Source is www.boardsource.org.

CHAPTER 3

1. Jim Collins, *Good to Great* (New York: HarperCollins, 2001), 195.
2. *New Oxford American Dictionary*, accessed April 6, 2012, http://www.oxfordreference.com.libezproxy2.syr.edu/views/SEARCH_RESULTS.html?y=9&q=collaboration&category=t183&x=14&ssid=934766213&scope=book&time=0.535255950223338.
3. As quoted in David McNally, *Even Eagles Need a Push: Learning to Soar in a Changing World* (New York: Delacorte, 1990), 135.
4. Samuel A. Culbert, "Get Rid of the Performance Review!" *Wall Street Journal,* October 20, 2008, http://online.wsj.com/article/SB122426318874844933.html#articleTabs%3Dcomments.
5. More information about ASCAP may be found at its website, http://www.ascap.com/about/about, accessed February 25, 2012.
6. Information about Broadcast Music, Inc. (BMI) may be obtained from its website at http://www.bmi.com/, accessed February 25, 2012. The website for SESAC is http://www.sesac.com/, and the website for ACEMLA is http://www.acemla.com/, accessed February 25, 2012.

CHAPTER 4

1. Used with permission. *The Poems of Emily Dickinson*, Thomas H. Johnson, ed. (Cambridge, MA: The Belknap Press of Harvard University Press, Copyright © 1951, 1955, 1979, 1983 by the President and Fellows of Harvard College).
2. Tom Adams, *The Nonprofit Leadership Transition and Development Guide: Proven Paths for Leaders and Organizations* (San Francisco: Jossey-Bass, 2010), 31.
3. William Bridges, *Managing Transitions: Making the Most of Change,* third ed. (Philadelphia: Da Capo Press, 2009), 3.
4. Sessions on transition and succession were presented at the Chorus America national conferences in 2010 and 2011.
5. The online seminar is located on the Members Only section of the Chorus America website, www.chorusamerica.org
6. Quoted from Sherry Schiller, August 20, 2009, in a phone conversation.
7. *Conductors Count: What Chorus Boards, Music Directors, and Administrators Need to Know* (Washington, DC : Chorus America, 2007), 43.

CHAPTER 5

1. http://oxforddictionaries.com/view/entry/m_en_us1244370#m_en_us1244370. Accessed March 2, 2011.

2. One example of this type of choir structure is the Hilton Head Choral Society, which sponsors the Youth Choir located on Hilton Head Island, South Carolina.

3. Miami Choral Academy (Shawn Crouch, academy director), founded in 2010, is an example of an inner-city after-school choral ensemble program formed under a parent ensemble, Seraphic Fire (Patrick Dupré Quigley, founder), a professional choir in Miami, Florida. A grant from the John S. and James L. Knight Foundation supported the creation of the Miami Choral Academy in cooperation with the Miami-Dade County Public Schools. Websites for both choral organizations are http://seraphicfire.org and http://miamichoralacademy.org.

4. http://oxforddictionaries.com/search?searchType=dictionary&isWritersAndEditors=true&searchUri=All&q=budget&contentVersion=US. Accessed March 17, 2011.

5. One such resource is *The Foundation Center's Guide to Proposal Writing* by Jane C. Geever and Patricia McNeill. The Foundation Center is a national service organization that provides authoritative information about grant writing, foundations, and corporate giving. Their website is http://foundationcenter.org/.

6. http://www.oxfordreference.com.libezproxy2.syr.edu/views/SEARCH_RESULTS.html?q=audit&category=t23&ssid=201265052&scope=book&time=0.0790277861885009. Accessed April 13, 2011.

CHAPTER 6

1. *Oxford Dictionary of English*, edited by Angus Stevenson. *Oxford Reference Online*, http://www.oxfordreference.com.libezproxy2.syr.edu/views/ENTRY.html?subview=Main&entry=t140.e0994345, accessed June 22, 2011.

2. Erik Qualman, *Socialnomics: How Social Media Transforms the Way We Live and Do Business* (Hoboken, NJ: John Wiley & Sons, 2010), xv.

3. Ibid.

4. "Social Media Revolution 3," http://www.youtube.com/watch?v=x0EnhXn5b0M, accessed July 3, 2011.

5. The Social Media A Cappella Conference (SMACC) was held at Syracuse University, April 1–3, 2011, and cosponsored by the Syracuse University chapter of the Public Relations Student Society of America and the Contemporary A Cappella Society (CASA).

6. National choral organizations such as the American Choral Directors Association and Chorus America are using Facebook and Twitter regularly to communicate with members and those who attend their national conferences.

7. Malcolm Gladwell, *Blink: The Power of Thinking Without Thinking* (New York: Little, Brown and Company, 2005), 12.

CHAPTER 7

1. This statement was made to a small group of choral conductors at Birch Lake, Wisconsin, in August 1990, and was later quoted in the March 1993 issue of the *Choral Journal*, p. 26, in an article by Linda Ferreira titled "Children's Choir: The Future, the Challenge."

2. The author of this classroom music assessment rubric for singers is retired music educator Janice F. Holbrook. This method was used extensively throughout her professional career to maximize accurate singing in the choral classroom context. Used with permission.

3. Lois Choksy, *The Kodály Context: Creating an Environment for Musical Learning* (Englewood Cliffs, NJ: Prentice-Hall, Inc., 1981), 98–103.

4. Audition components listed here but not included in the Choksy text come from various sources (anecdotal information, professional workshops, institutes, and convention sessions) collected over many years.

5. *The Oxford Graduated Round Book*, selected and arranged by W. Gillie Whittaker (London: Oxford University Press, 1937),13, includes "Ars longa, vita brevis," a canon by Beethoven. Whittaker states,

> Sir George Smart (1776–1876), a prominent English conductor and composer, visited Beethoven in 1825, and was welcomed with every token of friendship. He records in his diary his connection with the Master, and thus describes their farewell: "I gave him my diamond pin as a remembrance of the high gratification I received by the honour of his invitation and kind reception, and he wrote me that following droll canon as fast as his pen could write, in about two minutes of time, as I stood at the door ready to depart." Beethoven's dedication is "Written on the 16th of September, 1825, in Baden, when my dear talented musical artist and friend Smart (from England), visited me here." The original stands an octave lower, in the bass stave, and the number of voices is not stated. A canon on the same words was written for Hummel in 1916, but it is not given in Beethoven's complete works.

6. At the Adirondack Festival of American Music held for many years in Saranac Lake, New York, Gregg Smith would annually demonstrate how he voiced the Gregg Smith Singers, the New York City professional vocal ensemble in residence at the festival each summer in July. At the time of this writing, Gregg Smith, the only living founder of Chorus America, is also director of the oldest continually performing professional vocal ensemble in America, having performed for fifty-six years.

7. "Jubilate Deo" (translation: Rejoice in the Lord, Alleluia) (Psalm 65) is published by Boosey & Hawkes, octavo no. OCUB6350.

CHAPTER 8

1. Howard Behar, *It's Not About the Coffee: Leadership Principles from a Life at Starbucks* (New York: Portfolio, The Penguin Group, 2007), 28.

2. *The Chorus Impact Study: How Children, Adults, and Communities Benefit from Choruses* (Washington, DC: Chorus America, 2009), 7.

3. Ibid.

4. http://www.oxfordreference.com.libezproxy2.syr.edu/views/SEARCH_RESULTS.html?q=promotion&category=t23&ssid=412088877&scope=book&time=0.368591309649663, accessed August 14, 2011.

5. Matthew Sigman, *The Chorus Leadership Guide* (Washington, D.C.: Chorus America, 2009), 75.

6. More information about choral consortia may be found in the following article: Kelsey Menehan, "Choral Consortiums and the Local Advantage," *The Voice* 34, no. 4 (2011): 18–27.

7. Sigman, *The Chorus Leadership Guide*, 78.

8. As cited in Jerold Panas, *Asking: A 59-Minute Guide to Everything Board Members, Volunteers, and Staff Music Know to Secure the Gift* (Medfield, MA: Emerson & Church Publishers, 2005–2006), 10.

9. Ibid., 9.

10. Mary Deissler, *Four Fearless Fundraisers*, session, Chorus America National Conference (San Francisco, June 11, 2011).

11. SCC has often sent a summer postcard to donors while on tour or from chorister summer camp. Anecdotal information gathered when someone says how much he or she enjoyed receiving the card in the chorister's handwriting indicates that it is well worth the effort. And the choristers enjoyed writing them, often personalizing the cards by adding a small drawing, music note, or heart.

12. Chorus America, *Making the Case for Your School Choir: An Advocacy Guide*; TOOL: *Arts Education and Student Achievement: Quotes from Influential Leaders*, www.chorusamerica.org/choiradvocacyguide/free, accessed August 12, 2011.

13. *The Chorus Impact Study* (Washington, DC: Chorus America, 2009), 19.

14. This document and toolkit are available from the Chorus America website, http://www.chorusamerica.org/choiradvocacyguide/free.

15. Ken Robinson, *Out of Our Minds: Learning to Be Creative* (Chichester, West Sussex, UK: Capstone Publishing Ltd., 2011), 34.

16. Suggestions about large church choral music education programs were made by Stephanie Mowery, former director of the children's choirs at All-Saints Episcopal Church in Pasadena, California, in a phone interview on August 14, 2011.

17. Music educator Deborah A. Cunningham offered a description of her small church children's choir located in Manlius, New York, where a strong music education program exists in the surrounding school district.

18. Spoken by Isaac Stern on the occasion of the centennial concert at Carnegie Hall (1991).

CHAPTER 9

1. Erkki Pojhola with Matti Tuomistro, *Tapiola Sound*, trans. William Moore (Ft. Lauderdale, FL: Walton Music Corporation, 1993), 202.

2. http://www.merriam-webster.com/dictionary/impresario, accessed July 12, 2011.

3. Wayne D. Bowman, foreword in Doreen Rao, *Circle of Sound: Voice Education* (New York: Boosey & Hawkes, 2005), vii–viii.

4. Zoltán Kodály, *The Selected Writings of Zoltán Kodály* (London: Boosey & Hawkes, 1974), 125.

5. *Republic* 402a. In Edith Hamilton and Huntington Cairns, eds., *The Dialogues of Plato* (New York: Pantheon, 1966).

6. Gayle Ober, "The Live Concert—Your Next Recording?" *The Voice* 34, no. 2 (2011):3.

7. "The Rights Thing: A Chorus Guide to Getting the Proper Permissions," *The Voice* 34, no. 2 (summer 2011) provides detailed information about the legalities of performance rights, commissioning, recording, and distributing music.

8. D. James Tagg, "Helpful Hints for Singers in Sessions" (lecture, University of South Florida, Tampa, May 31, 2011).

9. http://www.oed.com.libezproxy2.syr.edu/view/Entry/1144?redirectedFrom=accompanist#eid, accessed July 13, 2011.

10. *Simpatico* is defined by the *Oxford English Dictionary* as "pleasing, likeable; congenial, understanding; sensitive, sympathetic," http://www.oed.com.libezproxy2.syr.edu/view/Entry/179943?redirectedFrom=simpatico#eid, accessed July 13, 2011.

11. Kurt Adler, *The Art of Accompanying and Coaching* (New York: DaCap Press, Inc., 1980), 240.

12. Comment made during an oral interview on July 13, 2011.

CHAPTER 10

1. http://blog.ted.com/2010/04/17/new_best_of_the_8/, accessed September 22, 2011. The performance may be found at http://www.ted.com/talks/a_choir_as_big_as_the_internet.html, accessed September 22, 2011.

2. http://blog.ted.com/2011/04/01/a-virtual-choir-2000-voices-strong-eric-whitacre-on-ted-com/, accessed September 22, 2011.

3. http://ericwhitacre.com/the-virtual-choir, accessed April 9, 2012.

4. Matthew Sigman, *The Chorus Leadership Guide* (Washington, DC: Chorus America, 2009), xi.

5. http://www.international-eisteddfod.co.uk/en/about-us/history, accessed October 2, 2011.

6. The weeklong Gregg Smith Legacy Festival, funded in part by the National Endowment for the Arts, was held at Saint Peter's Church in New York City in April 2008. SCC performed two concerts on Saturday, April 26, 2008. The ninety-minute afternoon concert was devoted to American music and presented solely by SCC. The evening concert included Cantori New York, the Choir of Saint Peter's Church, the Long Island Symphonic Choral Association, the Gregg Smith Singers, and SCC. Each choir sang individually, and the festival finale sung by the combined choirs was Gregg Smith's "Now I Walk in Beauty."

7. The work written by Libby Larsen and commissioned by SCC was based on research from an article titled "The Magic World of Hans Christian Andersen" in *National Geographic*, December 1979, 825–849.

8. *The Ballerina and the Clown: A Hans Christian Andersen Tale* is published by Oxford University Press.

9. The slides were made available from the publisher of the work, Oxford University Press.

10. Arden, Harvey, "The Magic World of Hans Christian Andersen," *National Geographic*, December 1979, 844.

11. Shape-note singing is a tradition that began in Colonial times and continues today throughout the United States and internationally.

12. *The Sacred Harp: The Best Collection of Sacred Songs, Hymns, Odes, and Anthems Ever Offered the Singing Public for General Use*, rev. by Hugh McGraw et al. The Music Committee (Bremen, GA: Sacred Harp Publishing Co., Inc., 1991), 13.

13. *The Sacred Harp*, 13.

14. http://www.fasola.org/singings/, accessed December 30, 2010.

CHAPTER 11

1. Additional repertoire for children's choir and orchestra may be found in the October 2000 issue of the *Choral Journal* in an article titled "Orchestral Repertoire for Treble Voices"

by Barbara M. Tagg and Jean Ashworth Bartle, and in Jean Ashworth Bartle's book *Sound Advice*.

2. Commissioned and premiered by SCC in December 2000.

3. Kelsey Menehan, "Choral Consortiums and the Local Advantage," *The Voice* 34, no. 4 (2011): 18–27.

4. http://www.canadianchildrensopera.com/about.php, accessed January 6, 2012.

5. *Rip Van Winkle: The Opera* was performed from a manuscript on loan from Gregg Smith, the composer of the work.

CHAPTER 12

1. The company Keynote Arts Associates, founded by James E. Dash in 1984, added a children's choir festival component in 1993 under the artistic leadership of Barbara M. Tagg. The first festival, held at Walt Disney World Resort, with additional performances given at the First Presbyterian Church in Orlando, was called Children's Holiday Choral Festival and was held in early December in 1993, 1994, and 1996. Additional festivals were added, including the Children's Celebration (held in California at Disneyland and the Crystal Cathedral in Garden Grove, California, over the Fourth of July weekend in 1996 and 1997) and the Children in Harmony festival (at Walt Disney World in Orlando, Florida, on Memorial Day Weekend from 1996 through 2009). David V. Patrick became executive director of Keynote Arts Associates in 1998 and served as president from 2001 until 2009. Distinguished composers who were commissioned by Keynote Arts Associates included Gregg Smith, Francisco Núñez, David Brunner, Stephen Hatfield, David J. Elliott, James E. Mulholland, Paul Brantley, Bob Chilcott, Nick Page, Z. Randall Stroope, Jackson Berkey, Ruth Watson Henderson, Vijay Singh, Allan E. Naplan, Stephen Paulus, Jim Papoulis, Paul Caldwell, Sean Ivory, and Eleanor Daley.

2. Both website addresses for travel information and passport information were accessed January 22, 2012.

Bibliography

CHILDREN'S CHOIR RESOURCES

Armstrong, Anton and Lucinda Allen Mosher. "The Children's Choir in the Church, Excerpts from ACDA Position Papers," *Choral Journal* 29, no. 8 (March 1998):46.

Bartle, Jean Ashworth. *Lifeline for Children's Choir Directors*. Rev. ed. Miami, FL: Warner/Chappell, 1993.

–––––. *Sound Advice: Becoming a Better Children's Choir Conductor*. New York: Oxford University Press, 2003.

Bourne, Patricia. *Inside the Elementary School Chorus: Instructional Techniques for the Non-Select Children's Chorus*. Dayton, OH: Heritage Music Press, 2009.

Chorus America, *Making the Case for Your School Choir: An Advocacy Guide*; *TOOL: Arts Education and Student Achievement: Quotes from Influential Leaders*, www.chorusamerica.org/choiradvicacyguide/free, accessed August 12, 2011.

Cooksey, John. M. *Working with the Adolescent Voice*. St. Louis, MO: Concordia Publishing House, 1992.

Goetze, Mary, Angela Broeker, and Ruth Boshkoff. *Educating Young Singers: A Choral Resource for Teacher-Conductors*. New Palestine, IN: Mj Publishing, 2009.

Hunt, Peter. *Voiceworks: A Handbook for Singing*. Oxford, UK: Oxford University Press, 2001.

Kemp, Helen. *Of Primary Importance: Information, Preparation, and Application—A Practical Guide for Directors of Younger Elementary Choristers*. Garland, TX: Choristers Guild, 1989.

Kodály, Zoltán. *The Selected Writings of Zoltán Kodály*. London: Boosey & Hawkes, 1974.

McRae, Shirley W. *Directing the Children's Choir: A Comprehensive Resource*. New York: Schirmer Books, 1991.

Page, Nick. *Sing and Shine On!: The Teacher's Guide to Multicultural Song Leading*. Portsmouth, NH: Heinemann, 1995.

Page, Sue Ellen. *Hearts and Hands and Voices: Growing in Faith Through Choral Music.* Tarzana, CA: H. T. FitzSimons, 1995.

Phillips, Kenneth. *Teaching Kids to Sing.* Belmont, CA: Schirmer, 1992.

Pohjola, Erkki, with Matti Tuomistro. *Tapiola Sound.* Trans. William Moore. Ft. Lauderdale, FL: Walton Music, 1993.

Rao, Doreen. *ACDA on Location, Volume 1: The Children's Choir with Doreen Rao and the Glen Ellyn Children's Chorus.* VHS. American Choral Directors Association.

–––––. *Choral Music Education Experience: Education Through Artistry.* 5 vols. New York: Boosey & Hawkes, 1987.

–––––. *We Will Sing: Choral Music Experience for Classroom Choirs.* New York: Boosey & Hawkes, 1993.

–––––, ed. *Choral Music for Children: An Annotated List.* Reston, VA: Music Educators National Conference, 1990.

Roach, Donald W. *Handbook for Children's and Youth Choir Directors.* Garland, TX: Choristers Guild, 1987.

Rotermund, Donald, ed. *Children Sing His Praise: A Handbook for Children's Choir Directors.* St. Louis, MO: Concordia Publishing, 1973.

Stultz, Marie. *Innocent Sounds: Building Choral Tone and Artistry in Your Children's Choir: A Personal Journey.* St. Louis, MO: Birnamwood Publications, 1999.

Swears, Linda. *Teaching the Elementary School Chorus.* West Nyack, NY: Parker Publishing, 1985.

Tagg, Barbara M. "Children's Choir." In *Women and Music in America Since 1900: An Encyclopedia.* 2 vols., 88–91. Kristine H. Burns, ed. Westport, CT: Greenwood Press, 2002.

–––––. "A Children's Choir Recipe for Success." In Alan J. Gumm, ed., *The Choral Director's Cookbook: Insights and Inspired Recipes from Beginners and Experts.* Galesville, MD: Meredith Music Publications, 2006.

"The Early History of the National Committee on Children's Choir 1981–1995," *Choral Journal* 52, no. 11 (June/July 2012):45–47.

–––––. "An Interview with Gregg Smith," *Choral Journal* 33, no. 8 (March 1993):19–20.

Tagg, Barbara M., and Jean Ashworth Bartle. "Orchestral Repertoire for Treble Voices," *Choral Journal* 41, no. 3 (October 2000):33–41.

Tagg, Barbara M., and Dennis Shrock. "An Interview with Helen Kemp," *Choral Journal* 30, no. 4 (November 1989):5–9, 11–13.

Wedel, Eva. "Music in Worship: A Selected List for Children's Choirs," *Choral Journal* 31, no. 4 (November 1990):45–47.

Welles, Joan. *The Board of Directors: How to Provide the Chorus' Business Needs.* vol. 1 of *Managing Young Choirs: Dynamic and Effective Planning, Promoting, Funding.* Deerfield, IL: J. Welles, 1995.

–––––.*Promoting and Fund-Raising: How to Market and Finance the Chorus.* vol. 2 of *Managing Young Choirs: Dynamic and Effective Planning, Promoting, Funding.* Deerfield, IL: J. Welles, 1995.

MUSIC AND ARTS-RELATED BUSINESS RESOURCES

Adler, Kurt. *The Art of Accompanying and Coaching.* New York: Da Capo Press, Inc., 1980.

Chorus America. *America's Performing Art: A Study of Choruses, Choral Singers, and Their Impact.* Washington, DC: Chorus America, 2003.

———. *Choral-Orchestral Engagements: Survey Results and Common Practices*. Washington, DC: Chorus America, 2004.

———. *Choral Survey Report*. Washington, DC: Chorus America, 2002.

———. *The Chorus Impact Study: How Children, Adults, and Communities Benefit from Choruses*. Washington, DC: Chorus America, 2009. Also at http://www.chorusamerica.org/system/files/resources/Impact09/ImpactStudy09_Report.pdf.

———. *Conductors Count: What Chorus Boards, Music Directors, and Administrators Need to Know*. Washington, DC: Chorus America, 2007.

———. *Education Outreach Toolkit: Chorus America*. Washington, DC: Chorus America, 2002.

Kaiser, Michael M. *The Art of the Turnaround: Creating and Maintaining Healthy Arts Organizations*. Waltham, MA: Brandeis University Press, 2008.

McCarthy, Devin F., Arthur Brooks, Julia Lowell, and Laura Zakaras. *The Performing Arts in a New Era*. Santa Monica, CA: Rand, 2001.

Menehan, Kelsey. "Choral Consortiums and the Local Advantage," *The Voice* 34, no. 4 (2011): 18–27.

Sigman, Matthew. *The Chorus Leadership Guide*. Ed. Robin L. Perry. Washington, DC: Chorus America, 2009.

———. *Leading the Successful Chorus: A Guide for Managers, Board Members, and Music Directors*. Ed. Robin Perry Allen. Washington, DC: Chorus America, 2002.

Wittry, Diane. *Beyond the Baton: What Every Conductor Needs to Know*. New York: Oxford University Press, 2007.

CHORAL AND MUSIC EDUCATION RESOURCES

Abrahams, Frank, Anton E. Armstrong, Joseph Flummerfelt, Graeme Morton, and Weston H. Noble. *Teaching Music Through Performance in Choir*. vol. 1, comp. and ed. Heather J. Buchanan and Matthew W. Mehaffey. Chicago: GIA Publications, 2005.

Bailey, Wayne. *Conducting: The Art of Communication*. New York: Oxford University Press, 2009.

Blackstone, Jerry, Heather J. Buchanan, Janet Galván, et al. *Teaching Music Through Performance in Choir*. vol. 2, comp. and ed. Heather J. Buchanan and Matthew W. Mehaffy. Chicago: GIA Publications, 2007.

Blocker, Robert, ed. *The Robert Shaw Reader*. New Haven, CT: Yale University Press, 2004.

Bónis, Ferenc, and Zeneműkiadó Vállalat, eds. *The Selected Writings of Zoltán Kodály from Visszatekintés I–II*. Trans. Lili Halápy and Fred Macnicol. London: Boosey & Hawkes, 1974.

Booth, Eric. *The Music Teaching Artist's Bible: Becoming a Virtuoso Educator*. New York: Oxford University Press, 2009.

Carter, Tom. *Choral Charisma: Singing with Expression*. Santa Barbara, CA: Santa Barbara Music Publishing, 2005.

Choksy, Lois. *The Kodály Context: Creating an Environment for Musical Learning*. Englewood Cliffs, NJ: Prentice Hall, 1981.

———. *The Kodály Method: Comprehensive Music Education from Infant to Adult*. 2d ed. Englewood Cliffs, NJ: Prentice Hall, 1988.

Conlon, Joan Catoni, ed. *Wisdom, Wit, and Will: Women Choral Conductors on Their Art*. GIA Publications, 2009.

Consortium of National Arts Education Associations. *National Standards for Arts Education: What Every Young American Should Know and Be Able to Do in the Arts.* Reston, VA: Music Educators National Conference, 1994.

Cooper, Irvin. *Teaching Junior High School Music: General Music and the Vocal Program.* 2d ed. Conway, AR: Cambiata Press, 1973.

Cutietta, Robert A. *Raising Musical Kids: A Guide for Parents.* New York: Oxford University Press, 2001.

Decker, Harold A., and Julius Herford, eds. *Choral Conducting Symposium.* 2d ed. Englewood Cliffs, NJ: Prentice Hall, 1988.

Deissler, Mary. *Four Fearless Fundraisers,* session, Chorus America National Conference (San Francisco, June 11, 2011).

Ehly, Eph. *Hogey's Journey: A Memoir by Eph Ehly.* Dayton, OH: Heritage Music Press, 2006.

Elliott, David J. *Music Matters: A New Philosophy of Music Education.* New York: Oxford University Press, 1995.

Ferreira, Linda, and Barbara M. Tagg. "Voices and Visions: An Interview with Eight American Choral Conductors," *Choral Journal* 38, no. 8 (March 1998):9–17.

Fowler, Charles, ed. *Conscience of a Profession: Howard Swan, Choral Director and Teacher.* Chapel Hill, NC: Hinshaw Music, 1987.

Glenn, Carole. *In Question of Answers: Interviews with American Choral Conductors.* Chapel Hill, NC: Hinshaw Music, 1991.

Gumm, Alan, ed. *The Choral Director's Cookbook: Insight and Inspired Recipes for Beginners and Experts.* Galesville, MD: Meredith Music Publications, 2006.

Haasemann, Frauke, and James M. Jordan. *Group Vocal Technique.* Chapel Hill, NC: Hinshaw Music, 1991.

Hegyi, Erzsébet. *Solfege According to the Kodály-Concept.* Kecskemét, Hungary: Zoltán Kodály Pedagogical Institute of Music, 1975.

Houlahan, Micheál, and Philip Tacka. *Kodály Today: A Cognitive Approach to Elementary Music Education.* New York: Oxford University Press, 2008.

Music Educators National Conference. *The Vision for Arts Education in the Twenty-first Century: The Ideas and Ideals Behind the Development of the National Standards for Education in the Arts.* Reston, VA: Music Educators National Conference, 1994.

Mussulman, Joseph A. *Dear People ... Robert Shaw, A Biography.* Bloomington, IN: Indiana University Press, 1979.

Neuen, Donald. *Choral Concepts.* Belmont, CA: Schirmer, Wadsworth/Thomson Learning, 2002.

Noble, Weston. *Creating the Special World: A Collection of Lectures.* Ed. Steven M. Demorest. Chicago: GIA Publications 2005.

Ober, Gayle. "The Live Concert—Your Next Recording?" *The Voice* 34, no. 2 (2011):3.

Parker, Alice. *The Anatomy of a Melody: Exploring the Single Line of Song.* Chicago: GIA Publications, 2006.

Rao, Doreen. *Circle of Sound, Voice Education: A Contemplative Approach to Singing Through Meditation, Movement, and Vocalization.* New York: Boosey & Hawkes, 2005.

R and S National Committee and Barbara Tagg, "American Composers and Arrangers: A List," *Choral Journal* 43, no. 8 (March 2003):43–46.

-----"Resources: Books, Articles, Organizations and Websites Related to American Choral Music," *Choral Journal* 43, no. 8 (March 2003):57–71.

Reimer, Bennett. *A Philosophy of Music Education*. 2d ed. Englewood Cliffs, NJ: Prentice Hall, 1989.

Robinson, Ray, and Allen Winold. *The Choral Experience: Literature, Materials, and Methods*. Prospect Heights, IL: Waveland Press, 1976.

Sándor, Frigyes. *Music Education in Hungary*. London: Boosey & Hawkes, 1975.

Snow, Sandra. *Choral Conducting/Teaching: Real World Strategies for Success*. DVD. Chicago: GIA Publications, 2009.

Spurgeon, Debra, comp. and ed. *Conducting Women's Choirs: Strategies for Success*. Chicago: GIA Publications, 2012.

Stanton, Royal. *The Dynamic Choral Conductor*. Delaware Water Gap, PA: Shawnee Press, 1972.

Swanson, Frederick J. *The Male Singing Voice Ages Eight to Eighteen*. Cedar Rapids, IA: Laurance Press, 1997.

Szőnyi, Erzsébet. *Kodály's Principles in Practice: An Approach to Music Education Through the Kodály Method*. New York; London: Boosey & Hawkes, 1973.

Tagg, Barbara M. "The Past and Future of ACDA's Repertoire and Standards Committee: An Interview with Colleen Kirk," *Choral Journal* 38, no. 8 (March 1998):47–48.

Tagg, Barbara M. and Linda Ferreira. "A Celebration of American Choral Music: Past, Present, and Future," *Choral Journal* 43, no. 8 (March 2003):7.

-----. "Fourteen Conductors Speak About American Choral Music," *Choral Journal*. 43, no. 8 (March 2003):9–25.

Thornton, Tony. *The Choral Singer's Survival Guide*. Los Angeles: Vocal Planet Publishing, 2005.

Vennard, William. *Singing: the Mechanism and the Technic*. Rev. ed. New York: Carl Fischer, 1967.

Webb, Guy B., ed. *Up Front! Becoming the Complete Choral Conductor*. Boston: ECS Publishing, 1993.

Weston Noble: Perpetual Inspiration. DVD. Houston, TX: Quaid/Schott Media Productions, 2006.

Whittaker, W. Gillies, sel. and arr. *The Oxford Graduated Round Book*. London: Oxford University Press, 1937.

GENERAL BUSINESS, LEADERSHIP, AND MANAGEMENT RESOURCES

Adams, Tom. *The Nonprofit Leadership Transition and Development Guide: Proven Paths for Leaders and Organizations*. San Francisco: Jossey-Bass, 2010.

Behar, Howard. *It's Not About the Coffee: Leadership Principles from a Life at Starbucks*. New York: Penguin, 2007.

Bridges, William. *Managing Transitions: Making the Most of Change*. 3d ed. Philadelphia: Da Capo Press, 2009.

Brooks, Arthur C. *Who Really Cares, The Surprising Truth About Compassionate Conservatism: America's Charity Divide—Who Gives, Who Doesn't, and Why It Matters*. New York: Basic Books, 2006.

Buckingham, Marcus. *The One Thing You Need to Know! ... About Great Managing, Great Leading, and Sustained Individual Success*. New York: Free Press, 2005.

Buckingham, Marcus, and Donald O. Clifton. *Now, Discover Your Strengths*. New York: Free Press, 2001.

Buckingham, Marcus, and Curt Coffman. *First, Break All the Rules: What the World's Greatest Managers Do Differently*. New York: Simon & Schuster, 1999.

Cockerell, Lee. *Creating Magic: Ten Common Sense Leadership Strategies from a Life at Disney*. New York: Doubleday, 2008.

Collins, Jim. *Good to Great: Why Some Companies Make the Leap ... and Others Don't*. New York: HarperCollins, 2001.

—————. *Great by Choice: Uncertainty, Chaos, and Luck—Why Some Thrive Despite Them All*. New York: HarperCollins, 2011.

Covey, Stephen R. *The Eighth Habit: From Effectiveness to Greatness*. New York: Free Press, 2004.

—————. *Principle-Centered Leadership*. New York: Summit, 1991.

—————. *The Seven Habits of Highly Effective People: Restoring the Character Ethic*. New York: Simon & Schuster, 1989.

Culbert, Samuel A. "Get Rid of the Performance Review!" *Wall Street Journal*, October 20, 2008, http://online.wsj.com/article/SB122426318874844933.html#articleTabs%3Dcomments.

Culbert, Samuel A., with Lawrence Rout. *Get Rid of the Performance Review!: How Companies Can Stop Intimidating, Start Managing—and Focus on What Really Matters*. New York: Business Plus, 2010.

Drucker, Peter F. *The Drucker Foundation Self-Assessment Tool: Participant Workbook*. Rev. ed. New York: The Drucker Foundation, 1999.

—————. *Managing the Non-Profit Organization: Practices and Principles*. New York: HarperCollins, 1990.

Gallwey, W. Timothy. *The Inner Game of Tennis: The Classic Guide to the Mental Side of Peak Performance*. New York: Random House, 1974.

Gardner, Howard, with Emma Laskin. *Leading Minds: An Anatomy of Leadership*. New York: Basic Books, 1995.

Geever, Jane C., and Patricia McNeill. *The Foundation Center's Guide to Proposal Writing*. New York: The Foundation Center, 1993.

Gladwell, Malcolm. *Blink: The Power of Thinking Without Thinking*. New York: Back Bay Books/Little, Brown, 2005.

—————. *Outliers: The Story of Success*. New York: Little, Brown, 2008.

—————. *The Tipping Point: How Little Things Can Make a Big Difference*. New York: Little, Brown, 2002.

Hanson, Peter G. *Stress for Success: How to Make Stress on the Job Work for You*. New York: Doubleday, 1989.

Iacocca, Lee. *Where Have All the Leaders Gone?* New York: Scribner, 2007.

Johnson, Spencer. *Who Moved My Cheese?: An A-Mazing Way to Deal With Change in Your Work and in Your Life*. New York: G. P. Putnam's Sons, 1998.

Jones, Laurel, Heather Peeler, and Morrie Warshawski. *National Endowment for the Arts Advancement 95/96*. N.p.: The Bay Group International, 1995.

McNally, David. *Even Eagles Need a Push: Learning to Soar in a Changing World*. New York: Delacorte Press, 1990.

Panas, Jerold. *Asking: A 59-Minute Guide to Everything Board Members, Volunteers, and Staff Must Know to Secure the Gift*. Medfield, MA: Emerson & Church, 2005–2006.

Peters, Thomas J., and Robert H. Waterman, Jr. *In Search of Excellence: Lessons from America's Best-Run Companies*. New York: Warner Books, 1982.

Putnam, Robert D. *Bowling Alone: The Collapse and Revival of American Community*. New York: Simon & Schuster, 2000.
Qualman, Erik. *Socialnomics: How Social Media Transforms the Way We Live and Do Business*. Hoboken, NJ: John Wiley & Sons, 2011.
Ryan, Rebecca. *Life First, Work Second: Getting Inside the Head of the Next Generation*. Madison, WI: Next Generation Consulting. 2007.
Shapiro, Ronald M., Mark A. Jankowski, and James Dale. *The Power of Nice: How to Negotiate So Everyone Wins—Especially You!* New York: John Wiley & Sons, 1998.

GENERAL TEACHING AND EDUCATION RESOURCES

Crew, Rudy. *Only Connect: The Way to Save Our Schools*. New York: Farrar, Straus, and Giroux, 2007.
Csikszentmihalyi, Mihaly. *Flow: The Psychology of Optimal Experience*. New York: Harper and Row, 1990.
Csikszentmihalyi, Mihaly, Kevin Rathunde, and Samuel Whalen. *Talented Teenagers: The Roots of Success and Failure*. New York: Cambridge University Press, 1993.
Gardner, Howard. *The Disciplined Mind: What All Students Should Understand*. New York: Simon & Schuster, 1999.
Kock, Kenneth. *Rose, Where Did You Get That Red? Teaching Great Poetry to Children*. New York: Vintage Books, 1990.
Levine, Mel. *A Mind at a Time*. New York: Simon & Schuster, 2002.
Pink, Daniel H. *A Whole New Mind: Why Right-Brainers Will Rule the Future*. New York: Penguin, 2006.
Robinson, Ken. *Out of Our Minds: Learning to Be Creative*. Chichester, West Sussex, UK: Capstone Publishing, 2011.

GENERAL MUSIC AND ARTS-RELATED RESOURCES

Arden, Harvey. "The Magic World of Hans Christian Andersen," *National Geographic*, December 1979, 844.
Becker, Howard S. *Art Worlds*. Berkeley, CA: University of California Press, 1982.
Bernstein, Leonard. *The Infinite Variety of Music*. New York: Simon & Schuster, 1966.
Burns, Kristine H., ed. *Women and Music in America Since 1900: An Encyclopedia*. 2 vols. Westport, CT: Greenwood Press, 2002.
Cameron, Julia. *The Artist's Way: A Spiritual Path to Higher Creativity*. New York: G. P. Putnam's Sons, 1992.
Clapp, Edward P. *20Under40: Re-inventing the Arts and Arts Education for the Twenty-first Century*. Bloomington, IN: AuthorHouse, 2010.
Gardner, Howard. *The Arts and Human Development: A Psychological Study of the Artistic Process*. New York: Basic Books, 1994.
Hamilton, Edith, and Huntington Cairns, eds. "Republic 402a." In *The Dialogues of Plato*. New York: Pantheon, 1966.
Jensen, Eric. *Arts with the Brain in Mind*. Alexandria, VA: Association for Supervision and Curriculum Development, 2001.
Johnson, Thomas H., ed. *The Poems of Emily Dickinson*. Cambridge, MA: The Belknap Press of Harvard University Press, Copyright© 1951, 1955, 1979, 1983.

McGraw, Hugh, music committee general chairman, Richard L. DeLong, Raymond C. Hamrick, David Ivey, Toney Smith, Jeff Sheppard, and Terry L. Wootten. *The Sacred Harp*. Rev. ed. Carrollton, GA: Sacred Harp Publishing Company, 1991.

Moses, Don V., Robert W. Demaree, Jr., and Allen F. Ohmes. *Face to Face with an Orchestra: A Handbook for Choral Conductors Performing*. Princeton, NJ: Prestige Publications, 1987.

The Oxford Graduated Round Book, selected and arr. W. Gillie Whittaker. London: Oxford University Press, 1937.

Rao, Doreen, "Children and Choral Music in ACDA: The Past and the Present, The Challenge and the Future," *Choral Journal* 29, no. 8 (March 1989):6–11.

Ross, Alex. *Listen to This*. New York: Farrar, Straus and Giroux, 2010.

Rudolph, Max. *The Grammar of Conducting: A Practical Guide to Baton Technique and Orchestral Interpretation*. New York: Schirmer Books, 1980.

Suesse, Gwen. *Womansong: Balance & Harmony in a Feminine Key*. Tryon, NC: Cantando Press, 2010.

Tagg, D. James. "Helpful Hints for Singers in Sessions." Paper presented at the Professional Choral Institute, University of South Florida, Tampa, FL, June 2011.

Tepper, Steven J., and Bill Ivey, eds. *Engaging Art: The Next Great Transformation of America's Cultural Life*. New York: Routledge, 2008.

Wall, Joan. *International Phonetic Alphabet for Singers: A Manual for English and Foreign Language Diction*. Dallas, TX: Pst ... Inc., 1989.

Wall, Joan, Robert Caldwell, Tracy Gavilanes, and Sheila Allen. *Diction for Singers: A Concise Reference for English, Italian, Latin, German, French, and Spanish Pronunciation*. Dallas, TX: Pst ... Inc., 1990.

Index

A

Accompanist
  as collaborator, 143–46
  hiring of, 40, 144
  perspectives of, 145–46
ACDA. *See* American Choral Directors Association (ACDA)
ACEMLA (La Asociación de Compositores y Editores de Música Latinoamericana), 42
Adams, John, 168
Adams, Tom, 44
Ad hoc committees, 27–28
Adirondack Festival of American Music, 249n6
Adler, Kurt, 143
Administrative rights, 81
Administrators, starting a choir, 12
Advertisements, 120
Advisory board members, 19
Agendas
  board of directors, 26–28
  committees, 27–28
Alumni committees, 41
Amahl and the Night Visitors (Menotti,), 168, 180
American Boychoir, 188
American Choral Directors Association (ACDA), 52, 100
  church context, promoting children's choirs through, 126
  first meeting of, 2
  leadership transition, 45, 46, 52
  National Board, 245n2
  National Committee on Children's Choirs. *See* National Committee on Children's Choirs
  Standing Committees for Choral Repertoire and Standards Annual Report 1988-1989, 245–46n7
American Guild of Organists, 45, 126
American Orff Schulwerk Association, 6
American Society of Composers, Authors and Publishers (ASCAP), 42
Ancient Voices of Children (Crumb), 180
Anderson, Hans Christian, 154, 185
Anima, 188, 211
Ann and Séamus: A Chamber Opera (Hatfield), 183
Announcements
  concerts, season announcements, 134–35
  founder's departure, 51–52
  new artistic director, 55–56
  rehearsals, 96
  tours, 195–96
Apollinaire, 37
Aristotle, 83
Armstrong, Kathy, 5

Art is lasting, life is passing, 108
Artistic director, planning, 129
Artistic vision, organization order chart, 208
Artistry, 37
ASCAP. *See* American Society of Composers, Authors and Publishers (ASCAP)
Audience surveys, 115–16
Audit, 80–81
    defined, 61
Auditions, 86–87, 99–101
    "blink" moments, 87
    conversation, 102
    echo clapping, 101
    echo singing, 101
    formal, 101–2
    leadership transition, 53–54
    reading sample aloud, 102
    recommendations from teachers, 86–87
    seating chart, 100
"Ave Maria," 112
Awards, 103

B

Baker, Ann Meier, 208–9, 212
Balance sheet, 61, 68
The Ballerina and the Clown: A Hans Christian Andersen Tale (Larsen), 185
Ballet companies, collaboration, 185
Banquets, 201
Bartle, Jean Ashworth, 5, 245n5
Bartók, Béla, 168
Basilica of San Marco, 207–8
Behar, Howard, 111
Beliefs
    creation of, 31–32
    statement of, 34
Bernstein, Leonard, 148, 168, 180
Bertaux, Betty, 5
Biebl, Franz, 112
"The Birth, Life, Death, and Resurrection of Lake Onondaga," 155
Bizet, Georges, 183
Bless the Lord (Carter), 168
"Blink" moments, 87
BMI (Broadcast Music, Inc.), 42, 247n6
Board handbook, 25

Board of directors
    ad hoc committees, 27–28
    advisory board members, 19
    agendas, 26–28
    appreciation for service of, 28–29
    chorister representative to the board, 21–23
    committees, 21, 27–28
    conflict of interest policy, 25
    development committee, 28
    director, overwhelmed feelings of, 37–38
    expertise of board, 19–20
    fiduciary responsibility, 19
    finance committee, 28
    founding director, 28
    handbook, 25
    honorary board members, 19
    insurance, 26
    leadership transition and, 46–47
    liability insurance coverage, 19
    meetings, 26–27, 70–72
    mentoring new board member, 21
    new members, inviting, 20–21
    personnel committee, 28
    removal of board member, 23–24
    retention of board member after completion of tenure, 24–25
    size of, 20
    structure of, 17–18
    tenure, completion of, 24
    term limits, 24–25
    terms of office, 24
    types of members, 18–19
    volunteer board members, 20
Board Source, 29
Boris Godunov (Mussorgsky), 168
Bowman, Wayne D., 133
Boys Choir of Harlem, 188
Bridges, William, 44
"Bring a Friend to Choir Day," 163
Britten, Benjamin, 168, 170, 182–84
Brochures, season concert, 116–18
Brontë, Emily, 59
Budget
    Account ID, 65
    Account Type, 65
    defined, 61, 62, 68
    expenses, 62, 67–68, 71
    first budget, 61–62, 69
    income, 62

income statement vs. annual budget, 70
monthly budget report, 71
new organizations, set up of budget, 62–63
ongoing budgets, 64–65
project budgets, 74–77
touring, 72, 75–76, 193–95
types of income, 63
uneven distribution of income, 71
Year to Date column, 65
Building community. *See* Community, building
Bylaws, 17

C

Canadian Children's Opera Chorus, 184
Cancellation insurance, international tours, 193
Canon (treble repertoire, suggested), 221–22
Carmen (Bizet), 183
Carmina Burana (Orff), 168
"Carol of the Child" (Lang), 182
Carter, Andrew, 168
Carver Center, 29
CDs, concerts, 136–37
Cell phones, 201
The Center for Association Leadership, 29
Challenges of program, 6–7
Chamber ensembles, collaboration, 182
Chanticleer, 112
Chaperones
  chorister summer camp, 92
  touring, 196–98
Chicago Children's Choir, 7, 188, 205–6, 211
Chichester Psalms (Bernstein), 168, 180
Children's author, collaboration with, 155–57
Children's choir development, history of, 4–6
Children's Chorus of Maryland, 5
Children's Crusade (Britten), 168, 183
Children's Holiday Choral Festival, 252n1
The Children's Plea for Peace (Wilder), 5
Choir development, history of, 4–6
Choir festivals, 8, 151–53
Choirs within choirs, 166
Choksy, Lois, 5, 102
Choral consortiums, collaboration, 182–83
Choral Impact Study, 112
Choral Journal, 6, 246n9

Choral Music Experience Institute for Choral Teacher Education, 5
Choralnet, 133
Chorister representative to the board
  full board member, returning as, 23
  generally, 21–22
  selection of, 22–23
Choristers Guild, 6, 45
Chorister summer camp, 90–93
  adult chaperones, 92
  challenges, 91
  facilities included, 91
  flag-lowering ceremony, 92–93
  medical care, 91
  staffing, 91–92
Chorus America
  board of directors, appreciation for service of, 29
  bylaws, 17
  Chorus Impact Study, 15, 112
  "The Chorus Leadership Guide," 29
  conflict of interest policy, 25
  leadership transition, 46, 52
  "Leading the Successful Chorus: A Guide for Management, Board Members, and Music Directors," 29
  Making the Case for Your School Choir: An Advocacy Guide, 124
  Navigating a Music Director Transition, 46
Chorus Impact Study (Chorus America), 15, 112
"The Chorus Leadership Guide" (Chorus America), 29
Church
  choir festivals, 8, 152
  promoting children's choirs through, 125–27
Clothing, recordings of concerts, 141
CME Institutes, 5
Cockerell, Lee, 60
Coffee can economics, 63
Cohen, Gerald, 182
Colbert, Stephen, 187
Collaboration
  accompanist as collaborator, 143–46
  ballet companies, 185
  chamber ensembles, 182
  children's author, with, 155–57
  choral, 150
  choral consortiums, 182–83

Index | 263

Collaboration *(Cont'd)*
  composer, with, 154
  dance company, with, 154
  international ensembles, 186
  librettist, with, 154
  multigenerational singers, with, 155–57
  music educators, 164–65
  opera, 183–85
  puppet theater, with, 155–57
  recruitment opportunity, as, 163
  starting a choir, 12
  types of, 181–86
  values and, 36–37
Collins, Jim, 30
Columbus Boychoir, 188
Commissioned work
  new work. *See* Commissioning new work
  project budgets, 74–75
Commissioning new work, 157–60
  components, 157–58
  fee for composer, 159–60
  initial contact with composer, 158
  premiering, 159–60
  selection of text, 158
  timeframe, 158
Committees
  ad hoc, 27–28
  agendas, 27–28
  alumni committees, 41
  appointment to, 21
  development committee, 28
  finance committee, 28
  parent committees, 41
  personnel committee, 28
Communication, social media, 84–86
Community-based children's choirs, 212
Community, building, 149–61
  "Bring a Friend to Choir Day," 163
  children's author, collaboration with, 155–57
  choir festivals, 151–53
  choirs within choirs, 166
  choral collaborations, 150
  commissioning new work, 157–60
  composer, collaboration with, 154
  dance company, collaboration with, 154
  hosting guest choir, 161–63
  hosting guest composer, 160–61
  librettist, collaboration with, 154
  multigenerational singers, collaboration with, 155–57
  music educators, collaboration with, 164–65
  puppet theater, collaboration with, 155–57
  recruitment opportunity, collaboration as, 163
  regional community, 151
  support messages, 165–66
  virtual choir, 149–50
  workshops, 164
Composer, collaboration with, 154
Computer security, 81
Concerts, 128–48
  accompanist as collaborator, 143–46
  artistic director, planning, 129
  CDs, 136–37
  dimmers, 138
  dress rehearsals, 135
  lighting, 138
  logistics, 135
  planning. *See* Planning, concerts
  professionals, performing with, 177–78
  recording. *See* Recordings, concerts
  repertoire selection, 132–34
  season announcements, 134–35
  timeline, 129–31
  unforeseen events, 146–48
  venues, 130
Confidentiality, 52
Conflict of interest policy, board of directors, 25
Consultants, 38
  leadership transition and, 46–47
Contracts, 39–40
Conversation, auditions, 102
Copland, Aaron, 168
Core values, 34–37
  artistry, 37
  collaboration, 36–37
  excellence, pursuit of, 35–36
  list of, 35
Covey, Stephen, 1
Coville, Bruce, 155–56
Crouch, Shawn, 209, 212

Crumb, George, 180
Cues, 176
Culbert, Samuel A., 41

D

Dance company, collaboration with, 154
Dash, James H., 252n1
Day camp, 93
Deissler, Mary, 122
Departure of founder. *See* Leadership transition
Development committee, 28
Dickinson, Emily, 43, 59
Director, overwhelmed feelings of, 37–38
Discounts, 114
Dolloff, Lori-Anne, 5
Domestic tours and festivals, 190–91
Donors, seeking, 120–22
Dress rehearsals, 176
Drucker, Peter F., 14

E

Eastman Children's Choir, 4–5
Eastman School of Music, University of Rochester, 4–5
Echo clapping, auditions, 101
Echo singing, auditions, 101
Eliot, T. S., 58
Employer Identification Number (EIN), 17
Entering and exiting stage, 177
Entrepreneur, choral conductor as, 60–61
Erie Canal, 155
Evaluation of staff, 40–41
Ewing Marion Kauffman Foundation, 59
Excellence, organizational as well as musical, 203–8
  artistic vision, organization order chart, 208
Excellence, pursuit of, 35–36
Expenses
  budget, 62, 67–68, 71
  professional recordings, 140
Expertise, board of directors, 19–20

F

Facebook, 84–85
Family groups, touring, 197
Fargo, Milford, 4–5
Feedback, staff, 41
Fees, commissioning new work, 159–60
Ferreira, Linda, 5
Festivals, choir, 151–53
  choir choirs, 152
  multigenerational, 153
  school choirs, 152
Fiduciary responsibility
  board of directors, 19
  definition of fiduciary, 247n3
Finance committee, 28
Finances, 60–82
  administrative rights, 81
  audits, 61, 80–81
  balance sheet, 61, 68
  board meetings, financial statements for, 70–72
  budget. *See* Budget
  coffee can economics, 63
  commissioned work, 74–75
  computer security, 81
  depreciation, defined, 61
  entrepreneur, choral conductor as, 60–61
  financial reports, 68–70
  financial statement, defined, 61
  fundraising opportunities, 76–77
  grants, 77–80
  income statement, 68–70
  invitation-only receptions, 76–77
  net income, defined, 61
  retention of records, 81
  revenue sources for choir, 65–67
  scholarships and, 72–74
  staff departures, 81
  starting a choir, 10–11
  tuition as source of income, 72–73
  year to date, 61, 65
Financial reports, 68–70
Financial statement
  board meetings, financial statements for, 70–72
  defined, 61
The First Art (radio program), 6

Five-year rule, starting a choir, 12–13
Flexibility, 172
Folk Songs of the Four Seasons (Williams), 168, 170
Foreign countries, unforeseen events, 147
Founder, departure of. *See* Leadership transition
Four-part treble (treble repertoire, suggested), 240–42
Fundraising. *See* Promotion and fundraising
Future of choral singing in America, children's choirs and, 208–12

G

Galván, Janet, 5
Gertrude McFuzz (Kapilow), 168, 180
Gift exchanges, touring, 200–201
Gladwell, Malcolm, 87
Glen Ellyn Children's Chorus, 2, 188, 211
Goals, 31
   creation of, 33
Golden Vanity (Britten), 183, 184
Grants, 77–80
   applications, 78–79
   types of, 79–80
Green Eggs and Ham (Kapilow), 168, 170
Greenspan, Alan, 123–24
Gregg Smith Legacy Festival, 153, 251n6
Gregg Smith Singers, 185, 207–8
Guest choir, hosting, 161–63
Guest composer, hosting, 160–61

H

"Hallelujah Chorus," 85
Hall, Tom, 203–4, 213
Handbook
   board of directors, 25
   touring, 198–99
"The Handbook of Nonprofit Governance" (Bard Source), 29
Handicapped accessibility, 10

Hansel and Gretel (Humperdinck), 183
Hansen, Morten T., 30
Hatfield, Stephen, 183, 252n1
Hege, Daniel, 209–10, 213
Holbrook, Janice F., 248n2
Holman, Derek, 182
Home-schooled students, 8
Honorary board members, 19
"Hope is the Thing" (Dickinson), 43
Hosting
   guest choir, 161–63
   guest composer, 160–61
Humperdinck, Engelbert, 183

I

Imagining America, 59
Impresario, defined, 128
Incidental movement, 175
Income statement, 68–69
   annual budget, vs., 70
Incorporation, 16
Influences by others, 203–14
   artistic vision, organization order chart, 208
   excellence, organizational as well as musical, 203–8
   future of choral singing in America, children's choirs and, 208–12
Insurance
   board of directors and insurance matters, 19, 26
   cancellation insurance, international tours, 193
   liability insurance coverage, 19
Internal Revenue Service (IRS), 17
International choirs, hosting, 162–63
International ensembles, collaboration, 186
International Society of Music Education, 6
International tours
   cancellation insurance, 193
   generally, 192–93
   government travel requirements for international travel, 193
   passport photos, 193
   unexpected events, preparation for, 201

Interviewing
  leadership transition, 46–47, 53–54
  staffing and, 39
Invitation-only receptions, 76–77

J

Jacobs, Ruth Krehbiel, 126
Job descriptions
  leadership transition, 48–49
  staffing, 38–39
Jones, Ann Howard, 204–5, 213
Jones, Samuel, 174
"Jubilate Deo," 109

K

Kapilow, Rob, 168, 180
Kemp, Helen, 6, 126
Keynote Arts Associates, 252n1
Kirk, Colleen, 100
The Kodály Context (Choksy), 5, 102
Kodály Envoy, 6
Kodály, Zoltán, 134

L

La Bohème (Puccini), 183
Lang, Rupert, 182
Larsen, Libby, 154, 185, 210, 213
Leadership transition, 43–59
  announcement of founder's departure to chorus, 51–52
  announcing new artistic director, 55–56
  anonymous chorister information, 54
  applicants, review of, 52–53
  auditions, 53–54
  board of directors and, 46–47
  confidentiality, 52
  consultant, hiring, 46–47
  contingency plan, 55
  evaluation of candidates, 54
  exit interview for departing director, 56
  interim, hiring of, 55
  interviewing, 46–47, 53–54
  job description, 48–49
  new director, timetable for arrival of, 56–57
  offer of position, 54–55
  orientation for new director, 57–58
  right person not found, 55
  role of departing founder or music director, clarifying, 58
  search committee, 47–48
  second search, lessons learned, 55
  thanking departing founder or director, 58
  timelines, 45, 49–51
  timing of founder's departure, 44–45
  touring, 57
  welcoming new director, 57–58
"Leading the Successful Chorus: A Guide for Management, Board Members, and Music Directors" (Chorus America), 29
Leck, Henry, 5
Levity, moments of, 142–43
Liability insurance coverage, board of directors, 19
Library, music, 103–4
Librettist, collaboration with, 154
Licensing agencies, 42

M

Mahler, Gustav, 168, 171
Mailings, summer mailing to parents, 93–94
Making the Case for Your School Choir: An Advocacy Guide (Chorus America), 124
Mathias, William, 182
Ma, Yo-Yo, 187
Mead, Margaret, 36
Medical considerations
  chorister summer camp, 91
  touring, 199
Meetings, board of directors, 26–27, 70–72
MENC. *See* Music Educators National Conference (MENC)
Mendelssohn, Felix, 183
Menotti, Gian Carlo, 168, 180
Metropolitan Opera, 143
Microphones, concert recordings, 141
A Midsummer Night's Dream (Mendelssohn), 183

Mission. *See also* Mission statement
creation of, 31–32
Mission statement, developing, 33–34
Moore, Christopher, 206
Mormon Tabernacle Choir, 85
Multigenerational choir festivals, 153
Multigenerational singers, collaboration with, 155–57
Musical America, 52
Musical matters, 99–110
auditions, 99–102
awards, 103
choristers singing for choristers, 103
first rehearsal, 108–9
music library, 103–4
rehearsal room setup, 104–5
structure of rehearsals, 105–8
voicing the choir, 109–10
Music distribution, rehearsals, 96–97
Music educators, collaboration with, 164–65
Music Educators Journal, 6
Music Educators National Conference (MENC), 6, 185
Musicians, hiring of, 40, 144
Music library, 103–4
Mussorgsky, Modest, 168

N

NAME. *See* National Association for Music Education (NAME)
National Anthem, 167
National Association for Music Education (NAfME), 126
National Committee on Children's Choirs
changes by, 5–6
conferences and conventions, 245–46n7
first meeting of, 245n2
leadership of, 5
report of, 245–46n7
National Endowment for the Arts (NEA), 59, 184
Advancement Program, 7–8
National Public Radio, 6
Navigating a Music Director Transition (Chorus America), 46
Navius, Geoff, 155

NEA. *See* National Endowment for the Arts (NEA)
Net income, defined, 61
Neuen, Donald, 205, 213
Newsletters, 119–20
New work, commissioning, 157–60
The Nightingale (Raminsh), 183
"The Nonprofit Board Answer Book" (Board Source), 29
Notes, handwritten, 122
Numbering system, rehearsals, 95, 96
The Nursery Rhyme Cantata (Page), 168
The Nutcracker, 168

O

Old American Songs (Copland), 168
Olympic Games, 8
Online surveys, 116
On the Transmigration of Souls (Adams), 168
Open Hand Theatre, 155
Open house for parents, 98
Opera, collaboration, 183–85
Orchestra rehearsal, rehearsal prior to, 173–74
Orchestra, rehearsal with, 175–176
Orff, Carl, 168
Organizational chart, 30–31
Organizational Self-Assessment Checklist, 7
Organizational structure, 14–29
board of directors. *See* Board of directors
bylaws, 17
daily work of organization, 27
incorporation, 16
Organization of American Kodály Educators, 5, 6

P

Page, Nick, 168, 205–6, 213, 252n1
Page, Sue Ellen, 126
Panas, Jerold, 121
Papoulis, Jim, 210, 213, 252n1
Parents
chorister summer camp and, 92–93
commitment, 88

committees, 41
open house for, 98
orientation, rehearsals, 96
registration and, 88–90
rehearsals and, 83–98
summer mailing to, 93–94
support groups, 125
Parker, Alice, 211, 213, 215
Passport photos, international
    tours, 193
Patrick, David V., 206, 213–14, 252n1
Paulus, Stephen, 59, 252n1
Paychecks, 40
Performance Today (radio program), 6
Performing with professionals. *See*
    Professionals, performing with
Personnel committee, 28
Photographers, touring, 201
Piano rehearsal, 174, 183
The Place of the Blest (Thompson), 171
Planning, 9
    concerts. *See* Planning, concerts
    recordings, advance planning, 139–40
    retreat, strategic planning, 32–33
    starting a choir, 9
    tour, 191
Planning, concerts
    artistic director, 129
    creative planning, 131
    success, planning for, 128–29
    timeline, 129–31
Pohjola, Erkki, 128
Powers, Anthony, 168
Practicum in Children's Choirs, 6–7
Praetorious, Michael, 109, 109
Presenting, costs of, 184
Professional recording, preparing, 139–41
Professionals, performing with, 168–86
    ballet companies, collaboration, 185
    chamber ensembles, collaboration, 182
    choral consortium, collaboration, 182–83
    concerts, 177–78
    cues, 176
    dress rehearsals, 176
    entering and exiting stage, 177
    flexibility, importance of, 172
    incidental movement, 175
    international ensembles, collaboration, 186
    music preparation, 171–72
    opera, collaboration, 183–85
    orchestra rehearsal, rehearsal prior to, 173–74
    orchestra, rehearsal with, 175–176
    piano rehearsal, 174, 183
    presenting, costs of, 184
    rehearsals, 172–76
    scores, use of, 174
    symphony orchestra, performances with, 169–71
    unanticipated events, 178–80
Project budgets
    commissioned work, for, 74–75
    fundraising opportunities, 76–77
    invitation-only receptions, 76–77
    tour budget, 75–76
Promotion and fundraising, 111–27
    advertisements, 120
    church context, promoting children's choirs through, 125–27
    complimentary tickets, 118
    discounts, 114
    donors, seeking, 120–22
    events, 122–23
    fundraising opportunities, 76–77
    marketing the choir, 114–15
    newsletters, 119–20
    notes, handwritten, 122
    opportunities, fundraising, 76–77
    parental support groups, 125
    revenue, additional, 120
    school choral events, promoting, 124–25
    schools, choral music education in, 123–24
    season concert brochure, 116–18
    social media, 118
    surveys, audience, 115–16
    ticket sales, analysis of, 114–15
    tickets, purchase of, 113–14
    value of choirs, 111–12
    visibility, 120
    websites, 113
"Psalm 150" (Britten), 182
Public relations, touring, 200–201
Puccini, Giacomo, 183
Puppet theater, collaboration with, 155–57

Q

Qualman, Erik, 84–85
Quigley, Patrick Dupré, 207, 214

R

Raminsh, Imant, 183
Rao, Doreen, 2, 5, 109, 211, 214, 245n2, 246n9
Reading sample aloud, auditions, 102
Receptions, hosting guest composer, 161
Recognition, staff, 41
Recommendations from teachers, auditions, 86–87
Recordings, concerts, 136–39
    advance planning, 139–40
    CDs, 136–37
    clothing, 141
    dimmers, 138
    distribution of, 137
    expenses, 140
    levity, moments of, 142–43
    lighting, 138
    microphones, 141
    professional recording, preparing, 139–41
    recording engineers, 137–38
    recording session, preparing for, 141–43
    selections, order of, 142
    slates, 141–42
Registration, 88–90
    after registration, 89–90
    in-person, 89
Rehearsals, 83–98
    announcements, 96
    community children's choirs, first rehearsals, 94
    dress rehearsals, concerts, 135
    facilities, 9–10
    first rehearsals, 94–96, 108–9
    importance of, 84
    materials for, 95–96
    music distribution, 96–97
    numbering system, 95, 96
    open house for parents, 98
    parent commitment, 88
    parent orientation, 96
    planning, excellence and, 205
    professionals, performing with, 172–76
    room setup, 104–5
    sample plan, 107
    scheduling, 84
    social media and, 84–86
    structure of, 105–8
    summer camp and, 90–93
    techniques, excellence and, 205
    transportation, 88
    volunteers, 97–98
Repertoire
    concerts, 132–34
    excellence and, 204–5
    selection, concerts, 132–34
    touring, 199–200
    treble repertoire. *See* Treble repertoire, suggested
Responsibility
    board of directors, 19
    excellence and, 205
Retention of records, 81
Retreat, strategic planning, 32–33
Revenue
    promotion and fundraising, 120
    sources for choir, 65–67
Rich, Kim, 184
Rip Van Winkle: The Opera, 184–85
Robinson, Ken, 124
Rotermund, Donald, 126
Rottsolk, Rebecca, 5
Rules, excellence and, 205

S

The Sacred Harp, 155–56
Salvatore Mundi (Mathias), 182
Sandburg, Carl, 128
San Francisco Girls Chorus, 7, 188
"Save the date," use of, 117–18
SCC. *See* Syracuse Children's Chorus (SCC)
Schaar, John C., 31
Schiller, Sherry, 207, 214, 247n6
Scholarships, 72–74
School choral events
    festivals, 152
    promoting, 124–25
Schools, choral music education in, 123–24

Scores, use of, 174
Search committee, leadership transition, 47–48
Season announcements, concerts, 134–35
Season concert brochure, 116–18
   photographs of choir, 116–17
   "save the date," use of, 117–18
   written narrative, 117
Seating chart, auditions, 100
Security, computer, 81
Self-Assessment Checklist, 7
Self-evaluations, staff, 41
SESAC (Society of European State Authors and Composers), 42
Sharing the Choral Experience (SCE), 164
Sharp, Timothy A., 5
Shaw, George Bernard, 120
Shaw, Robert, 149, 203, 205, 213
The Shoe Bird: A Music Fable (Jones), 174
"Simple Song" (Bernstein), 148
Sir Cristëmas (Holman), 182
Six Children's Choruses (Bartók), 168
Slates, concert recordings, 141–42
"Sleep," 149
SMACC. *See* Social Media A Cappella Conference (SMACC)
Smart, George, 249n5
Smith, Gregg, 109, 184–85, 207–8, 214, 252n1. *See also* Gregg Smith Legacy Festival; Gregg Smith Singers
Snow, Sandra, 211–12, 214
Snowstorms, 179–80
Social media
   promotion and fundraising, 118
   rehearsals and, 84–86
Social Media A Cappella Conference (SMACC), 85
Sparfeld, Ethelyn, 5
Sparfeld, Etheyln, 5
Staff departures, 81
Staffing
   accompanists, hiring of, 40, 144
   chorister summer camp, 91–92
   contracts, 39–40
   evaluation of staff, 40–41
   feedback, 41
   generally, 38–39
   interviewing, 39
   job descriptions, 38–39
   musicians, hiring of, 40, 144
   paychecks, 40
   recognition, staff, 41
   self-evaluations, 41
   starting a choir, 12
Starbucks International, 111
Starting a choir, 1–13
   administrators, 12
   alternate ways, 8–9
   challenges of program, 6–7
   collaboration, 12
   financial matters, 10–11
   five-year rule, 12–13
   Organizational Self-Assessment Checklist, 7
   planning, 9
   questions during, 4
   rehearsal facilities, 9–10
   staffing, 12
   timeline, 11–12
   volunteers, 11, 12
St. Louis Children's Choir, 5
Strategic planning retreat, 32–33
Summer camp, chorister. *See* Chorister summer camp
Summer mailing to parents, 93–94
Sunday in the Park with George (musical), 99
Support messages, 165–66
Surveys, audience, 115–16
Symphony No. 3 (Mahler), 168
Symphony No. 8 (Mahler), 168
Symphony orchestra, performances with, 169–71
Syracuse Children's Chorus (SCC)
   background of, 2–4
   beliefs, statement of, 34
   "The Birth, Life, Death, and Resurrection of Lake Onondaga," 155
   budget, 11
   choir festival, New York, 153
   chorister representative to the board, 21–22
   five-year rule and, 12–13
   founder, departure of, 44–45
   founding of, 6–7
   Golden Vanity (Britten), presentation of, 184
   leadership transition, 59
   mission statement, 34
   postcards to donors, 250n11

Syracuse Children's Chorus (SCC) (Cont'd)
  questions during start-up, 4
  rehearsal facilities, 10
  Sharing the Choral Experience (SCE), 164
  start of, 1–13
Syracuse University School of Music, 3

T

Tapiola Choir of Finland, 128
Taxation, retention of records and, 81
Texas Boys Choir, 207–8
Thompson, Randall, 171
Three-part treble (treble repertoire, suggested), 232–40
Tickets
  complimentary, 118
  discounts, 114
  purchase of, 113–14
  sales, analysis of, 115
Toronto Children's Chorus, 211, 245n5
Tosca (Puccini), 183
Touring, 57, 187–202
  announcing the tour, 195–96
  banquets, 201
  beginning to tour, 190
  budget, 193–95
  budget for years including a tour, 72
  chaperones, 196–98
  domestic tours and festivals, 190–91
  early touring, 188–89
  family groups, 197
  funding the tour, 195
  gift exchanges, 200–201
  government travel requirements for international travel, 193
  handbook, 198–99
  hosting guest choir, 162
  international tours, 192–93
  last night of tour, 201
  medical considerations, 199
  organizational details, 200–201
  organizing repertoire, 199–200
  payment schedule, 197
  photographers, 201
  planning tour, 191
  project budgets, 75–76
  public relations, 200–201
  selection of tour company, 191–92
  timeline, 198–99
  training sessions, 197–98
  travel, justifying, 189–90
Training sessions, touring, 197–98
Transportation, rehearsals and, 88
Travel, touring
  international tours, 193
  justifying travel, 189–90
Treble/adult and treble--multiple voicings (treble repertoire, suggested), 242–43
Treble repertoire, suggested, 215–43
  canon, 221–22
  four-part treble, 240–42
  skills resource, 243
  three-part treble, 232–40
  treble/adult and treble--multiple voicings, 242–43
  two-part treble, 222–32
  unison, 215–21
Tuition as source of income, 72–73
Two-part treble (treble repertoire, suggested), 222–32

U

Unforeseen events
  concerts, 146–48
  international tours, 201
  professionals, performing with, 178–80
Unison (treble repertoire, suggested), 215–21

V

Value of choirs, 111–12
Values
  core values, 34–37
  creation of, 31–32
Venues, concerts, 130
V'higad'ta L'vincha (Cohen), 182
Vienna Boys' Choir, 3
Virtual choir, 149–50
Visibility, promotion and fundraising, 120
Volunteers, 11, 12

board members, 20
rehearsals, 97–98

W

Walt Disney World Resort, 252n1
War Requiem (Britten), 168, 170
Websites, 113
Whitacre, Eric, 149
White, Benjamin Franklin, 155
Whittaker, W. Gillie, 249n5
Wilder, Alec, 5
Williams, Ralph Vaughan, 168, 170

Y

Yarbrough, Cornelia, 245n4
Year to date
  budgets and, 65
  defined, 61

Z

Zlata's Diary (Powers), 168